ONE MAN IN HIS TIME...

ONE MAN IN HIS TIME...

A Memoir

MICHAEL AUDAIN

Douglas & McIntyre

1 2 3 4 5 — 25 24 23 22 21

Douglas and McIntyre (2013) Ltd.
P.O. Box 219, Madeira Park, BC, V0N 2H0
www.douglas-mcintyre.com

Edited by Pam Robertson
Text design by Carleton Wilson
Jacket photographs by Ashia Bonus Photography
All other photographs courtesy Michael Audain
Printed and bound in Canada
Paper contains 100 per cent post-consumer fibre

Canada Council for the Arts | Conseil des Arts du Canada | Canada

British Columbia Arts Council | British Columbia

Supported by the Province of British Columbia

Douglas and McIntyre acknowledges the support of the Canada Council for the Arts, the Government of Canada, and the Province of British Columbia through the BC Arts Council.

Library and Archives Canada Cataloguing in Publication

Title: One man in his time . . . : a memoir / Michael Audain.
Names: Audain, Michael, author.
Identifiers: Canadiana (print) 20210289856 | Canadiana (ebook) 20210289872 | ISBN 9781771623001 (hardcover) | ISBN 9781771623018 (EPUB)
Subjects: LCSH: Audain, Michael. | LCSH: Philanthropists—British Columbia—Biography. | LCSH: Political activists—British Columbia—Biography. | LCSH: Businesspeople—British Columbia—Biography. | LCSH: Art objects—Collectors and collecting—British Columbia—Biography. | LCGFT: Autobiographies.
Classification: LCC HV28.A93 A3 2021 | DDC 361.7/4092—dc23

For Yoshi, who has given me so much happiness these past forty years.

Contents

PREFACE

WHEN ON A TOUR of Iceland recently, a guide told us in heavily accented English that one in ten Icelanders writes a book, the highest proportion of any nation in the world. She added that the book is usually about themselves. When I enquired as to what the motivation was, she answered, "Well, they usually say it's something for their grandchildren, but I believe that it also helps people to understand themselves better," adding that she planned to write a book herself, about training her gentle Icelandic horses.

I don't have the excuse of being Icelandic and am not sure I have anything to write about as interesting as horses, but I can certainly recommend the exercise on the basis of the guide's other point: writing this book has been very instructive for me.

Until fairly recently, I had not considered my own life something that others might want to read about. My thoughts have until now always been about the future, because you can do something about the future. A memoir is the opposite. What caused me to revise my thinking was when Robert Bernstein, the human rights activist who for twenty-five years was president of Random House, asked me, after dinner one evening in New York, whether I had thought of writing a book, because he found my transformation from a left-wing social worker into a residential developer rather intriguing.

"Some people could share my view," he observed, zipping up his fly in the men's room of the Ritz-Carlton Hotel. (I should note at the outset that I have scrupled to use actual names in all but a few rare cases where an alias seemed appropriate.)

In fact, others had suggested the same thing over the years, but I was impressed that Bernstein, having brought many thousands of commendable books into the world, would risk the same opinion. He knew I'd been jailed as a civil rights activist in the American South and that today I earn my living dotting the Vancouver area's landscape with condominiums. Many people find the apparent contradiction between once having had a demonstrable social conscience and later being successful in business something that wants explaining. It is one of the comments I am most used to hearing from those who have some familiarity with my history.

Interestingly, the next most common assumption I encounter is that such success as I have had wants no explaining at all, and must have come about as a matter of course owing to the fact my great-great-grandfather, the coal baron Robert Dunsmuir, and my great-grandfather, Robert's son James Dunsmuir, built a family dynasty that sprinkled the Vancouver Island landscape with coal mines, railroads and castles. Proponents of this theory seem undeterred by the fact that several generations of internecine wrangling and bad living had reduced the dynasty to a smoking ruin by the time I arrived.

For much of my life I was at pains to avoid identifying with my Dunsmuir ancestry. There are noted landmarks and important streets as well as towns in modern British Columbia and California that bear the Dunsmuir name, but for the most part it is linked with greatness gone awry. Although Robert and James were British Columbia's leading job-generators of their day, their hard-nosed management style caused them to go down in popular lore as enemies of the working class. A labour leader I knew once told me he spat every time he spoke the name "Dunsmuir." As a young leftist reformer I was not eager to enfold myself in this heritage, though now, having experienced some of the challenges of building and sustaining a significant business enterprise, I am inclined to be more appreciative of what the Dunsmuirs were able to accomplish after coming to the so-called New World with nothing.

Before settling in what is now British Columbia, the Dunsmuirs came from a Scots mining family that had been decimated by illness, and even after becoming the wealthiest family in the province they were not immediately accepted on equal terms by what passed for high society

Michael as a young teenager.

in the colony. Like many newly rich, they desired social status to go with their money. James Dunsmuir had eight daughters who survived to adulthood and, in the words of clan biographer Terry Reksten, his strategy was to marry them to "men who were attractive, high born and relatively useless. For the most part, they lived up to his expectations."

One of the results of this approach to estate planning is that it rapidly exhausted the dynasty's cash reserves. It is sometimes said the Dunsmuir story can be summed up as how to create a great fortune in one generation and lose it in three. By the time I came along there was almost nothing left of the fabled cash but still a good deal of the acquired class pretension. My grandmother Sara Byrd "Byrdie" Dunsmuir had been married off to Colonel Guy Audain, a Sandhurst-educated officer in the Indian army who happily resigned his commission to accept a generous annuity from his father-in-law and spent the rest of his days in relentless pursuit of pleasure. He toured Britain in chauffeured automobiles rented from Harrods, stayed at the best hotels, criss-crossed the globe with an entourage, went on hunting and fishing safaris lasting months, and generally showed the Dunsmuirs how to dispose of their wealth with style. My father, Jimmy, grew up as a bystander to this spectacle and inherited the style though not, unfortunately, the means.

In our home there was no talk of "trade," and my parents had absolutely no friends in the business world. My father had a horror of people who stooped to engage in trade, no matter how successfully. His contemptuous term for what I have become would be a *boxwallah,* originally an Anglo-Indian word for a peddler who went door-to-door carrying goods in a box, but in his lexicon it encompassed anyone who sullied themselves by engaging in commerce. It was drummed into me at an early age that the only respectable professions were in the military, the church and the law, and the latter only if you became a judge. Of course, farming was also respectable if you owned land.

These patrician sentiments persisted in my father's mind, undiminished by the lack of inherited wealth needed to support them. There was always a chronic shortage of money in our household, but it was considered gauche to talk about it. Dogs and horses were safer subjects

LEFT: Young Michael Audain did not distinguish himself academically or on the sporting field. On entering Glenlyon School at age ten with a broken wrist, his nickname was "Dumb Wing."

BELOW: Michael's father, Jimmy, with the stallion Supreme Verdict.

of conversation, which seemed strange to me at the time, as I knew my great-grandfather had been a businessman whose success the family had been coasting on ever since. However, Jimmy apparently took his cues from his own father and had great pride in the Audain line of descent. They were originally Huguenots, as French Protestants were called, and spelt the name "Audoen." When France revoked the Edict of Nantes, guaranteeing religious freedom, in 1685, Huguenots had to flee their homes or risk being burnt as heretics. One branch of our family ended up on the island of St. Kitts, in the Caribbean, where a notable antecedent, John Audain, a.k.a. "The Pirate Pastor," managed to combine the vocations of clergyman and privateer, suggesting my own habit of mixing unlikely professions may be something genetic.

Another branch of the family became comfortably established in Northern Ireland, where my great-grandfather Colonel John Willet Payne Audain was commander of the Bedfordshire Regiment, 16th Foot. Several of my father's aunts remained in Ireland, and he sometimes took me to visit them in the charming village of Portballintrae before we moved to Canada in 1947.

My grandfather Colonel Guy Audain was Indian army through and through. And Jimmy, who had spent his early childhood in India, made an effort to pass on some of that ethos to me as a child. For example, I was brought up on Rudyard Kipling, one of my favourite tales being *The Jungle Book*. Every night when I was home from school, if he wasn't drunk, my father would read me stories about the man cub Mowgli, who was raised by wolves, and the heroic mongoose Rikki-Tikki-Tavi, not to mention the tiger Shere Khan, Bagheera the black panther and Baloo the bear. Later, when I learnt to read, my favourite book was *Kim*, about the Lahore beggar boy who sets out with a llama on the Grand Trunk Road to play a role in the Great Game—for me, it's still the best spy novel ever written.

There were many Indian mementoes in our house: silver polo cups on the mantelpiece, surrounded by photos of unknown men in jodhpurs and white helmets; a footstool made out of an elephant's foot; on the walls, heads of mountain sheep shot up in the Hindu Kush; and a huge tiger-skin rug before the fireplace.

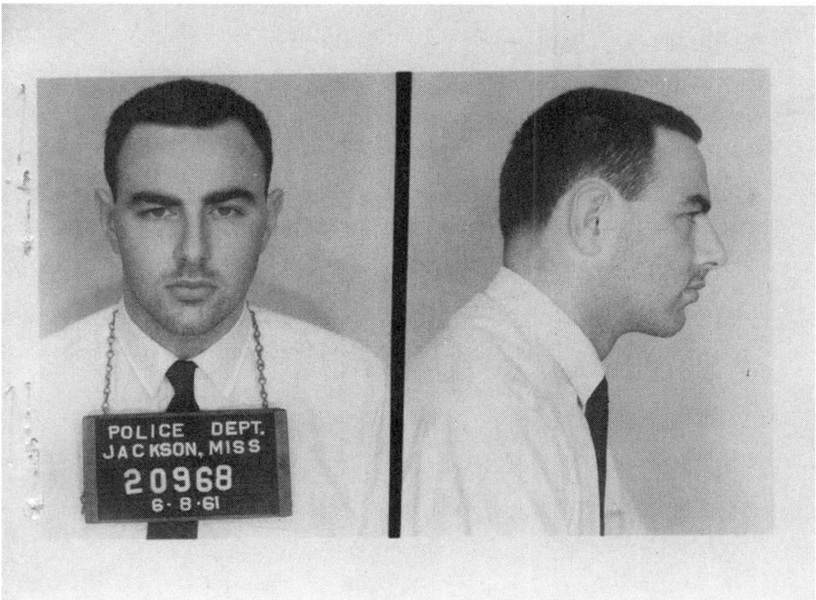

While a university student, Audain travelled to Mississippi to participate in the Civil Rights movement as a Freedom Rider—resulting in a stint in jail.

Michael with Tunya Swetleshnoff, March 1962. They met the year before at the New Democratic Party's founding convention.

The lingo in our home even tended to reflect that of the old Empire. One took a *chota-peg* of whisky at sundown, while Jimmy always referred to restaurant waiters as "bearers"—to their mystification. Curry was eaten at least twice a week, though it was made from leftover roasts of beef or lamb mixed liberally with spoonfuls of curry powder and ketchup. And, of course, it was always eaten with mango chutney. We even had fish khichuri every weekend for breakfast. The original Audain home on Foul Bay Road in Victoria, built in 1903, was designed by the architect Samuel McClure to resemble an Indian bungalow and was christened *Ellora,* after the famous caves near Aurangabad. I suppose the legacy continues, as our present home in West Vancouver is also called *Ellora.*

I recall when growing up in Victoria how much Jimmy respected the local Indo-Canadians.

"They are Sikhs, a brave warrior caste like the Rajputs; never call them Hindus," my father warned me.

Despite his professed respect, Jimmy didn't seem to have any Indian friends, his only contact being when a load of firewood was delivered by Indian drivers. When this happened, he would invite the truck driver and his mate into his study for a cup of tea, where he would show them photo albums of himself with his ayah, or nurse, as a child in India, plus pictures of his father, Guy, proudly seated in the front row of regimental photographs featuring hundreds of havildars, naiks and sepoys—all servicemen. The wood deliverers always seemed quite impressed and were very apologetic about having to take their leave. But, then, they may have been used to situations like this, as Victoria had so many retired Indian army officers and civil servants back in those days.

Strangely enough, when Jimmy attended my Vancouver wedding in 1962, he didn't say a word to my best man, Parkarsh Ram Mahant, until after the ceremony, when he enquired why he wasn't wearing his turban.

"Because I am not a Sikh, but the son of a Hindu Brahmin," Parkarsh advised him.

Jimmy seemed disappointed and said to me quietly, "Well, if your best man is really an Indian priest's son maybe he can turn himself into a tiger or an elephant. Why don't you ask him to have a go at it?"

Michael and wife Yoshi Karasawa, at the National Gallery of Canada (in front of *Leaves of Grass* sculpture by Geoffrey Farmer). *Photograph by Andrew Van Beek*

One of the realizations I have come to while pawing around in the dusty attic of my memory is how miserable, lonely and unhappy I was most of the time, from my early childhood through to my early twenties. I never felt physically abused, and the few hard knocks I endured I felt must have been common to most children at the time. And although I was blessed with a loving father, he was also one who wasn't shy about letting me know how I continually disappointed him with my poor academic and physical performance—to say nothing about his apprehension about my masculinity.

Another realization this writing has forced upon me is the degree to which I have been a loner all my life. Children who are loners tend to become quite impervious to being hurt, because they don't invest much in social relationships. Introverted people also tend to be more self-sufficient, though perhaps less compassionate than their fellow human beings. Loners, though, can be innovators and risk-takers because their instincts are not circumscribed by the herd. Never a team player, the only sport I somewhat enjoyed was amateur boxing.

I was fortunate that I was able to escape the slings and arrows of outrageous fortune by retreating to a private world of the imagination, which I inhabited as a child and teenager: a world of comic books, radio plays and good literature. This provided me with pleasant daydreams, in the classroom and on the soccer field, about Batman, Superman, my cowboy heroes Roy Rogers and Gene Autry, Tarzan, Ulysses, Richard Coeur de Lion, Kim of the Great Game, and David of the book of Moses. That's what sustained me.

Through my own experiences, and watching my children and grandchildren grow, what I have come to realize is that every child has the possibility to develop and accomplish marvellous things for themselves, their families and their countries, no matter how inadequate they may feel when they are young.

But perhaps such generalizations will make more sense after I relate some of the particulars of my story. The following pages contain a series of anecdotes from my life. Those that have been preserved here have been selected, with the assistance of my editor, as forming an admittedly

Established in 2016, the Audain Art Museum in Whistler, BC, was founded upon the philanthropic gift of Michael Audain and Yoshiko Karasawa.

one-sided account of one man's life journey, with its ups and downs, both in British Columbia and abroad.

Before getting on with the story proper, I feel I should add a word here about its prosaic title. I originally favoured the more poetic *My Bow of Burning Gold,* borrowed from the Anglican Church hymn "Jerusalem." Besides being my favourite hymn as a child, a couple of times it played a rather important role in my life, as the reader will discover. However, when I decided to try it out and see what it would conjure up in the minds of friends and family, the only response I got was a blank stare with an "eh?" from Canadians, a "huh?" from Americans, and a puzzled "what?" from a couple of Brits.

My search for something more serviceable continued until I shared the manuscript with a journalist friend, who said, "I am simply amazed that you have done so many different things in your life." I hadn't thought much about it, but considering that I attended eleven schools, five universities and had eight very different jobs by the time I was forty-three, I do seem to have been a bit of a rolling stone. For fun, I even counted up the number of homes I have lived in. The total came to thirty-three, excluding student residences!

After dwelling on that, one of the verses from Shakespeare's *As You Like It,* which I had to memorize at an early age in school, came to mind:

> All the world's a stage,
> And all the men and women merely players;
> They have their exits and their entrances,
> And one man in his time plays many parts…

The verse goes on to describe the seven ages of man, most of which I have now personally experienced, but what seems to be particularly appropriate to my own life is that I have, indeed, played many parts, even though at times I may have felt I was drifting through a dream rather than following my own script.

CHAPTER 1

"Stay Away from the Guns, Son: They Are Still Hot"

Royal Navy sailor, 1940

THE GRIZZLY-FACED SAILOR MOTIONED with his hand to an area where the little girl in the camel-coloured coat and I could play a game of hopscotch more safely than next to the pom-pom guns that had been so recently in action against the Luftwaffe.

"Stay away from the guns, son: they are still hot," the sailor said, not unkindly.

A fresh breeze blew between the half-clouded sky and the grey English Channel, speckled with whitecaps.

It was so bracing to be on the wood-clad destroyer deck after a long night below, where I had slept on the floor at my mother's feet as she sat in a noisy wardroom along with half a dozen other women evacuated at the last opportunity from Jersey, in the Channel Islands. She fed me digestive biscuits, for which I quickly developed a lifelong loathing.

Years later my mother, Madeleine, startled by my flashback from such an early age, filled in the rest of the scene. She had come to Jersey with my father in 1938 to escape British income tax. Although a British possession, Jersey was a tax haven that suited a man like my father, who received a meagre income from a Canadian-based family trust. Jimmy had started off well enough, following his father's footsteps to Sandhurst, England's finest military college, then moving on to an officer's commission with the 7th Queen's Own Hussars, which should have led to an elite military career. But after several years of increasingly wild drinking and carousing, which included two serious car crashes, he was forced to resign his commission. There followed several years of hanging out in the fleshpots of London. One of his favourite haunts was a trendy restaurant called the Eiffel Tower, operated by Rudolph Stulik, an Austrian bon vivant who had two attractive, well-educated daughters. Somehow Jimmy persuaded the elder one, Madeleine, to marry him.

Things didn't go well between my parents. In fact, after two months on Jersey, Jimmy ended up in jail, charged with arson for setting fire to our rented house during a drunken spree. He escaped a lengthy sentence by skipping his fifty-pound bail and fleeing the island, leaving my mother and me on our own in a small flat. That was until the war came to Jersey.

In 1940, my father went off to France with the British Expeditionary Force under the command of Major General Lord Gore. Jimmy cabled my mother that the German blitzkrieg was moving fast through Belgium and France so it was time to pack up our household goods and return home to England. Madeleine, however, dilly-dallied, believing that it was unlikely that the Germans would ever want to invade the Channel Islands, even though they are located much closer to the French coast than England. In any case, speaking perfect German (her father being Austrian), she felt that she had little to fear.

But as the days went by and the German juggernaut rolled forward across France, accompanied by furious air attacks, my mother began to have her doubts, particularly as the British government in mid-June told the people of the Channel Islands that it would be strategically impossible to defend them. Thus, passage was booked for us and our household effects on what was to be the last passenger ferry back to the UK.

Alas, when the port of St. Helier was bombed by the Luftwaffe on June 28, all ferry sailings were cancelled, though some people managed to escape in small boats. In desperation, several other evacuees, including my mother, managed to convince a lobster fisherman to ferry them out of the harbour, where just beyond lay a British destroyer. Fortunately, the naval captain agreed to take the women and children with British passports aboard. The fathers were forced to stay behind and would spend the war in German internment camps.

CHAPTER 1

I have no other memories of how we survived several days at sea, as the destroyer, under constant air attack, patrolled the English Channel on the lookout for an invasion fleet. Nor of how we got to London with only the clothing we were wearing, and where for weeks my mother and I, together with thousands of others, found refuge from the nightly blitz on the platforms of London Underground stations. Thankfully, we were soon able to reconnect with my mother's family.

CHAPTER 2

"Now the Sissy Is Blubbering"

Jimmy Audain, 1940

AS I STEPPED OFF the bus I was greeted by a tall, elegantly dressed woman with a serious-looking face. "*Mon Dieu,* what a big young man you are!" she exclaimed.

My father picked me up and hugged me, saying that I should call this lady "Aunt Marie." This was Marie Fagalde, the ex-wife of a French general, who he'd met while making the rounds in London. I had not seen Jimmy for some time but easily recognized him. He seemed to have grown fatter than the man I had last seen in an army officer's uniform. At the outbreak of World War II he'd volunteered, and was sent to France in the spring of 1940, but he ended up being court-martialled for being intoxicated and AWOL just before being evacuated with the rest of the British army prior to Dunkirk.

I had travelled the twenty-five miles from Farnham, Surrey, to Fleet, Hampshire, on the green double-decker bus, sitting wedged near the open door, where the female conductor said she could easily keep her eye on me, as my mother had requested early that morning when she had tearfully dispatched me for my obligatory monthly visit to my father. At the time, my mother and I were staying as refugees from the London bombing, with my father's sister, Laura Henderson, whose husband was serving with the Canadian Scottish Regiment.

After being shown the upstairs room in which my father and my new "aunt" were living, we rented a rowboat for a picnic on the River Thames.

Having never been in a small boat before I was thrilled at how easily my father rowed us against the stream, with its willow-clad shoreline. Finally, we pulled onto a muddy bank and lunched on a tablecloth spread on the nearby grass, after which it was time for bathing. My father and Marie retired behind some bushes to don their swimming suits, while I was left to pull on what my mother had provided. It was a powder-blue crocheted woollen suit that covered my chest, and around my waist was embroidered a ring of yellow ducks.

As soon as my father saw what I was wearing he started laughing, calling to Marie, "Oh my God, look what a sissy boy Madeleine has made my son!" Marie joined in the laughter, saying, "Your wife obviously doesn't have the slightest idea about boys."

I started crying. At that my father said, "Oh dear, now the sissy is blubbering. I need to put a stop to that."

He quickly ripped the offending clothing right off me and led me nude to the water. But there was no beach and I floundered, until my father started swimming on his back and held me with one arm on his chest. I was terrified as I had never done more than paddle in the shallows near Jersey's sandy beaches, so after a couple of minutes my father steered me back to land, where he popped me on the bank and told me to find a towel while he and Marie had their swim. By the time they returned, I was half dressed and had settled down, having found a big furry caterpillar to play with. But my fear of water would continue for some years.

On the return trip to the marina, we went under a dark bridge where my father told me a witch lived—not a very pleasant experience for a three-year-old whose head was filled with fairytale images of witches making meals of little boys and girls and puppy dog tails. For some years, whenever I encountered a bridge, I wondered whether it might provide accommodation for a wicked witch.

I suppose that it is common for children to develop irrational fears of different things. A similar experience occurred again on another picnic, this time with my mother. We were in the woods somewhere near Farnham when my mother said something to the effect of "Oh, look at those lovely foxgloves!"

I immediately burst into tears and implored her to take me home. I associated the flowers with the likely presence of foxes! And foxes were something to be afraid of, because they came in the night to steal chickens. As a Beatrix Potter fan, I also knew they were not friends of Peter Rabbit.

CHAPTER 3

"Here's a Boy Who Doesn't Know How to Spell Mat!"

Headmistress, St. George's School, 1941

THE HEADMISTRESS WORE STEEL-RIMMED glasses on a sharp, beaky nose as she stood over me and exclaimed in a very loud voice, "Here's a boy who doesn't know how to spell *mat*!"

My first day at nursery school was a terrifying experience that put me off school for life. Earlier the headmistress had ordered me to spell out "cat" using the wooden blocks, but I barely knew my ABCs let alone any spelling. The nursery school, called St. George's, was situated in a large room at the back of an old house on Castle Street, in the town of Farnham. Outside was a lawn and garden where the little boys and girls had to act out *A Midsummer's Night Dream* as the school play—something that permanently put me off Shakespearean comedies.

Even though my mother was allowed to sit with me that first morning, it was still quite terrifying. There was a dunce's stool, with a cone-shaped hat for children who misbehaved. And for more serious punishment, the headmistress wielded what appeared to be a long bamboo cane with a crooked handle.

As the morning wore on, I further drew attention to myself at the elevenses snack break by spilling my milk down my front. Every child in England received a half pint from Churchill's wartime government. At this school one apparently had to learn to drink it out of the bottle, no straws being available. How long I stayed at this nursery school, I have no idea.

Farnham was seldom bombed, but I do remember spending the odd night in air raid shelters, and in the morning going out with my mother—or on weekdays the older girl who had been put in charge of me while my mother worked—to look for the remains of shot-down airplanes, which sometimes could be seen roped off from us souvenir-hunting children. One morning we even witnessed ambulance personnel moving bodies from a still-smoking German bomber in a nearby park, while a tall, lanky, blond-haired flyer sat nearby, guarded by a sole British Bobby. As kids, we all aspired to getting hold of a Nazi dagger, or even a Luger pistol, but mostly we scavenged shell cases or pieces of silk parachute. The latter were hastily snapped up by the local girls, who reportedly made them into undergarments.

Nearby was nine-hundred-year-old Farnham Castle, with its ancient keep and grass-clad moat, where I enjoyed playing knights and squires.

As my mother and I moved around the Farnham area from one bedsitter to another, I briefly attended a couple other nursery schools nearby. My mother would take the train daily up to London, where she worked in a West End dress shop to supplement the five-pound monthly allowance she was paid by my father. Finally, not long after I reached the age of four, funds were secured from a trust set up by my grandfather for me to attend a boarding school.

CHAPTER 4

"Take Your Bags Down"

Headmaster Lynn-Jones, 1942

I WAS LEANING OVER an armchair in Headmaster Lynn-Jones's cluttered bedroom when I received the order: "Take your bags down." So, I removed the bags of knitting I saw on the chair to the floor beside it.

"No, you nitwit. I mean your trousers and drawers."

I complied, and the slippering I received was over swiftly. It was my introduction to corporal punishment at Melbreck, the first of seven boarding schools I attended.

I was at one school so briefly that its name has been blotted out of my mind. I thought that my brief tenure meant that I had been expelled, but later my father told me that I was simply sent home ignominiously because, during the war, remittances from the Canadian trust that paid my school fees were occasionally lost at sea due to submarine action, and my father lacked the wherewithal to make up the deficit.

Set in a large Tudor house not far from Farnham, Melbreck made quite an impression on me. I remember my first day there after being deposited by my mother. I was playing under the table with some other four-year-olds when we heard loud footsteps. One boy said, "Ssshh, Sir is coming."

"Sir" is what we called Headmaster Lynn-Jones, both to his face and when referring to him. He was a lean, tall man with a bushy moustache and a ruddy outdoor complexion, perhaps from chasing slow-moving boys like me around the soccer field with a swagger stick. I even remember what an impressive figure he made when he first paraded with the Home Guard, clad in plus fours with a shotgun over his shoulder. Anyway, to us, he was God.

Sir's method of motivating his thirty boys was literally a stick-and-carrot process. Each boy was obliged to carry a black conduct book in his grey flannel shirt pocket. We referred to it as the "plus and minus book" because when you did something particularly good, such as scoring a goal in a soccer game against another school or achieving first place on a class test, the teachers would put some pluses in the book. Likewise, you got minuses if you had infractions, such as forgetting to polish your boots, doing very poorly on a test, or joking in the dormitory after lights out.

Before lunch on Saturday, Lynn-Jones would balance our books. Pupils who had a balance of over a hundred pluses could receive sweets after lunch every day, whereas over a hundred minuses meant a visit to the headmaster's bedroom after lunch for a mandatory beating. There were also gradations of reward and punishment between those levels.

While I have many memories of this school, I only recall two staff other than the headmaster. One was a kindly matron whose young son also attended the school, and the other was a fearsome mistress known as Miss Tilly. It was Miss Tilly who doggedly forced me and Simon Burns, another slow reader, to read *Alice in Wonderland*, with its ridiculously hard words, out loud in the staff common room.

Simon was my closest friend and his was the only name I could remember from the school until I arrived at the University of British Columbia fifteen years later, when I heard an English voice call out behind me, "Well, if it isn't Audain the Madhatter!" The lanky blond-haired youth introduced himself as Desmond Alexander, informed me that he had been at Melbreck with me, and enquired whether I had forgotten the *Alice in Wonderland* nickname with which I had been dubbed at the school.

I have no idea whether Lynn-Jones was a kind man to his wife and children, or if he indeed had children of his own, but to us little boys he was a terror. I was a witness to three sadistic acts that stay with me to this day. The first may sound silly, but during the war we were always hungry. So, at the final school lunch before the Christmas holidays, the headmaster tantalized us by saying that the cook had made a special Christmas pudding full of fruits and nuts, which we would all enjoy. We sat there expectantly while with great ceremony a cloth-covered dish was brought to the table in front of Lynn-Jones and his wife. We were urged to start singing "Deck the Halls," at the end of which the cloth cover was lifted for all to see: a muddy, holly-clad soccer ball.

No one laughed, other than the teachers. Some of the boys actually cried. My young mind wondered at the headmaster's macabre sense of humour.

On another occasion, I was in a small dormitory with three other boys who had been confined to bed with one of those childhood diseases, either chicken pox or mumps. There was no heating in the dormitory, so staying in bed was necessary to stay warm. Apparently, Lynn-Jones had overheard two of the boys whispering during the afternoon rest period and he was determined to punish them. He did this, in front of the rest of us, by ordering them to kneel on the bed and lower their pajama bottoms so he could apply strokes of a leather slipper. I couldn't help looking, even though I felt badly witnessing their indignity and pain.

The last episode was more serious. An older boy, perhaps eight or nine, had a burst of temper and kicked Miss Tilly on the plaster leg cast that she was wearing. I had seen it happen at the edge of the playing field after the mistress had cuffed the boy on his ears for being cheeky.

While at lunch, Lynn-Jones made the boy stand on a chair and told the whole room that afterwards he was going to relish making an example of this child so that he would never lose his temper with anyone again. Later in the afternoon I had to visit the matron's room for some reason. There I saw the matron placing Dettol-soaked gauze pads on large red weals that criss-crossed the boy's back and buttocks. Some of the weals had formed scabs where the bleeding had stopped.

"What happened?" I asked naively.

"Sir took a dog whip to me, and now I have been expelled," the older boy replied.

"His mother is coming to pick him up this evening. It won't be a minute too soon to get him away from this place," the matron observed dryly. I often wonder what happened to that boy. Did he become a pillar of the British establishment, all the better for his encounter with Lynn-Jones? Who knows, but it was certainly a shocker, and in some ways worse cruelty than what I observed later in life in a Mississippi prison.

In the spring of 1943, I spent a long time in bed, first with flu, which developed into pneumonia. I couldn't move or eat anything other than a thin broth. As a consequence, the school matron took the initiative to write my father recommending that I be moved to a private nursing home, where I could receive a better level of care than she could give me.

My father swiftly made some arrangements. I was transferred for a week to the nearby home of my school friend Simon Burns. Simon's father was a senior officer with the British forces fighting the Japanese in Burma, while his mother, a former nurse, was doing voluntary service at a nearby hospital for wounded soldiers. With more care and somewhat better food, my strength started to come back, to the point that I could walk to the bathroom and sit in a chair for meals. A few days later I was on a steamer bound for Northern Ireland and, thankfully, was never obliged to return to the care of Headmaster Lynn-Jones.

CHAPTER 5

"Don't Be a Funker"

Jimmy Audain, 1942

IT WAS BECOMING DARK as we left the theatre in the naval port of Plymouth. *Peter Pan* was my earliest introduction to pantomime, and what a wonderful production it was to see Wendy flying through the air, Tinkerbell darting around the stage, all performed by very accomplished young actors. The character who impressed me most, though, was the indomitable Captain Hook as he stomped around the stage.

I also had a huge shock upon seeing what I thought was a real-life gigantic dog bounding up the aisle and found it difficult to believe my father's explanation that there were two people inside the Nana costume.

The bus home to Kingsbridge, the town in the south of England near which I now lived full-time with my father when not in school, stopped close to the theatre, but rather than wait in the rain my father decided it was time to "splice the main brace" and he took me in search of a pub. We hadn't gone far when the air raid sirens started to sound. Only a few minutes later the anti-aircraft guns opened fire on what we later heard was a lone German bomber sweeping in from the sea.

The lack of time between the onset of the sirens and commencement of the bombing, plus our lack of familiarity with Plymouth's air raid shelters, led to our being caught virtually in the open as bombs started to whistle into the now deserted streets. With great presence of mind, my father quickly shoved me up against a brick wall in a small alleyway and pressed his body tight against mine, enveloping us both with his long camel-hair coat.

"Don't be a funker," my father growled.

A gigantic explosion occurred just up the street, and a minute or two later all was quiet. An "all-clear" sounded a few minutes later, and we ventured out into the street just as clouds of dust were settling in the light rain. The fire brigade was already at the scene, where a hundred yards or so away the whole exterior wall of a building had come crashing down in a pile of rubble.

"Well, it seems God still wants me to find that pub," my father said laughingly.

I also felt I could use a drink, so I was delighted when a few minutes later we were seated in the warmth of an old pub, where I quaffed a stone bottle of ginger beer. Later we caught the last bus of the evening to Kingsbridge, and from there we were driven five miles home to the fishing village of Bantham by Crispen, my father's favourite taxi driver.

We learnt later that Plymouth, which had suffered so much bombing during the earlier Blitz of 1941, recorded that raid as one of the last of the war.

CHAPTER 6

"Get That Boy Right Back on That Bloody Animal"

Wasp Morehead, 1943

ONE DAY JIMMY DECIDED it was time for me to learn to ride. Some second-hand jodhpurs were purchased and a suitable pony sought. But the only one available was a small, strong-willed horse primarily used for pulling a "trap," a two-wheeled vehicle used for short journeys.

My father saddled up the animal with the help of his army friend Wasp Morehead. The latter had suffered a serious head wound in enemy action and was staying with my father as part of his convalescence. I was told from the first day that all I had to do was sit in my saddle and learn to hold the reins properly while my father led the pony around the field.

With Jimmy's help I mounted, got the hang of the reins, and was just thinking how much I was going to enjoy the experience when all of a sudden the horse decided that it had had enough. It lurched out of Jimmy's grip and started to canter across the field, with me leaning forward and holding tightly onto its mane for dear life. Then the horse decided it had had enough of me. Coming to a quick stop, it bucked me off over its head, hitting me with a glancing blow from a hoof in the process. For a while, all I saw were stars, then I was taken home in a local doctor's car and put to bed in a dark room for a couple of days with a splitting headache.

As soon as my headache diminished, I asked if I could take our dogs for a walk across the fields. But Morehead said, "Jimmy, there is only one place that he should go today. Get that boy right back on that bloody animal." And so, despite my protestations, that's where I went. This time, my father and Morehead, one on each side, walked the horse on lead reins around the field, and I was given a riding crop to urge it forward.

I rode that horse for two years, but never enjoyed it. Even using a bit, I was incapable of controlling the beast. I recall on one occasion, after fording a river, the animal decided it would be a good time to punish my father for inflicting his useless son onto its back. The horse gave Jimmy's leg a vicious kick and charged off in the direction of the village and its stable. It ran for several miles, heedless of my attempts to rein it in. In fact, all I could do was hang onto its saddle and mane, shouting "Help!" to startled passersby. The horse careened down the main street of Thurlestone village until an alert butcher van driver blocked the narrow road and managed to grab the horse's bridle.

After that experience, Jimmy, who was nursing a badly bruised leg, remarked, "What a horrible beast. We'll have to find you something better."

The experience didn't lead to me giving up riding. In fact, while I never had one of my own, I enjoyed horses during much of my younger life. As a teenager, I even worked for a couple of months at a dude ranch in British Columbia's Cariboo country, where part of my job was to look after the tack and occasionally escort guest rides when one of the resident cowboys wasn't available. But I never did forget my first day on a horse.

CHAPTER 7

"Here Comes the Toff"

Village boy, 1944

ON MY WAY HOME from Thurlestone's golf links, I was pedalling the new Raleigh bike I had received for my seventh birthday when I heard a youthful voice cry, "Here comes the toff."

This was followed by a volley of stones hurled in my direction from unknown assailants hidden behind the tall hedgerow that lined the narrow lane. I instinctively started to zigzag, recalling that's what merchant ships did when under U-boat attack. But my inexperience with a bicycle on loose gravel defeated me, so I toppled to the ground. Three or four boys of my age appeared, their faces masked by handkerchiefs. "And now we can see the toff is nothing else than a sissy boy," one of them said in a broad Devonshire accent as I sat there crying, blood spurting from my mouth and my right knee cap.

"Get away from him, you little bastards!"

Through my tears I recognized a tall blond girl named Eileen. Only twelve, she sometimes helped my stepmother, Marie, with housework. The boys scattered, and I tried to right my bicycle, but I seemed to have twisted the front wheel. Eileen announced that she had to go home, which was in the opposite direction to Bantham village, where I lived with Jimmy and Marie, but she enlisted the help of a teenager—a fisherman's son named Elliott. He slung the bike over his shoulder and took me by the hand so that I was able to hobble home in a daze. There I was put in a dark room and my wounds were washed with Dettol, which only stung slightly less than iodine. At Marie's suggestion that I needed some stitches, Jimmy scoffed, saying, "He will be all right tomorrow."

Like most youngsters, I did recover quickly, but ever since I have carried scars on my knee and lip, as well as having lost two front teeth.

After my bicycle accident I had a great fear of being attacked again by the village kids, so I told my father that I wanted to give up my golf lessons, since I hated the game.

"Nonsense," Jimmy said. "A gentleman must learn to play a decent round of golf. Not too decent, of course, or you are liable to show up your host." For my remaining golf lessons, I worked out a way of traversing the hilly fields, avoiding any habitations.

At the links there was a wizened old pro who endeavoured to teach me how to hit a ball straight. He invariably ended the hour on a disparaging note: "You are no more likely to make a golfer than I am to visit London." I asked Jimmy why the golf pro never intended to visit London. Laughing, Jimmy told me that the old man had never been further than the market town of Kingsbridge, which was only five miles away.

It was at this age that I became aware of the social class differences that prevailed in England in those days. Being sent to boarding schools far from my Devonshire home, I talked with a completely different vocabulary and accent than the local boys, who I frankly found hard to understand.

One Christmas morning, Jimmy invited a number of young village kids to our home, where he dressed up as Father Christmas. He handed out presents from under the Christmas tree as the local children mumbled their thanks and furtively glanced in my direction. I felt so shy and strange that this was happening in my own home, particularly as some of the boys were probably those who had stoned me.

During those days I never had an opportunity to play with the local kids. My father said, "It's best to not get too familiar with them or you will no longer speak the King's English."

There being no King's English-speaking children for me to associate with in that remote village, I played exclusively with our two cocker spaniels, Susan and Laura. Sometimes I wore a feathered headdress and yelled blood-curdling war cries at the dogs while brandishing my toy tomahawk. On other days, I was a cowboy practising quick draws with my cap gun and firing it off close to their ears. The dogs were tolerant of my antics, but not overly impressed.

However, as soon as I turned eight, Jimmy trained me to use a single-shot .22-calibre rifle (which had been his as a boy) and the dogs started to treat me with new respect. I only had to grab the rifle for them to start barking in wild excitement. However, in the early morning, when I would hunt rabbits, I would leave the dogs at home because they would disturb the game.

We shot rabbits purely for the pot. Jimmy's technique was to contact a boy from a nearby Romani camp, who would produce a malicious-looking white ferret from a wooden box on the back of his bicycle. First, all the rabbit holes on one side of a hedgerow would be netted to prevent the rabbits from escaping, while along the other side, the ferret would be introduced to the warren, and Jimmy would stand with his 12-gauge double-barrelled shotgun and blast away as the rabbits emerged in terror, attempting to escape the ferret.

What amazed me was how quickly the ferret's owner could pounce on the rabbits trapped in the nets on the hedgerow's reverse side. He would grab a struggling animal and bang its head over the back of his other fist and, presto, the rabbit was dead. With this method he would usually have a bigger bag of game than my father, who wasn't always successful in shooting the fleeing animals. The action was exciting and swift, but we sometimes had to wait a couple of boring hours for the ferret to re-emerge, having made a meal of its own in the rabbit warren.

My own rabbit-hunting technique consisted of stalking close enough to a group of grazing rabbits that I could hit one with my little weapon. That wasn't difficult. The challenge was to reload and get off another shot before the rabbits scampered back into their burrows. This was possible because of the tendency of rabbits to freeze at any sign of danger. Later in life, killing animals for sport held no interest for me, but the many rabbits I shot before I reached the age of ten seemed justified, both by their abundance and by hunger, there always being people in the village who welcomed a cleaned and skinned rabbit for their larder.

CHAPTER 8

"Would You Be Wanting After the Fish?"

Fisherman, Portballintrae, 1944

HE WAS A RUDDY-FACED giant of a man, with a pipe stuffed in his mouth and wearing the usual garb of an Ulster fisherman: blue sweater and a battered blue cap on his stock of white hair. I don't recall any names, but I knew that he was the father of one of that summer's playmates, boys who lacked shoes except to wear to school and to church on the Sabbath.

Like my new-found friends, I ran around shoeless in the daytime, though when the shadows started to lengthen I had to return to the Bayview Hotel, where Jimmy and Marie were staying, and don clothes other than a pair of shorts for what my parents called "high tea."

My summer friends were very welcoming, despite the fact they lived in two-room fishermen's cottages while I stayed for the summer at what was the only hotel in the small village of Portballintrae, on Ireland's County Antrim coast. So it was no surprise when one of my friends' fathers invited me to board his small fishing craft, saying, "Would you be wanting after the fish?"

Without thinking, I said, "Sure," and jumped aboard, helping my young friend to slip the mooring lines.

An old two-cycle engine fired us out from the quay, and within minutes we began to encounter the North Atlantic swells. Immediately the engine was doused and the large red sail hoisted, which stabilized the vessel somewhat as it sliced through the heaving waters.

I soon began to feel sick. The grizzled captain said with a smile, "Just get rid of your breakfast over the lee side, son, not on my deck!"

Once breakfast was gone, I was ordered, following the lead of my playmate, to start baiting the long mackerel lines. It seemed no sooner than the lines had all been run out, with their dozens of hooks, than it was time to bring them in again—this time heavy with long silver fish that flopped around energetically on the deck until they were tossed into one of the large wicker baskets. The afternoon wore on, and as dusk settled in we were handed large chunks of soda bread generously slathered with butter. The captain then announced that he was going to run down the coast to where he would moor for the night, so that he would be able to haul up his lobster pots at first light. I slept soundly on one of the single cabin's bunks, to be awakened in the darkness with a mug of tea.

"Time to go after the lobsters," grunted the captain.

Raising the lobster pots in the early dawn light was a back-breaking exercise, but we two boys managed it, pulling together on the line. Not being able to see properly in the early dawn, I was scared to put my hand into the pot lest I got a finger taken off, but my friend deftly showed me how it could be done by moving quicker than the lobsters' reflexes.

When we returned to the Portballintrae quay later in the morning, Jimmy was waiting with an angry expression on his face. I said that I was sorry that I hadn't got permission to accept the fishing invitation, as I hadn't known that we would be out all night. My father replied that he was not worried about me—I had been seen boarding the vessel—but he was furious that I had left our two cocker spaniels on the dock, where they had gotten sick from eating some rotten salmon.

Back in the hotel, Jimmy lashed me hard with his heavy leather belt and confined me to my room all the next day. But the following morning I was back on the beach and something of a hero among my friends after I showed them my bruised hindquarters.

My two summers in Northern Ireland were the highlights of my early life. It was easy to make friends, and there were so many caves and ruined castles to explore as we ran free up and down the coast, all the way from the Giant's Causeway to Portrush. We mostly travelled by what was known as the oldest electric railway in the British Empire as it trundled along the coast. We had no money for fares, so when the conductor came, we just jumped off into the heather or gorse. On one occasion, I fell rather than jumped off. My leg bled so much that it needed to be stitched up in the casualty ward of the Portrush Hospital.

I didn't even mind going with my father on Sundays to the Church of John the Baptist in Bushmills, where my great-grandfather Audain had married a girl by the name of Cassidy from the south of the country. I thought, though, that it was unfortunate that my stepmother, Marie, had to sneak down the back lane to a small, dilapidated Roman Catholic church because religious prejudice was so strong in those days. One Sunday when I accompanied her, my father being away, the word got out to my young friends that I had been spied going into a Papist den of iniquity. Their ragging, though, was good natured, as they knew that I came from Protestant stock. My father told me that one of the oldest tombstones in Dublin's Huguenot graveyard has our family name on it, though it is spelt the original way, "Audoen."

Only one incident really scarred my first summer in Northern Ireland. I witnessed an argument between my father and Marie, who was nagging him not to put on a shirt because she wanted to send it for washing. When she tried to grab it from him, he drove a fist into her face, breaking her nose. The hotel manager brought in a doctor, who after resetting Marie's nose said that he felt that it was his duty to report the incident to the local constable. At that, Jimmy disappeared out the back door of the hotel, and we didn't hear from him until a week later, when Marie received a very apologetic telegram from over the border in the Republic of Ireland, enquiring if it was safe to return. Marie, the strong woman that she was, forgave him, so he contritely returned, bringing her a present of a bunch of grapes, the first that I had ever seen.

Jimmy explained to me that he'd had a bad hangover that morning and that Marie's action had simply triggered an automatic reflex in him as a competitive boxer. Although I loved my father, I was always physically afraid of him—particularly as his drinking bouts seemed to be getting worse and more prolonged as I grew older.

CHAPTER 9

"You Are Riding for a Fall"

Marie Audain, 1945

IT WAS WHAT THE Irish call a "soft day": one that is not raining cats and dogs but has just a steady shower. With the wind sweeping in across the golf course, it could soon sodden your skin if you were wearing a light pullover, as I was that afternoon. My father and Marie were having an animated conversation as they strolled along. I had been reprimanded for eavesdropping, so I alternately tagged along behind or disappeared through hedgerows to surprise them when they rounded a corner. Annoyed, Marie warned me, "You're riding for a fall, young man. Yes, you are riding for a fall."

As I didn't quite know what that meant, I continued my skylarking while my parents sauntered across sundry stonewalled fields. I climbed up and ran along one of the high walls, but when I accidentally dislodged a stone, I received a strong verbal rebuke from a small old man who was plodding along the lane with his donkey.

"Come here," Jimmy shouted, "I have some medicine for you." Forthwith he forced me to take down my shorts and bend over, and he thrashed me with his belt until I was screaming for him to stop.

"I warned you, Michael, that you were riding for a fall. Why didn't you listen?" said Marie. And at that she and my father strode away, saying that I could find my own way home.

The old man, who had been watching the proceedings, put away his clay pipe and walked over and patted me on the head, saying, "Your people are strange. You'd think you had been knocking over gravestones.

These old walls have been falling down for centuries." When I shook my head after being asked if I knew my way home, the man said, "Well, I'll walk you halfway there. Me and my mate," referring to his donkey, "don't require tea for a while."

There was no tea for me that evening back at the hotel. Instead, I was sent to bed early with a glass of water and an empty stomach.

Corporal punishment was a feature of all the schools I attended, except the last one. I wasn't really bothered by it, because on the whole it seemed to be quite objective. You broke a school rule and then were punished, with all the boys suffering a similar fate. I had my share of slipperings and canings, but certainly less than boys who broke many more rules.

My father prided himself on being a modern parent, saying that he didn't believe in excessive corporal punishment. Nevertheless, I recall him lamenting that since I wasn't beaten enough at school, he had to do the job himself.

Somewhat surprisingly, only on one occasion was I beaten for a dismal report card—Jimmy said the schoolmaster should have done it himself. Instead, most of my beatings seemed to come out of thin air. Things seemed to be going along well, and then suddenly my father developed a rage that could only be expunged by him finding a reason to thrash me.

He claimed this once happened when we were sheltering in a London underground tunnel during the Blitz; I was too young to remember that. What I do recall was being five years old and calling to ask my father to help me do up the buttons on a pair of jodhpurs. He unexpectedly lit into me with a slipper for nagging.

On another occasion, when I was seven, we were out shooting snipe and I laughed at my father when he sank with his gumboots into some deep river ooze. He was so furious that I was given a prolonged beating that evening with his belt.

In every case, an hour or so after the beating, when Jimmy's anger had subsided, he would come to my bedroom almost apologetically to assure me that he still loved me and wanted me to know that the punishments I received from him were nothing as rigorous as was meted out by his father and schoolmasters. For instance, he said that at Wellington College, in his day, the prefects would beat the boys by having them kneel on a chair, then running up and swinging a cane, which severely marked them.

But as I grew older, the punishment at home became more ritualized, with Marie commenting to my father that it was time that I received a "good dose." On one occasion when my father wasn't home, Marie even beat me herself, with a riding quirt, having me lie on some pillows across my bed. Not only did it sting, but it left vivid red marks. And with Marie there were no kind words later. Instead, she warned me that I should expect my father to deal with me more severely when he returned—that's something that thankfully did not occur, because my father only struck me when he was enraged.

Finally, on one occasion when I was fourteen years old, Jimmy came into my room to strip me for a beating for complaining about Marie, after he had been doing the same thing. I told my father that I wasn't going to play his game any longer. He struck me hard on the head, to the point that I staggered onto my bed disoriented. After that he beat me through my pajamas with a heavy walking stick.

While I was showering after boxing training in the Victoria City Police gym, the boys mentioned the black-and-blue marks on my rear end to my trainer, Eddie Haddad, who asked to see them for himself.

This apparently led to a quiet talk between my father and the Victoria Police chief, after which Jimmy accused me of being a Nazi, because apparently in Nazi Germany children were encouraged to report their parents' wrongdoings to the authorities. Although he didn't speak to me for almost a week, that was the last time my father beat me.

To this day, I have never complained to anyone else about my treatment at home. I was well fed and clothed, and never lacked for the basics. Yet I lived in constant fear of my parents.

CHAPTER 10

"Henry Has Returned"

Marie Audain, 1945

WHEN I LOOK BACK and think about which adult I was most comfortable with as a child, it was not a family member, a schoolteacher or a sports coach. It was a man named Henry Baker, who lived in a Romani caravan parked on a verge near the village of Bantham.

Henry worked as a labourer for various farmers and also did odd jobs around the village—for us, he built a chicken coop and pigsty. He also had a reputation as a poacher, though I am not sure how lucrative that was because there were no big estates full of pheasants to poach in our vicinity.

My father was happy if Henry kept me occupied during the school holidays. He said that although Henry's mother was reputed to be a Romani, Henry was actually a gentleman. Having apparently served with some distinction in the 1914–18 war, he spoke with an accent different from the local West Country dialect. What I liked about Henry was that he accepted me as I was, asking the odd question about my background or schooling, but never offering the usual advice adults give to children. Sometimes I would accompany him to a nearby farm and watch him help with the birth of a calf or the treatment of a lame horse. He certainly had a way with animals, including the big farm horses that pulled the ploughs and hay carts. They relaxed when he would quietly speak to them.

When it was time to harvest the grain, I joined Henry all day threshing, usually snatching rides on the ricks full of sheaves to be fed into the noisy steam-powered machine, while our dogs chased the rabbits that emerged from the wheat sheaves stooked in the small fields.

Henry thought it important that I learn about nature, so he taught me how to recognize the songs of different birds and how to check their nests without disturbing the eggs. He also taught me how to sit totally still in the twilight and let the animals come close, saying that the badgers, hedgehogs and rabbits all talked to one another if you attuned your ears to hear their tiny voices. And then there were lessons on how to catch rabbits with snares, not guns. He taught me how to rig a snare and where to place it for a rabbit or mole, even though I thought it was a cruel way to kill an animal. Henry seemed to make much of his living selling fresh rabbits in the surrounding villages, as other meat was rationed in wartime.

Henry also taught me practical skills, such as how to chop wood, make a whistle from a willow and clear scrub. For the latter he used a large hand scythe, while giving me a small sickle to do my part. Anything to do with firearms he usually left to my father, though I did sometimes see Henry returning from the river's mouth in the early morning with ducks and a shotgun slung over his back.

Henry was a respected member of the community, but he kept mostly to himself, seldom dropping by the local pub for a pint.

As time went on, the highlight of my school holidays was spending time with Henry, who was usually invited to take his supper at our kitchen table. For my eighth birthday, my father asked Henry to build a hutch for a couple of reddish brown and white rabbits he had bought me. I was really looking forward to having such handsome rabbits as pets.

But then something terrible happened. On July 28, three days before my birthday, Henry was killed. He had been riding my father's bicycle, descending the steep hill that ran between Thurlestone and Bantham. My father took me to the scene the next morning. There was still some dried blood and brain matter caked to the blacktop at the start of a sharp turn where the road bed dropped downward at its steepest point. My father comforted me by saying that Henry didn't suffer, as he was killed almost instantly.

"He was likely singing a song in Romani about his mother and forgot to brake," Jimmy explained.

Just what really caused the accident I was never told. I asked if the brakes on the bicycle had failed, but the machine seemed to have already disappeared, never to be seen again.

We attended the sad service at the old All Saint's Church in Thurlestone a couple of days later. It was my first funeral. But when we arrived home in the late afternoon, Marie suddenly burst into the living room with a broad smile, saying, "Henry has returned. Come and see."

We trooped into the kitchen, where to our surprise a light grey pigeon was perched on the back of the very chair in which Henry normally sat for his supper. "What a coincidence," my father said laughingly.

"I was at the sink when the bird suddenly flew in the open door," Marie said. It didn't seem troubled by the dogs, who couldn't reach it anyway. Then the bird was hurriedly hustled out the door through which it came.

But the following afternoon the pigeon reappeared and perched on the back of the same chair.

"Oh my God," said my father. "This can't be a coincidence. It must be Henry's spirit returning to where he felt most comfortable. What should we do?"

"At least we can offer Henry something to eat," Marie said as she gingerly put half a scone on a plate in front of the bird. The bird ignored the food, and after ten or fifteen minutes simply flew out the kitchen door again, but this time it went through the open door of the garage, where we kept chicken food and implements, and up into the rafters.

The next morning the bird was gone, only to reappear in the kitchen in the late afternoon. I supposed that either Marie had recounted the story at the local village shop or my father had done so at the local pub, because a dozen villagers showed up and asked if they could witness Henry coming into the kitchen. Some thought it was a joke, and others were convinced they were seeing a ghost. After a few days, even the local vicar came to determine whether an unnatural phenomenon warranted some action. Henry was becoming quite famous, such that ten days later a police constable arrived on his bicycle. He said that he had been told by his inspector to apprehend the bird in case it had an important message attached to it. Carrier pigeons were used extensively by the French Resistance during the war.

I wasn't home for this event, but apparently Henry was caught in the kitchen with my butterfly net. No message was found on the bird, but the number on the ring around its leg was noted by the constable. Later we were told that there was no carrier pigeon registered with that number in the UK.

As summer faded into autumn Henry flew less often into the kitchen, as the door was seldom open, but each night the bird continued to roost in the rafters of the garage. I believe that my parents may have started feeding it some grain.

Alas, while I was at boarding school a few months later, father said that he had found Henry lying dead on the garage floor. He suspected that my cousin, a small boy named Peter, might have killed the pigeon with a stone, though that was strongly denied by his mother. Marie asked the vicar if Henry's grave could be reopened to accept what was generally believed to be his roaming spirit, but permission was abruptly denied. The bird was apparently buried at the bottom of our garden, with a simple wooden cross spelling out Henry's full name. A troop of villagers attended, and there were numerous toasts to Henry at the pub.

But that's not quite the end of the story. In 2014 I decided to surrender my unlicensed guns to the West Vancouver Police. This included the .22-calibre Winchester rifle of my boyhood; my grandfather's Mannlicher rifle, which had been used for big-game hunting in India; and a 12-gauge shotgun I had inherited from my father. On the wooden stock of the shotgun was a small engraved plaque I hadn't noticed before: "Presented to Henry Baker for valour in his rescue at sea of Women's Royal Navy Service members."

I have long treasured the memory of Henry and his kindness to me as a boy, and of course the strange return of his spirit. It's made me appreciate the impact that kind adults can have on children, particularly those feeling somewhat troubled. It also made me somewhat more open to the existence of the supernatural realm. I don't think Henry had any family, certainly none came to his funeral, so perhaps sixty years later his strong character and kindness are only remembered by me.

I did pay a visit to Henry's grave in 1958 and spent an hour cleaning the moss off the almost-covered headstone. I also went down to the village of Bantham to pay my respects where his spirit was laid to its eternal rest, but the cottage we had lived in had been replaced by a mansion-like house with new landscaping. There was no sign of a grave at the bottom of the sloping garden.

When my father was alive we would occasionally reminisce about our adventures during the war, and the story of Henry would inevitably come up. But one thing my father never adequately explained was how he ended up with that shotgun. Perhaps it was a quid pro quo for him paying for Henry's gravestone.

CHAPTER 11

"I'm Cutting These Flowers for the Altar"

Anne Wooten, 1946

FOR THE FIRST TWO decades of my life, I felt that I never really accomplished anything useful. I was a poor performer academically and an abject failure at sports, though my hard head enabled me to show some modest prowess at amateur boxing. I certainly didn't receive much positive feedback. It is only nowadays that one hears about the importance of finding certain accomplishments to praise so that children have a feeling of self-worth.

Fortunately, I don't recall ever feeling totally depressed as a child. Through books I was able to retreat into the rich world of the imagination, where I was alternatively a Spitfire pilot, cowboy or commando.

But there was one exception. Most of the boys in Eagle House School had victory gardens. Three times a week we donned overalls, called "boiler suits," and tended our gardens, supposedly to help feed the nation. Most boys grew things that sprung up quickly from seed, such as radishes, lettuce and carrots, even peas and beans. I, however, went in for slightly more exotic produce, transplanting wild strawberries that I found in a nearby meadow. I grew them under glass jam jars so that the small, sweet fruit ripened early. I also grew flowers, transplanting daffodils and bluebells that I found during an excursion in the woods outside school bounds.

One day, I spied a tiny lupine plant growing in a crack along a flagstone pathway. When no one was looking, I dug it up with my trowel and transported it to my garden, wondering whether it would thrive. I gave it the best of care, including some manure that I pinched from a barn. And thrive it did, by next July becoming huge—it was, in fact, the largest lupine that I had seen before or have since. It thrust its many long-bodied flowers, thickly covered with rich red petals, upward in an exuberant display. Other boys joked to me about my lupine and threatened to destroy it, but I knew that they were just envious of my growing such magnificent flowers.

I don't know how word got around, but while I was tending my strawberries, I heard a woman's high-pitched voice: "You there, what's your name?"

"Audain," I replied.

"Well, Audain, I'm cutting these flowers for the altar," said Anne Wooten, the headmaster's wife.

Without another word the cardigan-clad woman bent down and cut the long-stemmed flowers. She then tramped off with an almost inaudible "Thank you," to which I just nodded. But that Sunday in chapel, I was privately ecstatic to see my magnificent lupines arranged in two vases on a white cloth on either side of the altar's silver cross.

No one said anything to me as we muttered our prayers and belted out the hymns, but I kept gazing at those flowers, privately knowing that I was the one who helped that neglected little lupine plant achieve such fame and glory.

I went to Eagle House in the spring of 1944. It was, my father told me, one of the best preparatory schools in England and I was lucky to go there—something he had been able to arrange because he was a graduate of nearby Wellington College, the famous public school with which Eagle House was associated. Wellington boys mainly went into the British army, which Jimmy said would be my destination unless the war ended soon, then I could go into the Canadian navy.

My opinion about a career was never solicited, though my father did occasionally emphasize how lucky I was not to have been living with my mother, in which case, according to him, I would likely have ended up as a pageboy at the Savoy Hotel. I'm not sure how my father contrived to end up with my sole custody, but I believe it may have been arranged by his sister Laura's solicitor. Laura was the sole trustee of the trust that Colonel Audain had left for my education, and she would have arranged matters to suit my father's wishes. My mother was not in much of a position to object because she had no means at this time beyond a three-pound-a-week retail job. Later, after she and my father divorced, she married a respectable barrister named George Carmichael.

Eagle House was actually a great improvement on Melbreck, my first boarding school. There were about sixty boys aged between seven and eleven. I cannot recall much about the academic side, except that we read a lot of Homer and Virgil. Homer because how else could one understand the New Testament if you couldn't read it in ancient Greek? And Virgil because the Romans were considered history's best soldiers—next to the British, that is.

There were, of course, a few unique customs. Every morning all the boys in the school formed a naked line to spend half a minute under a cold shower. The matron stood there with a stopwatch, saying "in" and "out." In summer, you could substitute the cold shower with swimming the length of the unheated outdoor pool, which had green slime cladding its walls.

A curious custom after breakfast was "tectum," which involved doing your "No. 2" in a series of unheated toilet stalls. You were only allowed to flush once you had reported to the matron at the door, "Been." If you couldn't perform, you had to force down a spoonful of Milk of Magnesia from a large bottle that she carried. On one occasion, a boy apparently said "Been" and the matron checked—he hadn't. Whether the after-lunch caning actually improved his constipation, I never learnt.

The school had some good points. There was a scout troop, though Jimmy didn't allow me to join since he was convinced that most scoutmasters were pedophiles. Also, I remember the headmaster's wife would invite "new boys" to tea on Sunday afternoons and afterwards read out loud to us. *The Wind in the Willows* seemed to be her favourite book. The school also had a small museum in which I took an interest. It was full of wondrous objects: bird nests, bones, and even a shrunken head from the

Amazon. Paul Wooten, the headmaster, was an ardent naturalist with a special interest in ospreys.

I found the food to be the most disagreeable part of my Eagle House experiences. It wasn't that there was just a lack of it, but its quality was often disgusting. The porridge was lumpy, the potatoes had often already started to sprout, the baked beans were cold, and the bread was regularly mouldy. Our elevenses treat often consisted of a mug of cocoa accompanied by a slice of bread smeared with meat fat called dripping. There were plenty of root vegetables: parsnips, swedes (rutabagas), beets and, on occasion, mangels (fodder beets). The latter was a vegetable I later discovered was usually grown for consumption by cattle, not humans.

Of course, you had to eat what you were given, whether you liked it or not. And invariably, we were hungry enough to swallow down whatever appeared on the table. One boy, though, drew the line at eating his monthly boiled egg, stamped "Canada," which when he peeled the shell away revealed the beginnings of a chick embryo. The master at the table told him to swallow it down as it wouldn't do him any harm. He did—then dashed away to vomit.

In the dining hall, there was a French table presided over by a master named Watson, who insisted all conversation be in that language. At the other tables it was the rule that you could only ask for something to be passed to you in Latin. The same rule applied for permission to leave the class, and 101 other things that one needed to communicate from time to time. Starting at my first Canadian school the next year, I was considered quite exotic when I assumed the same rules applied.

A good part of my childhood unhappiness could be attributed to my aforementioned poor performance in both the academic and sports fields. At Eagle House, I was invariably in the bottom one or two members of the class when academic results were pinned up on the noticeboard, as was the custom in those days. My mathematics and languages (French, Latin and Ancient Greek) were abysmal, only just balanced by a slightly better score in English and higher marks in history and geography.

At some of the schools I attended it was the custom to hand out prizes on the annual speech day, as it was often called, but on only one occasion was I called up to the podium to receive an award, and that was in grade seven for scripture. After the event, my father remarked, "Well, I suppose if you aren't good for anything else, the church will take you."

In fact I greatly enjoyed scripture, or Bible study, and was thrilled with stories in the book of Exodus as well as the Gospels. To me the Bible was a great treasury of adventure stories that I relished reading over and over again. And, of course, it's the King James version to which I am referring, that great bastion of the English language.

However, at all the boarding schools I attended, performance on the playing field seemed to matter more than success in the classroom. Yet, in sports, my performance was even more abysmal than it was in my academic studies. After attending a sports day at my school back when I was seven years old, I recall my father remarking that he would never bother to come again, having watched me come last in the consolation race and also collapse on my partner during the three-legged race.

Sports were compulsory, so I was obliged to play them all: rugby, soccer and cricket. When we had pickup practice games, I was always chosen last by the captain, even though he may have been a personal friend—this was an unavoidable indignity. In return, I actually hated playing the games. I considered rugby to be idiotic and resented having to charge backwards and forwards in the scrum while the halfback had the opportunity to do interesting things with the ball. In soccer, I was likewise bored with kicking what was originally a pig's bladder around a muddy field in the rain. And when fielding in cricket, I used to silently pray that the ball wouldn't be hit in my direction. When batting, I just held my bat firmly in front of the wicket. That technique didn't score me any runs, but at least it made it difficult to get me out, except on a LBW (leg before wicket). Even though severely chided by the coach, it didn't take me long to become known as Stonewall Audain.

At Eagle House, we also used to do cross-country runs, in which I would invariably come in last or second last. The leaders often had already showered and changed by the time I arrived. One day the presiding master remarked, "Audain, did you happen to stop for tea on the way?"

"No, sir," I replied. "I had a pint in a pub."

Headmaster Wooten was keen on beagling. All the boys had to chase a pack of beagle hounds cross-country, presumably chasing a hare. On one occasion, my pal Michael Cope and I surprised Wooten by being among the first to arrive at the kill. What we had done was sit in some hedgerows while the hounds chased off over the hill and dale only to circle back almost twenty minutes later almost in front of us.

Perhaps a reason for my ineptitude at sports was revealed after I reached the age of seventy and needed orthotics to insert in my footwear. When the supplier videotaped my walking test to determine the correct orthotic construction, it was plainly visible that my left foot meanders out of kilter with my right.

CHAPTER 12

"One Day You Are Going to Be a Governor"

Romani woman, 1946

IT'S FUNNY HOW THE mind works. We all have our own ways of dealing with stress. When I was studying social work, I learned about Freud's defence mechanisms, which are so fascinating and are still considered by many as essential to understanding human behaviour. Now that I am looking back on my life, I recall that for the most part I was fairly adept at creating my own defence mechanisms, which allowed me to carry on in the face of rejection at home and with very little self-esteem at school. I did it by developing an active imagination. Despite my low status among my peers, I was confident that one day I would surprise them.

For example, when I was eleven years old, I attended a Sunday morning service in Victoria's Christ Church Cathedral with my father, and during a boring sermon I recall daydreaming that one day I would shock the stodgy congregation in their Sunday suits by galloping on my white horse right up the centre aisle to the altar to arrest the dean for embezzling funds from the collection plate. At that age the radio program *The Lone Ranger* was my favourite.

Radio programs such as *The Roy Rogers Show* and *Gene Autry's Melody Ranch* stimulated my imagination and helped me withdraw into fantasy land. There was also an actual occurrence a couple of years earlier that gave me some confidence, despite my overwhelming feeling of unhappiness.

It happened in Devonshire in 1946. I had accompanied my father to a fair in the nearby market town of Kingsbridge, an outing that I had greatly looked forward to: riding the merry-go-rounds and trying my luck at the coconut shy and, who knows, perhaps receiving some special treats to eat. I was therefore disappointed when I found out the fair was actually just an area for the local farmers to offer their livestock, mainly cattle and pigs, for sale. My father said that he had come to find a piglet to fatten up on table scraps, but he then decided he had an appointment in a local pub, leaving me free to wander around on my own for an hour or two.

Not far from the fairgrounds, I found a paddock on which were parked half a dozen gaily covered Romani caravans—not the motorhomes the travelling people live in nowadays, but the old-fashioned horse-drawn-type vehicles.

Despite my early riding mishaps, I have always had an affinity for horses, so when I spied a couple of small ponies, I climbed over a paddock fence and spent half an hour or so petting them. Suddenly I heard an accusing voice behind me say, "Oy there, whatcha doing? My ma wants you." A gangly youth clad in what looked like a very stained brown suit waved towards a thin woman with white braided hair, a long, colourful shirt and a black shawl across her shoulders.

Somewhat frightened, I walked slowly over to the woman, and she gestured to a stew pot bubbling over a fire in front of her caravan. "Do you know what I am cooking?" the woman asked me. I just shook my head.

"Well, it's not a hedgehog," she said. "All you townspeople seem to think we travelling folk only eat hedgehogs. Anyway, have you ever been inside a Gypsy caravan?" she asked. I shook my head again.

"Are you scared of me?" she asked. Again I shook my head, though I certainly was!

Motioning me to follow her, she climbed up the wooden steps into the front of the caravan, with its circular roof, then sat me down on a stool. In front of her she had her proverbial crystal ball. Looking at me with her dark eyes, she extended her right palm inches from my face and said, "Cross my palm with silver and I'll tell you your luck."

I finally had to speak. "I'm sorry. I don't have even a penny on me."

Then she smiled, showing me surprisingly gleaming teeth. Her dark eyes sparkled. "Oh, I was just pulling your leg. I didn't bring you here as a customer. I just wanted to meet a very special young man."

"What do you mean 'special'?" I enquired.

"Well, I was watching you with the horses. You are a natural with them. By the way, not many boys would dare venture into the middle of a Gypsy camp, particularly a young gentleman like yourself," she explained.

"Why?" I asked.

"Oh, the townies often accuse us travelling people of stealing young children, and I know that there are even stories about us cutting them up and adding them to our cooking pots along with the hedgehogs," she said with a chuckle.

"Anyway, let's get on with it. Show me your hand," she ordered. I stuck out my palm.

"No, it's the back of your hand I want to see," she said. She turned it over and after a minute of silence she let go of it. "Well, I know you are lonely and unhappy at the moment. I don't need to see your hand to tell you that. But your hand tells me other things. What it tells me is that you are indeed a very special young man and one day you are going to be a governor, yes, and a famous one. And when you grow up you will be able to cross my palm not just with silver, but with gold," she said confidently.

"Beyond that, what I sense is that you have the special gift of reading people, like what was given to me." She took my hand again and said, "Let me tell you a few things about how we read hands." She spent a few minutes explaining what you can learn from the size and the shape of the hand, the fingers and the various mounds one finds on a palm.

I can only recall two or three points she made, but I confess that it did pique my curiosity to the point that in my teenage years I bought a couple of books on palmistry—a practice I never entertained seriously, though to this day I confess to collecting impressions about people by slyly looking at the shape of their hands.

Saying that I had to meet my father, I thanked the old Romani woman for her advice, scrabbled down the steps and ran back to the fair. After some enquiries, I discovered my father slumped down at a nearby pub table, in a terrible mood for being kept waiting.

"I am going to have to take a taxi home now," he said, "as I have had far too much cider. You can get home on my bike. I can promise you, though, that you are going to get a beating later."

Feeling very hungry, I biked the five miles back home and told my stepmother, Marie, what had happened. "Well, if your father was really that drunk he probably won't remember his promise to beat you for showing up late," she said.

She was right: Jimmy arrived home in a deplorable condition later in the evening and passed out on the living room sofa. The next day all he did was complain about a dreadful hangover and the effects of the local cider.

For decades, I never recounted my visit to the Romani camp, and indeed today my encounter with the fortune teller and her crystal ball seems more like a story out of a fairy tale than one that could have actually occurred.

But her assertion that one day I would eventually become a leader secretly served to buck up my spirits in the bleak times as I grew up.

CHAPTER 13

"You Better Look After Your Gov, Son"

London taxi driver, 1947

As MY FATHER AND I alighted from the boxy old London taxi with its roof luggage rack, the burly cloth-capped driver gratefully acknowledged the sixpence tip I gave him, saying, "You better look after your gov, son."

Jimmy was already ringing an electric bell at the bottom of some steep stairs inside the maze of Shepherd Market, where in distant times sheep were penned prior to slaughter. Upon entering the smoky flat upstairs, we were surrounded by women in various stages of undress. My father waved me to a seat, saying, "I won't be long. I just have some quick business to attend to in the room next door."

I couldn't find anything decent to read so I had to make do with a pictorial magazine that highlighted some of the current Paris fashions, with their amazingly short frocks. Meanwhile, the women, seemingly dressed in undergarments, cooed around me, asking innumerable questions, which I politely answered in what they considered my quaint upper-class voice. When they pried too hard for details about my father, I simply said I didn't know.

Meanwhile, they favoured me with a glass of strange-tasting lemonade.

True to his word, my father soon re-emerged, doing up his fly buttons while a slip-clad red-haired woman of indeterminable age helped him on with his suit jacket. Swigging a taste of my lemonade, he hurled the glass at the wall, saying, "Who told you to spike my boy's drink with gin?"

The woman fled in terror to the corner of the room, scared of what damage my father might wreak. But he abruptly left, pulling me down the stairs with him.

"We had better find a place to duck before the heat arrives," Jimmy said, pulling me roughly into a philatelic shop in a nearby arcade.

"I want to see your best South African stamps," my father ordered the proprietor, who said that he needed to send an assistant to the cellar, where the stamps had been stored for safety during the war. After five minutes wait my father grew bored.

"We don't have all night," he yelled sharply.

Nudging me, he intoned, "I think we should be safe to make a dash to the hotel up the street. In the meantime, is there anything you want?"

Despite what aspirations the proprietor may have initially felt about his fairly well-dressed customer, all we ended up doing was paying nine pence for a package of three triangular colonial stamps.

Prior to the brothel visit, the whole day had been quite extraordinary. I had left Eagle House for good that morning to shouts of "Good luck! Send us a postcard of the Rockies!" from schoolmates sentenced to another five weeks of purgatory before their summer holidays. We were moving to Canada: Jimmy had decided to return to Victoria and there attempt to make a fresh start.

My father met me that morning at Waterloo Station and sent my brown leather suitcase with a porter to Brown's Hotel, where we would apparently stay that evening, then he and I rode in a taxi to the Tower of London. There, we tramped through room after room, with special attention to the chamber where Anne Boleyn had spent her last days, and the staircase that had been used to snuff out the life of the little princes. We also visited Traitors' Gate, which my father claimed had been the last port of call for William Joyce, a.k.a. "Lord Haw-Haw," the Irish-American turncoat whose melodious voice brought Nazi propaganda to our radio in the dark days of war. He was hanged in January 1946.

When Jimmy, who was considerably overweight, decided that he was tired of walking, albeit in a jovial mood, he chose to collapse on some steps leading down to the chamber in which the Black Prince rode splendidly in armour on his wonderfully sculpted steed. I am not sure what motivated him, but my father then considered it auspicious to sing Danny Boy before a Beefeater advised that lolling on the steps and singing was not appropriate behaviour for visitors to the Tower of London.

"But I am one of Robin Hood's merry men," my father told the somewhat bemused guard.

"What's more, if you don't mind your manners I may have to give you a good thrashing with the sword the Black Prince took into battle," Jimmy added.

At that the Beefeater quickly disappeared, blowing a whistle. He returned with two mates. Two men grabbed my father, and the other grabbed my arm. Thus, we were somewhat unceremoniously thrown out the back door of the Tower of London. This incident spawned a story that has been recounted with great mirth on many family occasions.

But let me get back to this incredible day. For dinner I found myself with my mother at the legendary Trocadero restaurant, in London's West End. Though the food was nothing to write home about, my mother did confess years later that the occasion impoverished her for months.

Two things at dinner, though, I do recall. One, that I was fascinated with a Turkish gentleman wearing a fez, who pushed a cart around offering coffee to the diners. I urged my mother to buy one of these coffees so that I could witness the whole ceremony that accompanied it. The other was an invitation from my mother to dance with her to the music of the dinner-jacket-clad orchestra. I observed the men and women sashaying around the floor to the music. At nine years old I felt just too embarrassed to be paired with this much taller, though not unattractive, woman whom I hadn't lived with for five years, so I stubbornly said, "No thanks."

I found out later that this created great sadness, because my mother lived for dancing. While she claimed to hate Jimmy, she admitted that he was an ace on the dance floor.

Back at the hotel that night, my mother put me to sleep in a small room that adjoined Jimmy and Marie's. Earlier I had seen my father sitting cross-legged on the floor in the hotel corridor, playing poker with the hotel valet, using some miniature playing cards my mother had given me for the pending journey. It must have been a sad evening for Madeleine, as she was not to see me again for many years. But for me, that day was the start of a new period of my life.

The next morning, we arose at dawn and, accompanied by twenty-six pieces of luggage, as well as our two cocker spaniels, Jimmy, Marie and I took the boat train to Southampton, from where we sailed for Halifax aboard the yacht-like liner RMS *Aquitania*, with its four raked-back funnels. We were en route to the Canadian west.

CHAPTER 14

"Make Sure You Don't Become a Drunk Like Papa"

Deputy chief of police, 1947

NOWADAYS, YOU CAN FLY from London to Victoria, British Columbia, in the space of eleven hours, including a brief change of planes at Vancouver International Airport. Travelling with Jimmy and Marie in 1947, the trip took over two weeks, including a three-night stopover in Montreal.

The train trip from Waterloo Station south to Southampton was uneventful. However, boarding the RMS *Aquitania*, one of the world's great ocean liners, was like entering heaven for a nine-year-old boy. Having found my cabin down the companionway from my parents, I was desperate to explore. But when my father said that the first order of business was to get a good lunch in the first-class dining salon, with its snowy linen-clad tables and mirrored walls, I truly felt that I had entered the Elysian Fields. The greatest thrill at lunchtime wasn't the food we were served, but the bowl full of warm white dinner rolls, which to my amazement were accompanied by a heaping dish full of butter balls. I had neither seen nor tasted pure white rolls in my life, let alone as much butter as I could slather on them.

After lunch I climbed up to the upper decks to visit our spaniels, ensconced in their comfortable kennels. I gazed across the harbour at the huge RMS *Queen Elizabeth*, which at that time was the biggest passenger ship in the world. It was then and there that I decided that what I wanted to do when I grew up: be a kennel boy on the *Queen Elizabeth*.

That afternoon, after we cleared port and dropped the pilot, the *Aquitania* began to slice into the North Atlantic rollers. I stood on the upper deck watching Eddystone lighthouse fade as we left the last of England behind. I felt that I was embarking on an adventure as wondrous as Kim's Great Trunk Road. I loved every hour aboard the ship and explored it from stem to stern: the engine rooms, the kitchen's wine cellar, the massive chain lockers, the lifeboats. Because a letter had come from father's uncle, Sir Rupert Bromley, a Gentleman Usher at Buckingham Palace, the Cunard Company captain told my parents that I could have the run of the ship and could even be a guest on the navigating bridge at any time except when entering harbour.

Thinking back on it, the ship was divided, like British society, into numerous classes, all of which seemed to have their own quarters, especially for dining. There was a small first-class salon, and lower down a larger one for cabin class, and then a dining area for tourist class, which seemed to be occupied by a hundred English war brides, many with babies. Below them, in the bowels of the ship, was a large crowd of former Polish soldiers who had elected to live in Canada instead of returning to Soviet-occupied Poland. They slept on steel bunks three tiers high. The captain told my parents that his main challenge was keeping the sex-starved Poles from assaulting the war brides, and vice versa. Come morning, some brides could be seen emerging from the Polish troops' deck.

The crew's quarters were even more cramped than those of the Polish troops. The stewards seemed to have bunks, whereas the seamen and stokers made do with hammocks. This was a sleeping arrangement which, to my surprise, they told me they preferred, as hammocks sway naturally with the ship's movements.

As the ship experienced an unusual summer gale, it turned out that, like my father, I was a good sailor, never missing a meal in the dining salon. With the games of shuffleboard and table tennis in the more sheltered part of the deck, my frequent visits to the kennels, films from a 16-mm projector in the evening, and the *Aquitania*'s steady twenty-two knot speed, the days passed quickly, but I was elated when the captain told me that if I came to the bridge at dawn the next morning, I could be among the first passengers to see the Canadian coastline.

And how different the conifers surrounding the entrance to Halifax harbour looked from the British countryside, and how exciting it was to land at Pier 21, be processed quickly through Canadian immigration, and board the Canadian Pacific train for Montreal. The only kerfuffle was when the baggage master on the train insisted that we buy muzzles for our dogs, with Marie adamantly lying that they had never bitten a single human being.

The dinner in the train's dining car was magnificent. But what intrigued me more was the men's washroom, with its two brass spittoons in which water sloshed around. When I asked my father what they were for, he suggested it was where cigars went when you were finished smoking them. The sleeping car porter later told me otherwise. It turned out that the porter, a Black resident of Halifax, was actually a great source of information, answering my myriad questions about Canada and, in particular, its trains. After dinner, I was delighted to find that the porter had made up my upper bunk, hidden as it was behind heavy green curtains, and he showed me how to enter and exit it without having to call for the ladder. My father and Marie had a drawing-room compartment further down the train.

In Montreal, we had adjoining rooms in the Windsor Hotel. The only difficulty occurred when one of the spaniels peed on the dark green carpet in the long corridor from the elevators. I recall Marie profusely apologizing to the maids and asking Jimmy to tip them generously.

There was something my parents hadn't told me about Canada: the people seemed to speak mostly French, which I could generally understand but was timid about speaking. To my surprise, on arrival in Montreal, Marie insisted on only speaking French, even to my father and me, something that created a little difficulty when we went to lunch at a posh golf club the following day and the waitress couldn't speak French. Marie had the girl on the verge of tears, with my father kindly intervening to say, "*Poulet* means chicken." After the meal, we went for a drive in an open calèche around the Old Quarter of Montreal.

The next morning, Marie woke me for breakfast and told me that my father hadn't come home last evening. She was not too concerned, simply saying that he would probably turn up later in an untidy state. In the afternoon, Marie took me to a movie theatre. When she was told that they couldn't sell a ticket to a child, she demanded to see the manager, who in turn advised her that children under sixteen were not allowed to attend films in the city of Montreal. Marie was furious. She knew that the church was powerful in Canada, but never imagined that it could be so intolerant. Later we learned that the Quebec government's prohibition followed a movie theatre fire in which a great many children had died.

When we returned to the hotel, my father still had not been sighted, so Marie got the concierge to telephone the police. They confirmed that they were indeed holding a Monsieur Audain, who was charged with damaging a Saint Catherine Street nightclub. Marie immediately left me at the hotel, in charge of the spaniels, while she went off to visit my father. She returned an hour later and told the concierge that she needed the best lawyer in Montreal to get him out of jail. I went to sleep to the sound of her sobbing in the next room.

The next morning Marie disappeared after breakfast, for most of the day, telling me to order whatever I wanted on the room service menu. When she finally returned in the late afternoon, she was smiling, and said, "Everything's been arranged and you will see your father tomorrow."

In the morning, we walked next door, to Windsor Station, to board the transcontinental CPR train. Jimmy still wasn't apparent, but ten minutes before the train departed, he arrived shackled in handcuffs, escorted by two Montreal policemen and an officer with gold braid on his cap, apparently the deputy chief of police. The deputy chief sternly addressed Marie and admonished her to never let her husband visit Montreal again, because police records indicated that he had gotten into the same kind of trouble there nine years previously. To me, he kindly said, "*Bon voyage*. Make sure you don't become a drunk like Papa."

Years later, Marie told me that she had gone to the chairman of the Royal Trust Company for help, and he, together with a senior lawyer, had brokered a deal whereby the charges were dropped in return for the

Royal Trust making good for the damages that my father had caused. The trust company was not out of pocket, as they simply deducted the sum they paid, plus interest, from the legacy that was due to my father on the next death of one of his Dunsmuir aunts.

The trip across the country was rather boring at first, as mile after mile of trees and lakes rolled by the windows. But at every station where at least a five-minute stop was scheduled, it was my job to retrieve the dogs from the baggage car and walk them. After a day of crossing the Prairies, we reached Calgary, and the excitement started to build again as an extra engine and an open observation car were added for the trip through the Rockies. To my delight, between Banff and Lake Louise, I was given permission to ride on the footplate of the lead engine with the engineer and the fireman, where I could be first to see any deer or elk as we traversed the national park.

Jimmy behaved like a perfect gentleman throughout the rest of the trip, saying that he had sworn off alcohol forever. That wasn't too difficult for him: in those days the dining and observation cars on the trains were completely dry! Marie was shocked when she couldn't get a glass of wine at dinner. And she was surprised that she hadn't heard a word of French since leaving Montreal.

The final day of the trip was the most exciting. At dawn, I watched as we wound our way down beside the surging Fraser River, arriving at 7:30 a.m. in Vancouver, followed by a brisk walk with the dogs over to the CPR pier to board the *Princess of Victoria,* which sailed at 9:00 a.m. Standing on the deck as we pulled away from the pier, with my father pointing to the Marine Building and the Hotel Vancouver, I wondered why he hadn't told me that Vancouver had skyscrapers, just like New York City.

"New York is an important city, whereas Vancouver is just an ugly town run by lumber barons. With mountains around it, it rains most of the time and doesn't compare in beauty to Victoria—where we will thankfully be in a few hours," Jimmy explained.

I don't recall our arrival in Victoria harbour, except that my father's cousin Joan Humphreys was there to meet us.

Later that afternoon, Jimmy took me across the Gorge Road from the San Sebastian Auto Court, where we were staying, to a corner grocery store, where I vividly remember two things: the Chinese man at the counter, as I had never seen an Asian person before, and the stacks of comic books that could be purchased for a dime. As we settled in that evening, I greedily commenced reading about the exploits of Superman and the Lone Ranger.

CHAPTER 15

"Your Thighs Are Too Thick"

Eddie Haddad, 1950

IT'S STRANGE HOW ONE tends to remember certain innocuous remarks and forget others. I was lying on an exercise mat in the top-floor gym at the Victoria City Police Station when my boxing trainer Eddie Haddad, a British Empire champion, said to me, "Your thighs are too thick. We need to get some weight off them."

I must have been about thirteen years old at the time, for I had already been a member of the Victoria Police Boxing Club for a couple of years.

"Every night you come in here, I want you to lie on your back and roll the medicine ball up and down the back of your legs. Also, whatever amount of rope you have been skipping daily, double it," Haddad said.

He was a good trainer who put up with me even though I lost two-thirds of my fights. Totally useless at other sports, I didn't mind boxing because there was no team involvement, it was just you in the ring with an opponent.

I'd learned by then that many people, especially women, were dissatisfied with their bodies, or at least parts of them. But up to that point in my life, I hadn't had a complex about my thighs. And I had never even thought about comparing mine to anyone else's!

It was at my father's instigation that I started boxing. When I was eleven he drove me in his car to a small boxing club near Victoria. There was no choice in the matter for me. I was told by Jimmy, "You're a disaster at all the sports you have attempted, so the least you can do is stand up, take some punishment, and then learn to defend yourself."

Many years later my father told me that the reason he insisted on my embarking on an amateur boxing career was that he was afraid I was becoming a homosexual. He added, "When I saw that you were able to stand and take a good hiding in the ring, I realized that you weren't a latent pansy." I recall being more astonished than hurt at this disclosure.

Thus, for three or four years I trained twice weekly at the Victoria City Police gym and fought bouts at least monthly during the winters. They had the Bronze Gloves, Silver Gloves and Golden Gloves, and I was in them all. On one occasion, I was even put into the Buckskin Gloves, a competition for First Nations youngsters, as they were short of kids in my weight class.

I liked two things about the boxing experience. The first was that it allowed me to meet a whole range of boys outside those I encountered at the exclusively White private schools I attended. Paul, the son of a celebrated Vancouver Island wrestler called Chief Thunderbird, became one of my closest friends. Somehow I achieved a bit more respect, perhaps because of my ability to take a good battering without being knocked out. Even if I got knocked down, I bounced up right away without waiting for the referee's count. I recall one occasion, in Port Alberni, when the referee stopped a fight because I had an under-eye cut that was bleeding profusely, and I was absolutely furious about it.

The other aspect I enjoyed about amateur boxing was the travel we did with the team, all up and down Vancouver Island, and to Seattle, Portland and, of course, Vancouver. When we went to Vancouver, we would fight in the Exhibition Gardens building at the Pacific National Exhibition, but the morning weigh-in would be at Fillipone's Diamond Taxi gym, which would later be incorporated into the infamous Penthouse nightclub.

I always had trouble making my weight. When I ended up as a welterweight at 156 pounds, I had to starve myself for a day or two before the weigh-in, after which I would be allowed poached eggs on toast to give me a little strength for the fight. But after fights we would be taken for thick pan-fried steaks at one of those ubiquitous cafés that served "Chinese and Canadian Food."

CHAPTER 15

On February 27, 1948, Jimmy was given a new lease on life. He gave up drinking and became an ardent member of Alcoholics Anonymous, helping other problem drinkers by telling of his harrowing experiences in prisons and mental hospitals. To keep sober, every week, and sometimes twice a week, he would attend Alcoholics Anonymous meetings. He had never been able to keep a job for more than a month after being court-martialled out of the army in 1940, but in Victoria he took up a series of jobs, eventually becoming a provincial civil servant. It was at this time that my father developed an interest in becoming an amateur boxing official, first a referee and then a judge. It was soon afterwards that he dragooned me into the ring.

To my surprise, "Mike Audain," as I was called on the billboards, developed a bit of a following in Victoria, particularly among the zoot-suited youth who at times rumbled with the young naval recruits at HMCS *Naden*, perhaps because one of my victories at the age of fourteen was winning a fight against a twenty-year-old sailor. I was big for my age, so I invariably fought men considerably older than me, as they were in the same weight class. Amazingly I won my class in the Vancouver Island Silver Gloves one year, perhaps because it only took one bout to do so, but when it came to the BC Golden Gloves I was eliminated in an early round. I had won boxing cups at my schools, where boxing was compulsory, but the fights weren't anything as combative as those that I encountered while boxing for the Victoria City Police Club.

By the age of sixteen, when my sight had deteriorated to the point that I couldn't clearly see my opponents' eyes, Jimmy reluctantly conceded that I had had enough boxing.

CHAPTER 16

"It Could Be a Bear Becoming a Man or Perhaps a Man Becoming a Bear"

Chief Mungo Martin, 1951

COMING HOME FROM SWIMMING lessons at the Crystal Gardens pool, I had often seen the carvers working in Thunderbird Park. Most people in Victoria knew that Kwakwa̱ka̱'wakw chief Mungo Martin, from Alert Bay, and his apprentice sons had been hired by the provincial museum to replicate the ancient totem poles whose wood was rotting away.

One day I finally became bold enough to ask a question of the small-statured man chiselling away on a big cedar log. I slipped under the rope meant to keep the public away.

"Excuse me, sir, is that a human face or a bear you are carving?" I enquired.

The old carver stopped his work and looked at me for a minute in surprise, then with a twinkle in his eye said, "Hmm, it could be a bear becoming a man or perhaps a man becoming a bear."

Mungo Martin went on for fifteen minutes, telling me about the original peoples of the Northwest Coast, who believed that animals could transform into humans and vice versa. He said, summing up, "After all, we all came from the raven. That's why we are all connected and should respect one another."

I was impressed by that and went home and asked my father that evening if it was likely that our dogs could become human beings in their next life. To which Jimmy replied, "It's more likely you will become a worm if you don't pull up your socks in the classroom and on the playing field."

In recent years, I have often been asked how I became interested in art. Was there art in our home? Was I any good in art at school?

The answer to those questions is a resounding "No." There was no art on the wall in our house except the heads of dead animals shot by Colonel Audain and heaps of photos of family members with their horses and dogs. In my grade-five art class, I recall distinguishing myself by getting four out of ten as my painting of a maple leaf wasn't realistic enough. I had never visited an art gallery during my UK days, assuming that there were indeed some open during the war, and Victoria lacked a public art gallery when I was young. That's why Emily Carr left most of her painting inventory to the Vancouver Art Gallery.

But from the age of ten, I had been fortunate to attend Saturday morning lectures at the Royal British Columbia Museum, where director Clifford Carl exposed us not just to European art, but to that of the Northwest Coast, where the First Nations peoples had been creating significant art for thousands of years. Not only did Dr. Carl show us magic lantern slides of totem-poled villages he had visited, but he would talk at length about the creative genius he had found up the coast, in carving and weaving of all dimensions. Afterwards, I would often drift upstairs to the glass-topped display cases full of masks, rattles and other strange objects, which occasionally Dr. Carl would give us access to and even let us handle while wearing pristine white museum gloves.

Those images were reinforced by a book that I was given with colour photographs of Northwest Coast art, which I remember taking to my Ontario boarding school in grade ten. On occasion, I thumbed through it to remind myself of the images I associated with home.

Later in life, I was delighted to find that my first wife, Tunya, was interested in art, the more challenging the better. After we were married, in the early 1960s, we started to gingerly buy works of art. I believe that fifty dollars was our limit, because I recall that we missed out on a wonderful bunch of Claude Breeze drawings that had a seventy-dollar price tag.

I bought art occasionally through the 1970s and 1980s, but didn't really start collecting in earnest until I felt financially stable enough to do so, in the 1990s. As the first decade of the twenty-first century arrived, my acquisitions became more oriented to the work of the First Nations of the Northwest Coast, and my fascination with the art of our region came full circle, back to the day my interest was piqued by that small, bright-eyed old man with the headband in the Victoria carving shed, who was busy creating a bear that was becoming a man, or perhaps a man becoming a bear.

CHAPTER 17

"Don't Bother Coming Back Tomorrow"

Television shop owner, 1951

A MONTH BEFORE I turned fourteen, Jimmy decided that it was time I got a summer job. He said that although our family obviously didn't need the money, it was a good idea for a lad like me to do some hard physical work.

So the next day, I put on my army cadet boots and filled in some forms at the National Employment Service in downtown Victoria. When it came to experience, I lied, saying "farming and fishing," though it's true that I had picked strawberries for one day and also fished with my father. I sat on a bench at the back of the employment office for a couple days waiting to be assigned to a job, but nothing happened.

The next morning my father came with me, saying that he was going to fix it. He had a word with someone he knew in the back office, and then I was told to stand across the street from the employment office and to immediately show up when this man signalled from the second-floor window. Sure enough, it worked, and I was assigned to report the same morning to a shop that sold televisions.

Not having operated a television, since we didn't have one at home, I was a little apprehensive about how I was going to sell or perhaps even repair them. "Don't worry," the shop owner said. "You just have to deliver the sets and install the aerials on the roof." When I told the owner that I didn't have a driving licence because I was only fourteen, he seemed a bit taken aback. "Well, then, I will deliver the sets and leave you with a ladder to secure the aerial on the roof. Just point it at Seattle's KOMO station," he said, giving me a small compass and the correct bearing.

The first house we arrived at was a bungalow with an aerial already installed on the roof. All I had to do was climb up and attach a new cable out through the people's living room window, which I was able to do. Whether it worked or not couldn't be determined, because until late afternoon the station apparently only broadcast a static signal.

The next home was more challenging, since it was two storeys and lacked an aerial. I ascended to the roof with a rather heavy and ungainly aerial in my left hand. Once there, I found the steepness of the pitch and the cedar shakes impossible to climb in my army cadet boots, so I gently put the aerial down on the roof, only to see it plunge all the way down into a flower bed.

When I ascended again, this time in my socks, I was somehow able to scramble up to the roof peak with the aerial, but then I couldn't figure out how to secure it with the screwdriver that I had been given. The flange at the base wouldn't fit over the shakes. Somehow I got it secured on one side and innovatively used one of my bootlaces to temporarily prop it up on the other side while I loosened the fitting to rotate the aerial spokes to the compass direction that was supposed to produce a picture once the cable was connected.

By now, the shop owner was back with his truck and seemed unimpressed with how I had temporarily rigged the aerial with my bootlace. "I've got lots of fittings in this truck for every type of roof. Why didn't you select the correct ones in the first place?" he said, giving me a fitting and screws for cedar-shake roofs. It took me another forty-five minutes to install the aerial correctly, and magically it produced a signal down in the homeowner's living room.

Back at the shop, with half an hour off for a late lunch, the owner told me that after such an exciting morning, he felt it best that I spend the afternoon sweeping out the shop. When I had completed the job he issued me a cheque for $6.25, telling me that the remainder was deducted for unemployment insurance and income tax. "And don't bother coming back tomorrow," my employer added.

CHAPTER 17

The next day I actually landed a much better job through my father's contact at the National Employment Service, on the Victoria docks. It paid $1.37 an hour, a considerable sum in those days. But that job only lasted a week. Fortunately, I was then taken on for the rest of the summer by a family friend, Ian Ross, who operated Victoria's world-famous Butchart Gardens. There I was paid fifty cents an hour for wiring advertising signs called "bumper stickers" onto the rear of visitors' cars.

CHAPTER 18

"Most Men Are Gullible"

Michael Garthwaite, 1954

IN THE COURSE OF a life one is likely influenced by many people, but when looking back there are usually a few people about whom one can say that, without having come across them, you would have been a different man or woman. In my case, I believe that four people fall into that category: my father, Jimmy Audain, Vern Paulus, Reuben Baetz, and Michael William Gladwin Garthwaite.

While I have written about my father, and later in the book will do so about Vern Paulus, I don't really have any particularly fascinating stories to tell about Reuben Baetz, who was executive director of the Canadian Council of Social Development when I worked in Ottawa in the early 1970s. Suffice it to say that Reuben, who later became an Ontario government minister, had a masterful way of dealing with public officials, which helped me immensely while I was in Ottawa and in the years that followed. His advice was to never ask anything of them until you have forged friendly personal relationships over a meal or, even better, at the hockey rink or on the golf course.

But perhaps I should tell you something about Michael Garthwaite, who came into my life when he arrived at Trinity College School, in Ontario, at the start of the summer term in 1953 and became my roommate the following term. A tall, fine-featured, handsome lad who distinctively combed his hair straight backwards, he was, I suppose, more patrician than rugged in appearance. Michael was the son of British shipping and sugar magnate Sir William Garthwaite. While he was patrician in his speech and attitude, there was nothing florid or particularly overbearing in his manner. The boy arrived mid-term because there had been "a bit of difficulty," as he put it, at his Swiss boarding school. Prior to that he had put in a year or two at Downside, the large Catholic school in the UK.

At first, Garthwaite seemed to be a bit lost, so Housemaster Angus Scott asked me to show him the ropes, and I suppose we clicked because I knew what it was like to have been sent to a British boarding school. So that's why the following term we ended up sharing a room, despite Garthwaite's assertion that it would have been his preference to have a private bedroom.

Some years ago I came across a letter from Headmaster Philip Ketchum to my father saying that Garthwaite was the most extraordinary boy he had ever had in his school. I believe that Jimmy must have been complaining about Garthwaite's influence on me.

Well, in what way was this sixteen-year-old so vastly different from the rest of us? In the first place he made it clear that he wasn't the slightest interested in things Canadian. Saying that he considered ice hockey a "colossal bore" was heresy to us back then. And he made it clear that he considered Montreal and especially Toronto provincial towns full of inconsequential "bourgeois" (yes, he used that word) people. He had no opinion about Victoria, where I lived at the time, except to speculate that it must share the common characteristics of most colonial capitals.

You might think that a boy like Garthwaite, with his superior airs, might come in for a good deal of bullying. Actually, he was circumspect in those to whom he confided his opinions, and his proficiency at academics won him respect, though like me he abhorred team sports. But he was a reasonable performer on the squash courts and in the pool, and he excelled on the tennis courts and ski slopes.

Garthwaite's attitude to the masters at TCS was one of amused contempt. He was as deferential as he needed to be, but at the same time privately said he regarded none of them as scholars because they had got their jobs with a reasonably clean war record, a mediocre degree or a liking for rugby. The boy was totally fluent in French and Latin, and he claimed his knowledge of English literature far exceeded that of our masters. Only in mathematics and science did he have to swot up before pulling off a first-class mark in examinations.

Garthwaite did indeed come from another world—one situated in Monte Carlo, New York, Nassau and various venues in between. He consorted with a crowd that they used to call the café society, headed by the Duke and Duchess of Windsor and made up of sundry members of royal households and show business. While it was fascinating to hear him talk about it, I wasn't in the least bit envious, because it was a group that appeared to have achieved so little.

"Don't worry about achievement," Garthwaite would say. "That's not the purpose of life."

When I asked him what was, he was less clear.

"If I were you, I wouldn't worry about such questions," he would advise. "Instead, just be aware of what the great religious leaders and philosophers had to say so that you will never be surprised or duped by those who want to have power over you. To me, what I value above all is freedom—the four freedoms mentioned by Franklin Delano Roosevelt. And at the moment I feel shackled by my father's requirement that I attend school in order to collect my allowance. I just can't wait until I am twenty-one to dispense with this nonsense."

When asked what he planned to do with his life, and did he have a career in mind, Garthwaite was again vague. "Nothing special," he would say with a chuckle. "Just be free."

Years later, watching *Brideshead Revisited* on television, I wondered whether Garthwaite had actually modelled himself after the character Charles Ryder in Evelyn Waugh's novel, as there seemed to be so much resemblance, with the exception that I never saw Garthwaite carrying around a teddy bear.

Garthwaite was certainly a man of style. His Savile Row suits were immaculate. He explained to me how to tell the difference between a tailored jacket and one off the peg. He bought his shoes at Lobb's, on Jermyn Street in London, and his hats at Dobbs. Like many of us at school, he smoked furtively, but only Balkan Sobranie cigarettes. His favourite drinks were ones we never knew existed, such as daiquiris or Bellinis, a specialty of Harry's Bar in Venice. He didn't shave with a Gillette blade but used a self-sharpening razor that he described as the Rolls Royce of safety razors. For a couple of months he even hid a Jaguar roadster near the school for weekend assignations. Hollywood films were not worth watching unless you were a friend of the producer or director. Rather, Garthwaite introduced me to the French New Wave cinema, to the point that I became enthralled with films by Truffaut, Resnais and Godard.

When it came to culture, Garthwaite was full of opinions. He found the British painters gloomy, but seemed very conversant with the Old Masters, being particularly drawn to Caravaggio. In music, he claimed familiarity with all the classical composers. He even loved Wagner. But I believe it must have been from Garthwaite that I developed my aversion to Mozart.

You can imagine that as a small-town boy, and Victoria in those days was a very small town, it was easy for me to fall under Garthwaite's influence, and if I repeated even a small portion of his opinions at home, I must have indeed sounded insufferable.

When it came to religion, despite his Roman Catholic affiliation, Garthwaite claimed to be agnostic, not because he necessarily believed in any particular faith, but rather because he claimed that atheism was a religious choice and therefore one that he wasn't interested in making.

As a fairly devout Christian, though not a person inclined to take every word in the Bible as the revealed truth, I used to argue long and hard with Garthwaite after lights-out about the presence of a higher power who had sent prophets such as Moses, Jesus and Mohammed down to Earth to teach mankind morality and correct behaviour. But argue as I might, I felt I was always on the losing end of the discussion.

After Garthwaite left the school, in June 1954, I only saw him once again, when I visited him at his McGill University residence. I recall that we returned there in the early hours of the morning after partying in some Saint Catherine Street nightclubs. Garthwaite had to lower the fire escape so that I could scramble up the outside of the building to his room, where I was billeted comfortably on the floor.

I wrote him once or twice, and on one occasion in the 1950s received a note back from the Beach Club in Palm Beach, Florida, telling me to post him there or at the Beach Club in Monte Carlo. Since then he seems to have vanished, other than a very brief entry in Debrett's noting his birth.

As to Garthwaite's influence on me, I don't believe that he turned me into a dilettante. He did endow me, though, with a certain sense of cynicism about the claims of people in authority or with special expertise. He also gave me more of an international perspective, realizing how small and mostly incidental to world history our country of Canada has been. On the other hand, I didn't envy him for his family wealth, believing from my early days that it was always preferable to make one's own way in the world.

One Saturday in Toronto, after playing in a soccer match against Upper Canada College, I went off with Garthwaite to watch a film starring Brigitte Bardot. I can't recall any of the plot, but I was certainly enamoured with the actress, particularly as it was the first time I had seen nudity on screen.

Coming out of the theatre, Garthwaite decided we needed a drink. "I understand they have just opened cocktail bars in this ghastly town. Let's try our luck at the Royal York Hotel."

When I reminded him that I was still only sixteen, Garthwaite, who was just eleven days older than me, responded, "Wonderful, that's exactly my age."

As we entered the large bar on the ground floor of the hotel, Garthwaite muttered, "Let me do the talking."

"But I don't know what to order," I said.

"Don't worry about that. Just shut up and I'll do the talking."

We hadn't sat down for more than a couple of minutes when a red-jacketed waiter scurried up saying, "Do you boys know there's a minimum age of twenty-one here?"

"That's what I am," said Garthwaite. "Now, my good man, kindly send me the manager."

Shortly after, a splendidly uniformed gentleman appeared, saying, "Excuse me, but you young gentlemen need to leave."

"I'm not leaving until I've had a drink. Bring me a daiquiri and a Manhattan for my friend."

"Where's your ID?" asked the bar manager.

Garthwaite replied, "I don't happen to have my passport with me at the moment. But here's my card and, by the way, I wanted to speak to the hotel manager—not someone of your station."

The man stalked away, muttering and staring intently at the card.

We waited in silence for almost five minutes before a short man in striped trousers and a black jacket appeared, gingerly handing over Garthwaite's card.

"Excuse me, sir, but should I address you as Lord Garthwaite?"

"You can call me anything you want, but I am desperately in need of a drink!"

"My Lord," said the manager, "we're honoured to have you and your guest at the Royal York Hotel. I'm sorry if you are being inconvenienced by my staff, but we seldom have the opportunity to entertain gentlemen related to the Queen, who may not be familiar with our local liquor laws in Canada."

And then to the waiter he said, "Bring these gentlemen what they need. And by way of apology, the first drink will be on the house."

Garthwaite stood and shook the manager's hand. Keeping a straight face he said, "Sir, you can be assured that Buckingham Palace will hear of your hospitality."

When he sat down, Garthwaite said laughingly, "You see, Michael, a little bit of bluffing can get you far in this world, as most men are gullible."

When I asked if that was a fake card, he said, "No, it was in fact my father, Sir William Garthwaite's, card. But he didn't do very much to get his baronetcy. Prime Minister Lloyd George was practically selling them back then, though it's true that an awful lot of our family's ships were sunk by enemy action in the First War."

I didn't at all enjoy my first Manhattan, but after the second I began to acquire the taste, and for the rest of my association with Garthwaite that's the drink I dutifully ordered, with my roommate, of course, always insisting on paying the tab.

CHAPTER 19

"I Would Expel You if You Didn't Live 2,500 Miles Away"

Headmaster Philip Ketchum, 1955

PHILIP KETCHUM, HEADMASTER OF Trinity College School in Port Hope, Ontario, seemed like a distant figure during the three years I spent in his school. A tall, greying man, he had an understated manner—generally serious but with a slight twinkle in his eye. He was widely respected by staff and students alike.

I believe that Ketchum vaguely knew who I was. He had met my father the day I arrived at the school in September 1952, but I can only recall one occasion on which he spoke to me during my first couple of years at TCS. That was when he bade me "Merry Christmas, Audain" at breakfast the morning after I had been sorting mail all night in the Port Hope post office. There were no funds that year to take me back to Victoria for Christmas and, anyway, I needed to make some money on the side. I joined two boys from Chile as the only ones left behind at the school during the Christmas vacation. But the following day I was invited to stay with Phil Spicer, a friend who lived near Hamilton, Ontario.

As with all the schools I attended, I loathed TCS. It was four and a half days by train and ferry away from my home in Victoria. There was a strong emphasis on sports, at which I was still wretched, other than boxing. At TCS, the most important sports were Canadian football and ice hockey. Having played rugby for years, it was incomprehensible to me seeing boys put on helmets and shoulder pads to toss a ball around. And as for ice hockey, I had never been on skates, nor seen a hockey game.

CHAPTER 19

My father's sister, Laura, was still the trustee of the fund left by my grandfather to provide for my education, and her husband, Ivo Henderson, had attended TCS in the 1920s. Laura persuaded my father that by attending the school I could meet future members of the Canadian elite.

Not knowing a soul—but being a veteran "new boy," with TCS being my eleventh school—I just kept my head down for the first year and tried to be as inconspicuous as possible. The inevitable hazing and fagging system at school didn't bother me much, nor did the sports that I elected to take part in: soccer and swimming. It was compulsory to play a sport every afternoon.

In my second year I began to get a bit of attention for the roles that I played in the school dramas, seeming to have the capacity to evoke a good deal of laughter, but when Speech Day came around in early June, I failed to receive any recognition—which may have had something to do with my parents' lack of involvement in school affairs. At least, that was my theory at the time, because quite a few boys seemed indignant that I wasn't given a drama prize.

Around this time I started to take an inept interest in the opposite sex, inviting a particularly attractive usherette from the Port Hope Theatre to the annual dance, amid hordes of girls from Branksome Hall and Havergal College, two of Toronto's all-girl private schools.

In my final year there were thirty-one boys in sixth form, thirty of whom were appointed to some position: school prefect, house prefect or house officer. I was the odd chap out. Thus, I was never given the privilege of wearing anything other than the regular school tie.

Given the circumstances I decided to go underground and form my own status system. Together with close friends Phil Spicer and Tony Martin, I started a group called the Black Thumb Society, which was a bit of a parody of the Black Hand organization that operated in Serbia prior to World War I. We adopted titles for ourselves; I became Minister of Revolts, Revolution and Spontaneous Demonstrations. Membership cards were issued with our pictures on them and a form of Fascist salute, with the bearer's black thumbprint on the opposite side. These we sold for a dollar each.

The whole thing was considered a joke until the May 24 fireworks celebration, held on a terrace next to the school. It was the custom to invite the mayor and members of the Port Hope Council, as well as school staff and their families, to our celebration of what in Ontario in those days was still referred to as Queen Victoria's birthday.

As dark fell and the rockets started to be fired off into the night sky, suddenly my voice boomed out from loudspeakers hidden in the ivy that climbed high on the school's brick walls. I don't recall exactly what I said, but I believe that my message was something to the effect that now was the time for TCS students to take over the world and imprison the adults who had done such a poor job of running it! I had prerecorded the message on tape. As the message droned on, my friends and I keeled over in fits of laughter. The fireworks stopped, and staff members convened about how to stop this booming voice calling for world revolution.

Finally, there was a banging on the door. It was the housemaster, Mr. Denning, who demanded entry. But the boy we had enlisted to guard the door refused to open it until I gave the order. When I did, in charged Denning, accompanied by two other masters, who yanked the cord out of the tape recorder. The fireworks started again a few minutes later.

The next morning at breakfast there were cheers and clapping as I walked into the dining hall, but a lot of scowling from the staff. Later that morning I received a summons to report to the headmaster's office. People said goodbye to me on my way, convinced that I would be expelled.

Philip Ketchum asked me to sit down. He said to me, not unkindly, "You are an extraordinary boy, Audain. I have just found out that you have taken more books out of the library than any other boy in the school. Was that also a prank or did you actually read them?"

I assured him that it wasn't a prank, and that I read extensively because I felt it was the best way to get an education. Also, I found most of my class work boring.

Ketchum continued: "But you've had books like *Das Kapital* and *Mein Kampf*. How can you read complicated tomes like that?"

I told him that *Das Kapital* was indeed very complicated, but necessary if you wanted Marx's take on dialectical materialism. I also suggested to him that if he wanted to understand communism better, without all the theory, a reading of Karl Marx and Friedrich Engels's *Communist Manifesto* would provide a synopsis.

And as for *Mein Kampf*, I said that it was extremely repetitive and contained many factual errors because Hitler had left school early and hadn't travelled extensively. But I added that if more people had taken *Mein Kampf* seriously in the 1930s, they might not have been surprised by the genocide that accompanied the Nazi era.

Ketchum looked bewildered and said, "Michael, I would expel you if you didn't live over 2,500 miles away."

The headmaster then told me that for the remainder of my school year I would be "gated to the grounds" and that every afternoon I had to run ten rounds of the school track. I thanked him for not expelling me and we never spoke again.

Later, when Angus Scott became headmaster at the school, I wrote him a letter of congratulations. He was a likeable man and had been one of my drama coaches. At the same time I told him how unhappy I had been at the school and recommended that a counsellor be appointed, someone students could talk to in confidence about their problems. I received a brief reply curtly telling me that counselling was the job of the school chaplain—a genial old bald chap named Canon Lawrence, affectionately known as "Boom Boom."

To my surprise, in 2010 I was approached by the current TCS headmaster to fund a new visual arts building on the school campus, one that could be named after me. It didn't take me long to graciously decline. I have never been back to a reunion at any of my schools, which I am told are often sad affairs, as those who were heroes in their school days often discover that prowess in the classroom or on the playing field does not always prepare one for the challenges of life.

CHAPTER 20

"Way to Go, Kid"

Paul Newman, 1955

The Wendy Barrie Show was a popular morning television program on the Westinghouse Network. It was hosted by the genial Wendy Barrie, and a guest spot on it had been obtained as part of publicity for the publication of my father's book *From Coalmine to Castle: The Story of the Dunsmuirs of Vancouver Island.*

Against all odds, Jimmy had made good on his fresh start in British Columbia. After being hospitalized in 1948 for the effects of his acute alcoholism, he went on the wagon and stayed there, greatly inspired by a personal encounter with Bill Wilson, the founder of Alcoholics Anonymous, who had passed through Victoria on one of his lecture tours. In his newly sober existence he decided he wanted to be a writer and spent several years researching and writing a history of the Dunsmuir family. But like so many other would-be authors, he discovered he still required a day job to support himself, and he became a civil defence instructor. He eventually did manage to publish several books, beginning with his Dunsmuir history, with Pageant Press, in New York, in 1955.

I arrived at New York's Pennsylvania Station from Toronto early the morning of the show and took a taxi to the studio, where I waited off set for my father to do his thing. Also in the room were two somewhat chunky young men, one of whom I recognized as former middleweight champion Rocky Graziano. The publicist told me that the other was a young movie actor named Paul Newman, who was playing Graziano in an upcoming film titled *Somebody Up There Likes Me*. They ignored me while chatting and drinking their coffee.

It turned out that Jimmy became a bit tongue-tied in front of the camera, so all of a sudden Wendy Barrie called out, "Where's that good-looking son of yours?" I was then hustled onto the set.

Wendy didn't want to discuss the book. She was more intrigued about the life of a seventeen-year-old Canadian boy with a "cute" accent. She even asked me where I bought my suit and bright pink shirt, which was a bit of a surprise because the program was only broadcast in black and white. And then she got into boxing, asking me who my all-time favourite was. "Joe Louis," I quickly replied, to her satisfaction.

When I was finally called off the set for a commercial, both Graziano and Newman stood up to congratulate me on my performance, with Paul Newman saying, "Way to go, kid." Of course, later I went to see their film—more than once.

After lunch at Jack Dempsey's restaurant in Times Square, the former heavyweight champion came over to our table to shake hands, and I told him how I still treasured the miniature boxing gloves he had signed for me eleven years earlier. That evening we went to dinner with my father's aunt, Dola Cavendish, who lived on Park Avenue.

"Jimmy, this is the first time in years that I have had to get up before lunchtime," Dola said. "I even rented a television set because I don't have one."

Dola spoiled us with a dinner that was served on silver platters by three red-jacketed waiters at the 21 Club. Besides Dola, in attendance were three of her retainers: Frances Carpenter, a small-statured, elegantly dressed Britisher, who apparently ran errands and specialized in obtaining theatre tickets; housekeeper Mrs. Denham, from Vancouver Island, whose main job was to look after Dola's several Pekingese; and a young, zoot-suited Puerto Rican, whose role I wasn't so clear about, as he sat slumped against the wall in an apparent drug-induced trance.

Despite being his aunt, Dola was younger than my father, and they had grown up together as children in Victoria. Eventually she had married a naval officer named Cavendish, commonly known as "Dish." But the real love of her life was the actress Tallulah Bankhead, who wasn't there that night but had been part of her circle for years.

My father told me that Tallulah had been a drinking companion of his in the 1930s, and that it was at my christening party in London that she had agreed to become my godmother. Once, when referring to that occasion, Tallulah confided to me, "Oh darling, I must have been really tight that day."

Tallulah did see me from time to time, likely on the prompting of her "companion" Dola. I recall a romp as a child on the lawn of Windows, Tallulah's house in Westchester County, with a lion cub called Winston, and one Sunday afternoon in the early 1950s I went and saw her at NBC studios in Rockefeller Center, where Tallulah did a two-hour live radio program called *The Big Show*. It was a radio precursor of Ed Sullivan's television program, with a mix of celebrities and performers in front of a live audience.

I was astonished that even though it was on the radio the orchestra's members were dressed in tuxedos. After the program, Tallulah was a bit nonplussed on how to entertain a fifteen-year-old boy after I turned down a gin and tonic.

"Well then, darling, I must find a girl to take care of you, or would you prefer a boy?" she enquired.

I was enthralled when middleweight boxing champion Sugar Ray Robinson joined us for dinner at the Stork Club that evening, a treat arranged by Tallulah.

Tallulah was undoubtedly one of the more colourful characters that I ever met. Although I was obviously boring to her, she didn't stint in her advice. When I confessed to hating my schools, I recall her commiserating with me: "I read Shakespeare and the Bible, and I can shoot dice. That's what I call a liberal education." Tallulah, of course, became famous for this advice—as well as dancing wildly on tables without any underclothing.

CHAPTER 21

"I'm Not Going to Get Killed by That Idiot"

Captain Charles Hill, 1957

WHEN I ARRIVED IN Norman Wells, a settlement located on the Mackenzie River just south of the Arctic Circle, a lot of people at the Canadian Pacific Airlines base were mystified as to why I had voluntarily chosen such a remote location as an assistant station agent.

"Because it's a place where I can save money," I replied.

I had another motive, however, and that was to become a commercial airline pilot. I had been working towards this goal since obtaining my private licence in the air cadets and had built up enough hours flying single-engine rental planes to qualify for a commercial licence. While I was stationed in Edmonton, I had gained some twin-engine training on a DC3, so I was put on a reserve list for flying freight out of Norman Wells. However CP Air lost its contract for supplying the massive DEW Line project, building military radar stations across the Arctic, soon after I arrived, so my flying ambitions didn't get off the ground.

An old Arctic hand once told me that you can only save money if you never play poker. And so I declined to play poker the night I arrived and every time thereafter. It was one of a number of personal traits that soon had people in the settlement talking about me as a real oddball. Among other things that apparently distinguished me negatively in their eyes was playing classical and jazz records on the portable gramophone in the company staff house. A preference for Scotch rather than rye whisky, and my genuine friendships with the

Indigenous girls who worked in the staff house, apparently made me even more exotic.

"This Mike guy was bushed on the day he arrived here," I couldn't help overhearing my boss say to a visiting aircraft pilot.

Nevertheless, station manager Ronald Willis had to put up with me, as there were only two of us to run the airline base. He tried in vain to get me to request a transfer out by giving me the toughest jobs to do, such as hauling staff-house garbage to the dump and loading aircraft in weather as cold as minus 48 degrees Celsius, when our casual labourers were supposed to do those jobs.

Actually, hauling the garbage was quite exciting because in the spring there was often the odd grizzly bear patrolling the dump. The trick was to slip out of the driver's seat onto the truck bed to dump the barrels full of garbage and get safely back in the cab before the bears decided to include you in their meal.

I had only been in Norman Wells a few days when I was asked to drive the legendary Captain Charles Hill from the airport to the staff house in the company's red International Harvester Travelall.

Charles Hill, "Cappy," as he was known, was one of Canada's earliest bush pilots. He had started out flying Noorduyn Norsemans in northern Quebec, where he had become a pal of CP Air's president Grant McConachie. From Norman Wells he flew nine-passenger single Otters, on floats in the summer and skis in the winter, to a whole slew of remote settlements along the Mackenzie River.

While I was driving Cappy home I took a curve on the icy road at too high a speed and ploughed into a snowbank on the side of the road, from which I couldn't extract the vehicle until I was able to secure a tow from a passing army truck. Cappy was quite shaken and didn't say much at the time, but at dinner that evening he announced, "I have been flying for over thirty years and I'm not going to get killed by that idiot."

He vowed that he would never drive with me again. Of course the word spread quickly around the settlement that I was in the doghouse.

Pretty well all the White community in Norman Wells felt sorry for my boss, Ronald, and decided not to have anything to do with me.

Invitations to curling parties, film shows and other events in the Imperial Oil community centre didn't come my way. But that was fine, because the Indigenous members of the community I got along with were also excluded from those social gatherings. One fascinating individual was a sixty-year-old northern Cree man named Joe Dillon. Joe had been recruited in 1914 to go to France as a sniper. Later, he told me that he got the first contract to deliver the mail with a dog team, travelling hundreds of miles down the Mackenzie River from Hay River to Aklavik. During World War II he became a professional grizzly bear hunter, selling the pelts to members of the Canadian and American armies stationed up north. The Americans actually built a pipeline to carry oil overland from Norman Wells to Fairbanks in order to supply the US army in case of a Japanese invasion of Alaska.

When Joe wasn't doing odd jobs around the settlement, he would take me hunting. There was no sport to shooting a moose, because during the winter they would simply inhabit corrals along the river, which they made by stamping down the snow. You just snowshoed up to a corral and fired away. Caribou were more of a challenge in that they had to be tracked by a dog team. On one occasion we came across half a dozen freshly shot caribou whose livers had simply been removed for consumption by the local people, and the frozen carcasses left for the wolves. There was plenty of caribou for the residents of Norman Wells to eat that week, even though consumption by White people was officially illegal.

I managed to avoid hunting any bears with Joe, but in the spring we bagged a whole boatload of white snow geese. I recall that as we approached an island where they were resting on their way further north, the whole island seemed to rise into the air with tremendous honking sounds.

Joe also taught me something about driving dog teams. He said it all depends on your relationship with the lead dog, which has to be the biggest and toughest of the bunch. Joe's theory was that all the other dogs hated the lead dog because he was the one you spoiled by giving him extra food, and that the motivation for the other dogs to move the sled was to overtake the lead dog and kill him. Certainly I noticed that, when we stopped, the first thing the lead dog did was to turn his snarling muzzle to the others, while Joe rushed forward to stake the other dogs so that they wouldn't become involved in a free-for-all. Not very elegant, but it worked after a fashion.

On one occasion, I volunteered to drive the Catholic priest's dog team forty miles, from Norman Wells to Fort Norman, with an RCMP constable going in front with a sled team to break the trail. The police dogs were magnificent, the biggest and best bred in the North, but the constable was just as unfriendly as the other Whites in the community.

"You better hang onto the back of your sled," he said, "because if you fall off I am not turning around to look for you."

Halfway along the trail we had to stay together overnight in a small lean-to by the river, where we each cooked our own rations over a Primus stove, the cop not saying a word to me until the next morning, when he shook my sleeping bag, saying, "Feed your dogs, then get moving."

It was, though, an exhilarating experience to be clipping along, standing on the runners at the back of the sled as the dogs did all the work, except when there was some rough ice to traverse and the sled had to be manhandled in the faint light of the Arctic winter.

There was just one person in the settlement who didn't seem to mind oddballs. He was a radio operator from Dublin named Peter O'Brian. We got along famously and later I visited him in Ireland for some wild times. Without his support I believe that I would have retreated home earlier. As the months went by my unconventionality became more accepted. Captain Hill even allowed me to transport him back and forth to the airport once again, but by then my thoughts were elsewhere.

CHAPTER 22

"What the Hell Is Wrong With You?"

Mary, 1958

UNTIL I WAS TWENTY-SIX years old, I hadn't even a passing acquaintance with psychology, my studies all having something to do with history and sociology. But at the University of British Columbia it was a requirement at the School of Social Work that all students take a course in what was called "case work." And the redoubtable Muriel Cunliffe, our case-work professor, said that in order to be effective, one needed to obtain a grounding in Freudian psychology.

The textbook she selected was very popular at that time: *Childhood and Society*, published in 1950 by Freud's student Erik Erikson. I actually found the book, which describes in detail what the author believed to be the eight stages of the development of the human personality, to be absolutely fascinating. I had never given an earlier thought to, say, the function of toilet training in character development. To this day, I believe *Childhood and Society*, along with Emil Ludwig's biography *Napoleon*, Harold Laski's *A Grammar of Politics*, Adam Smith's *The Wealth of Nations* and James Cook's *A Voyage to the Pacific Ocean*—and, of course, the King James version of the Bible—to be among the books that have most influenced my life.

But it was not enough for me to just read a book by one of Freud's students; I wanted to understand why the Austrian founder of psychoanalysis was so celebrated. So I read Freud's *The Interpretation of Dreams*, which deals with the role of the unconscious in determining human behaviour, after which I immersed myself in *Civilization and Its Discontents,* which speculates on how natural instincts such as aggression and sex can be at variance with the needs of a compatible human community. Absolutely fascinating!

One of the reasons for taking the course was supposedly to prepare me to become a counsellor, a career in which I had no interest. But instead it turned out to be an opportunity to understand myself slightly better through recognition of the role that a satisfying sex life can play in human well-being. This dimension of my growing up had been confusing and worrisome.

Compared to today's children, I had been quite shielded from sex in all respects. Around the age of eleven I recall asking my father if babies were created in condoms, because I had heard some chit-chat to this effect from one of my schoolmates.

"Condoms!" Jimmy exploded. "You must mean French letters, those things which are made out of sheep's guts. They are for preventing disease, not for making babies. But you don't need a French letter if you mate with a clean woman."

I duly passed on my father's advice to my still-bewildered friend.

At the urging of my friend, who was too timid to ask his own parents, I further enquired where babies come from.

Jimmy smiled and said, "Babies are made by rogering. You have seen dogs and horses do it. Well, people do it exactly the same way. And you have seen puppies being born. Well, babies drop out of their mother's stomachs exactly the same way. Although usually only one or two at time."

One mysterious aspect of my early adolescence was my father's horror of masturbation. Jimmy often warned me about the evils of "playing with myself," saying that it could ruin my life. Just what he meant by "playing with myself" I wasn't exactly sure, as I had no desire to touch myself for anything more than urination. While at school, I had heard some locker-room chatter about "whacking off," but didn't have a clue what that meant.

It wasn't until I was about fifteen that I started to have some interest in girls. I went out on the occasional double date with school friends, an aspect of which involved pleasurable kissing and petting, but absolutely giving no thought to "going all the way," which in middle-class Victoria we understood wouldn't happen until our wedding night.

I likewise had never heard of oral, let alone anal, sex. It's hard to believe how much North American teenage awareness of sex has changed over the last sixty years.

Until I was eighteen, I stumbled along in ignorance about sexual matters. That all changed when an attractive Kelowna girl I had been dating said that she would be happy to meet me for a weekend in a Vancouver hotel. Stationed in Edmonton at the time, I flew down to Vancouver and registered at the Devonshire Hotel under the name Mr. and Mrs. Audain. That evening, after a wonderful spaghetti and meatball dinner, highly excited, I decided that it was time to take Marguerite's virginity. Positioning her over a towel on the bed, I mounted her from behind, in what I assumed from my father's explanation was the correct procedure. Somehow it didn't work, and after a prolonged session of fumbling, Marguerite collapsed on the bed, laughing hysterically.

"Perhaps we should try in the morning, the other way around," Marguerite offered kindly.

My ego shattered, I agreed. But the following morning, though I started off determined to redeem myself, I was so nervous and insecure I wasn't able to do my part. Utterly chagrined, I begged off the rest of the weekend and went home to Edmonton, determined to avoid sexual trysts for the foreseeable future. At work I was surrounded by very attractive flight attendants who worked for the airline, and occasionally I got up enough nerve to go on dates, but I was too terrified to chance another close encounter.

Living alone in Edmonton, I was very unhappy and started to change my lifestyle by drinking excessively. I would drink before I went to a party so that I wouldn't feel shy and awkward dancing with girls during the course of the evening. I continued to drink excessively so the feeling of elation wouldn't wear off. I recall that at the company's Christmas party I ended up dancing with full glasses in each jacket pocket for fear of not being able to get a drink after the bar closed. That got me a written reprimand from the regional general manager, after which I sought some counselling for my drinking from the Alberta Alcoholism Foundation. They diagnosed me as simply an occasional heavy drinker, rather than an alcoholic, because I never touched a drink the following morning.

The Norman Wells staff house, maintained by CP Air, had twenty-six beds for passengers who were transferring from the larger C46 or DC3 aircraft to travel to smaller settlements along the Mackenzie River. To look after the rooms, in addition to the cook and her handyman husband, there were four or five girls of Inuit or northern Cree ancestry, recruited directly from residential schools. A friendly and hard-working bunch, they were not treated particularly well by male members of the staff and were required to tolerate what today would be called sexual harassment, as well as groping and other activities I wasn't directly aware of. But, I was eager to learn about their culture and the girls seemed to be especially friendly to me, perhaps as I too was not well regarded by other members of airline staff.

I did fantasize about becoming intimate with a couple of the girls but felt that it would be inappropriate, given my supervisory position and the likelihood that I could be even further derided in the predominantly White community. But late one evening, Mary, the least inhibited of the girls, surprised me by slipping into my bed close to midnight. She had been drinking and told me that she knew that I had been wanting some "poontang" time with her and this was my chance, then shrugged off her clothes. I thought to myself, "What the hell! I may as well have a go." Relaxed as I was, in near sleep, and encouraged by her enthusiasm, we got off to good start, but just as I was starting to think I might have finally mastered the art of poontanging, she grasped my loins and shouted, "Deeper, harder. You need to make that little cock of yours really work!"

With that I immediately lost my mojo. Knowing there was no use going on, I rolled off her and stood up. Mary said, "I'm so horny, what the hell is wrong with you?"

Angry at myself, I apologized to Mary and begged her to leave me to my misery, then pulled on some clothes and staggered out of my cabin down towards the river, distraught about my lack of performance and the realization that the story would likely have made its way around the settlement by morning. I was in utter despair. It might be difficult for anyone who hasn't experienced it to understand the absolute desperation felt by someone in the position I found myself in, but it would not have surprised Freud, who of all people understood the power of sexual frustration, especially in adolescent males. If only I had read him earlier, perhaps I might have handled my situation better. At that moment, I felt that if I couldn't have sex I wouldn't be a man, and therefore life wasn't worth living.

Full of such thoughts, I rushed down to the riverbank and plunged up to my chest in the icy water. The Mackenzie River was so wide at this point that it was hard to see the other bank, even with the midnight sun just below the horizon, but I saw large chunks of ice floating by, as it was breakup time. It flashed through my mind that no one would care if I just disappeared into that water, and even if my parents might shed a tear for me they would soon get over it. As I waded a bit deeper and started to feel a loss of sensation in my legs, rather than moving further from the shore, I decided it was time to just let the icy cold water take its course.

As I started to sit down, with the water up to my neck, I imagined I heard something strange. It sounded like a choir singing high in the sky. What was it? *Oh my God!* It was my favourite hymn, "Jerusalem," instilled deep in my subconscious from my earliest days as a child attending church in Devonshire:

And did those feet in ancient time
Walk upon England's mountains green?
And was the holy Lamb of God,
On England's pleasant pastures seen?

And did the Countenance Divine,
Shine forth upon our clouded hills?
And was Jerusalem builded here,
Among these dark Satanic Mills?

Bring me my Bow of burning gold:
Bring me my Arrows of desire:
Bring me my Spear: O clouds unfold!
Bring me my Chariot of fire!

I will not cease from Mental Fight,
Nor shall my Sword sleep in my hand
Till we have built Jerusalem
In England's green and pleasant Land.

Although to me the whole Arctic sky seemed full of angels singing in a celestial choir, perhaps the singing was my own, or an intensely vivid vision brought on by my agitated state. In any case I was released from my despair and soon found myself clambering up the riverbank and staggering towards my cabin, pathetically cold and stiff.

At breakfast in the mess hall, Mary looked at me quizzically and just smiled, putting her finger to her lips to indicate that she wouldn't be saying anything about our experience. Nevertheless, as soon as I got to my office at the airport I sent a telex to Vancouver HQ resigning from the airline. They asked me to stay on for another two weeks until they could send a replacement, which I did.

After that very deflating experience with Mary, I questioned whether I would ever have satisfactory sexual relations with a woman. My mind was willing, but my body seemed to conk out at the crucial moment. As a result, I just avoided intimacy for the next three years, during travels through Central America and Europe and a year back at college in Victoria. I would date occasionally but always stopped short of climbing into bed. I wondered if I was perhaps more suited to the priesthood than to secular life.

CHAPTER 23

"One Anything Coming Up"

Bartender, Rotterdam, 1958

IN THE MID-1950S THERE was constant press coverage about a small group of guerillas, under the leadership of Fidel Castro, who were fighting in the mountains of Cuba to remove Fulgencio Batista, a henchman of Washington's foreign policy and one of Central America's most ruthless dictators.

It's indicative of my state of mind at this time, desperate as I was to make a radical break, that I got the idea to join Fidel's group and become part of the Cuban Revolution. However, I wasn't sure what I could accomplish, because I had limited military experience. It's true that I had been a member of the cadet corps of all three of Canada's military services, but the only useful abilities I had gained were how to strip down a Bren gun in army cadets, plot a course with a sextant in the navy, and, most importantly, qualify for my private pilot's licence under the auspices of the Royal Canadian Air Force.

But at the age of twenty, I had the romantic view that if my life needed to be sacrificed as part of a people's revolution, so be it.

I had been told that the best way to reach Fidel's forces was to make contact with his supporters in Panama, so I made my way down to Panama City. A day or two after my arrival, in the Hilton Hotel bar, I was offered a three-week job flying a DC3 for Imperial Oil, as one of their first officers was on vacation. I had pretty much given up on becoming a pilot, but the opportunity to fly a DC3—the most versatile commercial aircraft ever built, which I had received training on but never got to fly (regularly), was too much to resist. As a temporary first officer I just sat quietly and reviewed checklists with the captain and was never given a chance to land the bird. Probably just as well, as some of the airfields were quite basic and we often lacked local weather information. The three weeks were soon up, and that was the end of my flying career.

Despite my enquiries using my very basic Spanish, I didn't come across any Cuban connections. But one evening in a waterfront bar I met the chief steward of a British freighter, who told me that his ship's next port of call was Santiago, Cuba, to take on a load of sugar. Santiago happened to be close to the Sierra Maestra mountain range where Fidel's forces were concentrated. So the next day, for a modest fee, I was aboard a Furness Withy Line freighter as we transited the Panama Canal and steamed into the blue Caribbean towards Cuba. We hadn't gone more than a day east of the Canal Zone, though, when the British captain was told that the guerilla war had become much more fierce as Fidel's forces engaged the government in some major battles and that the owners had decided that the ship wouldn't call in Cuba.

"So, my boy, you now have a free passage all the way to Rotterdam ahead of you," the captain told me.

"Rotterdam? How about London?" I asked.

"Certainly, you are welcome to stay with us until we reach London, but we will have to call at Rotterdam and Antwerp first."

The freighter was licensed to carry twelve passengers, but only half a dozen were on board—all of them over sixty except for myself. The meals weren't bad and I got a lot of suntanning in as we ploughed through the tropics. Fortunately, a modest library in the saloon contained a whole set of Dickens volumes.

One day the chief steward said to me before dinner, "The drinks are on us tonight."

When I enquired why, he replied, "Well, we know from your passport that it's your twenty-first birthday! I wish I could join you in a drink or two, but that will have to wait until we get into port."

Sure enough, when we finally arrived under leaden skies in the port of Rotterdam, the chief steward and a bunch of junior officers from the ship said, "You are coming with us tonight."

Our first port of call was a large waterfront bar with a huge variety of colourful bottles. It was located in the Katendrecht area, a sailor's district, where we were told the police never ventured alone. From behind the bar, a broad-shouldered woman, built like a female version of a Sumo wrestler, said to me, "So, what's your birthday drink?"

Nothing came quickly to my mind, so I simply said, "One anything."

"One anything coming up," the woman cried as she took a large glass and began to pour portions from a range of bottles into it. She gave it a stir and put it in front of me while my companions grinned in expectation.

Since I had spun the dice I knew that I couldn't do anything but plunge ahead. I raised my glass and said, "Good luck to you all. *Viva la revolución!*"

That's actually all I remember about that night. When I regained consciousness, I was in my bunk on board ship with a throbbing headache and limbs that would barely move. A matronly British stewardess appeared, saying, "Here, what you need is a good cup of tea." Sitting up in my bunk I raised the mug to my lips, but I was shaking so much that I felt I couldn't drink it without biting the chinaware. Later that day I staggered into my shower, and as the cold water cascaded around me I felt a paper napkin attached to my arm with Scotch tape. Tearing it off, I discovered a beautiful butterfly tattoo in red, blue and green.

When I met my shipmates the next day, they had black eyes and were limping. Apparently, as they were taking me back to the ship in a taxi, the driver felt that he was being intimately accosted by the radio officer, so he pulled everyone out of the car and belted them all, except me, because I was already totally out of it. The radio officer was so beat up that the ship had to stay an extra day in Antwerp until a replacement could be flown over from England.

When I arrived in London, I stayed a few days with my mother and her husband, after a six-year separation, then bought a Vespa motor scooter and proceeded to look for a job. It wasn't easy to secure employment. I was told that my Canadian airline experience counted for nothing in the UK, so for three months I settled for a position in the paperback department of the huge Foyles bookshop on Charing Cross Road. My pay, which was £5.10 a week plus lunch vouchers, barely covered the rent of my single room, let alone anything else.

One of the reasons I was attracted to London was the so-called Angry Young Men movement in British literature, theatre and film, starring such individuals as Kingsley Amis, John Osborne and Tony Richardson, who were so popular in the late 1950s. Being painfully shy, I never got close to any members of this group, though I did discover that not all of them were angry, most were not young, and one or two members were not even men.

It was during that London sojourn that I discovered ballet. I was dragged to my first couple of ballets by my father's cousin Victoria Bromley, fondly known as "Mouse." She took it upon herself to give me an introduction to culture. Being a ballet fan, she enlisted me to tag along as her escort at Covent Garden. I felt terribly out of place in my Harris Tweed jacket among theatregoers in dinner jackets and long gowns. As Mouse was the daughter of Sir Rupert Bromley, a Gentleman Usher at Buckingham Palace, she seemed to have an inexhaustible supply of theatre tickets. That's because the Lord Chamberlain, who licensed theatres, required that two tickets for every performance be sent to Buckingham Palace, where they were distributed to staff.

Even though I visited some of the lovely British countryside on my motor scooter, this was actually a woefully unhappy period in my life. Mouse endeavoured to remedy this by holding a small cocktail party to introduce me to some British debutantes, but I felt that they looked down their noses at me as an uncouth colonial.

I did confess to my stepfather, George Carmichael—who, together with my mother, was on leave from their post in what was then called British Guiana—that I had no idea what to do with my life.

"Well, you can't get anywhere in this world unless you have a qualification—and since you don't seem to want to be a bus driver in the sky, you need a piece of paper other than your pilot's license," said George.

He told me that coming from a poor Scottish family he had no funds to go to university, but having shown promise at school he had been able to get a job as a clerk in a barrister's office. He said it then took him ten more years of night study to get admitted to the bar.

When I told George that I didn't think I could get a university degree in Canada because I was so hopeless at written French, he said, "Do something about it. Go and stay for a few months in a French town, where you will be forced to learn the language." And so that autumn I found myself as a foreign student at the University of Lyon.

CHAPTER 24

"And How Did You Get Into This Kettle of Fish?"

Special Branch detective, Dublin, 1958

THE IRISH WEATHER WAS blessedly fine the morning Peter O'Brian met me in Dublin. A man of short stature with long, dark, combed-back hair and piercing eyes, he had been about my only friend while I was stationed in Norman Wells, in Canada's Arctic. Peter had told me that he would be spending his leave at home in Ireland and invited me to visit him there.

"I want to introduce you to the finest girls in all Ireland," he said. Thus, the afternoon of the day that I arrived at the Dun Laoghaire quay, we set off towards Ireland's West Country in a rented Morris Minor.

Peter seemed to despise maps. His idea of navigating the confusing country road network was to call at the various pubs along the route and ask for directions. As we journeyed west, we seemed to spend more time sampling the local ales than we did motoring along. But eventually, after a night in a farmhouse B&B, we arrived at Achill, a rugged island on the west coast joined to County Mayo by a narrow bridge.

By day, we explored Achill on foot, again going from pub to pub. Most of the island's inhabitants seemed fluent in Gaelic, and we enjoyed the lively music that was a feature of pub life every evening. But there seemed to be a scarcity of those "finest girls" Peter had promised. That is until we went to a dance in a church hall one evening, where there were indeed plenty of girls, many redheaded and quite entrancing.

It was a strange way of socializing. In the first place, neither beer nor hard alcohol was available—only lemonade and ginger beer. Also, the men seemed to gather on one side of the hall, the girls on the other. One had to be intrepid enough to cross the floor to ask a girl to dance. The girls seemed eager enough to accept our invitation, but we first had to undergo interrogation from an older woman, apparently a mother or grandmother.

"Why have we never met you before? Where did you come from? What's your occupation?"

Peter had warned me about this and claimed that we would have no trouble, because the mothers would likely see us as better prospects than the many part-time farm workers and fishermen on Achill. Anyway, we had plenty of exercise dancing. Fortunately jiving was permissible, as my ballroom steps have always been somewhat wobbly. I had said thank-you to my third partner and was about to approach a fourth when a florid-faced man in priestly garb intervened, saying, "Who do you think you are? Are you shopping for fish? You have already annoyed two of my parishioners by failing to offer their daughter so much as a glass of lemonade, so I believe it's time that you be off."

With that I retreated to the other side of the room and consulted with Peter, who advised me that I had already started to cause some animosity among the local men lounging around. "It might be safer if we quietly retreat before they get organized to waylay us outside," he said.

As we walked swiftly back to our lodging, I remonstrated to Peter that he should have briefed me more fully on the local social customs.

The next morning we returned to Dublin via a circuitous route, again stopping at various pubs. By late afternoon, we had both run out of cash, so we ended up having a restless sleep under the car in a farmer's field. A shaggy-looking cow with pointed horns woke us up at daybreak. The beast's coat was so long that we couldn't tell whether or not it was a bull—we just jumped in the car and drove off.

Back in Dublin, Peter invited me to sleep on the couch of the one-bedroom flat he had rented on the top floor of a semi-detached house. Downstairs were a bunch of young men who played loud Elvis music on their gramophone for much of the night.

After waking up late the next morning, we went for a fry-up breakfast at a pub where we had been told the author Brendan Behan frequently put in an appearance. His book *Borstal Boy* had recently made the best-seller list. A couple of hours passed without the author showing up, then Peter established that Behan was taking his early libation at another pub, to which we promptly dispatched ourselves.

The author was already in good form. When I told him that I was Canadian, he said, "Oh, you come from that strange country where your parsimonious CBC radio interviewers don't even offer their guests a drink."

After a couple more drinks, Peter decided it was time I saw the sights. So we trekked through the rainy city to the library of Trinity College, Peter having gone on at great length about how I must see the *Book of Kells,* which proved that Ireland was a place of enlightenment when England was in the Dark Ages.

That evening, back at the flat, just when I was preparing to doss down for another night on the couch, all of a sudden I heard the music downstairs subside and a moment or two later a loud pounding on our door. Since I was closest, I opened the door, only to be pushed backwards by some green-uniformed gentlemen, one pointing what looked like a machine gun in my face. It only took a moment for Peter and me to be handcuffed and hustled out of the house, then a sack was placed over my head and I was wedged into a vehicle.

The sack was not removed until I found myself inside a bleak police cell, with no one saying anything to me. I was quite bewildered about the situation and demanded to speak to someone of authority. After five minutes, a warder came along and told me, "You will be called for when you are wanted. In the meantime, you better get some kip."

An hour or so later, I was taken to what appeared to be an interrogation room, sat down and offered a cup of tea by a couple of tweed-suited men who said that they were Special Branch detectives.

"And how did you get into this kettle of fish?" one of them enquired.

"What offence am I being charged with? Can I get in touch with a lawyer?" I asked.

The heavy-set man who seemed to be the boss said, "As of now you are not charged with anything, so you don't need a lawyer. We have special powers to hold you here in Phoenix Park until you are charged."

In response to his many questions, I endeavoured to account for practically every hour that I had been in Ireland, and my answers were taken down in a notebook by the other detective. I noticed that he checked the date of arrival on the Canadian passport found in my luggage.

After half an hour or so, the older man said, "Well, it's high time for us to go home to bed. See you in the morning."

I was awakened in my cell a few hours later and offered some tea plus thick slices of bread and butter. I was told that a shower wasn't available but was given a safety razor in what the warder called my "luxury cell." The warder was actually a genial fellow who told me he had a son in Toronto—he hoped to visit next year and take in Niagara Falls. He slipped me a newspaper and said, "Do you want to read about yourself?" He pointed to a story about a Garda raid on a house in the Drumcondra neighbourhood, where half a dozen suspects had been detained for possession of explosives.

When my interview with the detectives resumed a couple of hours later, I told them straight away that I had nothing to do with any explosives, and they seemed elated. The more senior one exclaimed, "Well, you obviously knew that explosives were there, or why would you mention them?"

"Because I read it in this morning's *Irish Times*," I retorted.

The questioning continued for another hour and a half, drilling me again and again on what I knew about the other people in the house.

"I didn't even learn the names of the people downstairs. The only thing I know about them is that they are Elvis fans," I told the detectives.

The questions then focused on my friend Peter, who they were obviously holding elsewhere in their cells. Did I know that he had IRA connections? What were my own views about the IRA? Had I met any IRA members in Dublin?

I told them that while I was certainly sympathetic to the idea of a united Ireland, as were most of the supporters of the Sinn Fein political party, I didn't believe that it needed to come about through the use of violence.

"Did your friend Peter share the same sentiments?" they asked.

After more volleys of questions along this line, suddenly the senior detective (whose name I never caught) said, "And what do you think of Lord Nelson?"

Stunned for a minute, I said, "Do you mean Admiral Lord Nelson, hero of the Battle of Trafalgar, who as he lay dying on the deck of his flagship said, 'Let every Englishman do his duty'?"

He nodded, so I said, "Well, I believe that's a brave statement if you substitute the word 'Irishman' for 'Englishman.'"

Both detectives laughed and then followed up by asking, "So why did you walk so slowly around Nelson's Pillar yesterday?"

Realizing that I had been followed from the pub at which we met Brendan Behan, and possibly before, I said, "Well, we were simply on our way to view the *Book of Kells*." And with that I was taken back to my cell for a lunch of potatoes, mutton stew and custard, plus another cup of tea.

Shortly afterwards the senior detective came by my cell, handed me my passport and said, "Thank you for your assistance. We think it best you leave Ireland immediately and take care not to get in the wrong company again."

Five minutes later, a couple of policeman I had never met before escorted me out the rear door of the police station into a paddy wagon, on the bench of which I found my battered suitcase, with all my worldly possessions therein. We drove for about an hour until we came to Dublin Airport, where I was speedily checked in and given a brown manila envelope containing my wallet and traveller's cheques, and put on an Aer Lingus plane to London, apparently courtesy of the Irish government.

It wasn't until I opened my passport to go through UK immigration that I noticed an inside page had been stamped: "No Readmission to the Republic of Eire."

It was eight years later that I read in the newspaper that the Nelson's Pillar statue, which had stood for 150 years on O'Connell Street in front of Dublin's General Post Office, had been blown up by a group of men associated with the IRA. When I wrote to my old friend Peter at his parents' address, my letter was returned stamped "unknown."

CHAPTER 25

"Come to Church on Sundays"

British consul, Lyon, 1958

In November, a cold wind that hails from the north blows down the Rhône River through the centre of Lyon, France. Walking home through the dimly lit streets from the student restaurant on Quai Claude Bernard, where a meal could be bought for a hundred old francs, the equivalent of twenty cents, my thoughts turned to the upcoming weekend.

I planned to take a trip to Geneva's lively student quarter on my Vespa motor scooter rather than stick it out in the centre of dour and grimy Lyon. I cannot say that I enjoyed the Lyonnaise. I lived with a family on the fourth floor of a walk-up apartment building in Place Jean Macé. Judging by my landlady and her friends, the Lyonnaise seemed to be a self-absorbed lot, wary of foreigners and chiefly interested in food. Madame Durand shopped twice a day in the local markets, first before her postal clerk husband returned for his two-hour lunch break, and again in the early evening. Other than being offered a bowl of café au lait to start me off in the morning, I didn't share their complicated and lengthy meals. Instead, the student restaurant supplied me with a basic though meatless diet. Meal tickets were inexpensive enough if you were a registered student or faculty member.

Madame Durand was horrified that as a Canadian I couldn't speak fluent French when I arrived. But she beamed when I emphasized my Irish background—she claimed that the English were a contemptible race and had always made nothing but trouble for France. She said that the Americans were even worse because they had actually bombed the outskirts of Lyon one night during the war. Whereas, to my surprise, she asserted that the Germans had behaved very "correctly"—no doubt ignoring the exploits of Lyon's notorious Gestapo chief, Klaus Barbie.

Anyway, while walking briskly home that evening, I was crossing a cobblestoned street at a marked crosswalk when a car came swerving at speed around a curve, its yellow lights flashing and horn sounding. I instinctively stepped backwards, but apparently not fast enough for the driver, who had to slam on his brakes to avoid hitting me. He then rolled down his window and shouted some vindictive remarks.

Seeing the illuminated taxi sign on the vehicle's roof, I decided that I had had enough and stepped forward, wrenched the door open and yanked the driver out of his seat by the scruff of his leather jacket.

He was a short, middle-aged fellow with a rotund face and wearing a typical French beret. I didn't hit him, but his eyes bulged, looking terrified as I slammed his shoulders against the car and held him there while I went through my repertoire of swear words, which included more German than French, plus a certain four-letter Anglo-Saxon word.

I had only held the driver there for what seemed less than a minute when I felt a sharp prod in my back and heard, "Hands up!" Quickly turning my head around, I found myself staring at two submachine guns being pointed at me by men in black uniforms. I automatically did what I was told. When I turned around again, I was amazed to see that a small crowd had gathered, all offering comments of one variety or another.

Walking around Lyon in those days, I was used to seeing armed military police stationed behind sandbags at the entrances to public buildings, as there was a fear of a coup from French paratroopers stationed in Algeria. Apparently, the two soldiers had been stationed in front of a small post office just across the street and had witnessed what had happened. A few minutes later, a police car arrived and many of the onlookers started giving their versions of what had occurred. I stood there almost tongue-tied because my French was still rather basic. One of the policemen addressed me first in German, which I couldn't understand at all, and then turned to the driver I had attacked. He had lots to say and hurled abuse at me.

A man on a bicycle tried to explain that the taxi driver had almost run me over, while the driver indignantly claimed that he had given me lots of warning by flashing his lights, and that I had no business holding up traffic by not getting out of his way. All the while, one of the policemen took copious notes in a large book he carried. He then went around gathering everyone's name, even though the street corner had appeared deserted at the time of my crossing.

Eventually, the police told me, not politely, to get in the back of their car—they were going to detain me for assaulting a French citizen. They needed to verify my identity and status in France, my student ID card apparently not being good enough for them.

Five minutes later, we arrived at what appeared to be the neighbourhood police station on Rue Raoul Servant, and without further adieu I was ushered into a large cell full of dark-skinned men, some of whom seemed to be sleeping, others smoking while playing cards. One of the policemen who had arrested me told me that it was too late to investigate the case any further that evening, but in the morning someone would drop by my lodging to obtain my passport and visa documents.

There seemed to be no bunk for me, and I was wondering if I was going to have to spend the night on the floor, when suddenly a wiry man with tousled blond hair emerged from the darkness at the back of the cell, introducing himself in good English as Johann. He quickly explained that you had to pay for everything, including meals and a bunk. "But how can I pay for anything," I asked, "when my wallet, which only contains a few francs, was taken from me when I was checked into this hotel?"

"Oh, don't concern yourself with that. The jailers will give you credit for everything, and don't worry, they never have any trouble collecting," Johann explained.

"By the way, how long are you staying?" he asked. Johann said that most of our fellow inmates were Algerians awaiting deportation and some had been there for months. He had been there for three weeks, also for assault.

"My embassy won't do anything for me, because I was a freedom fighter and escaped Hungary," he said. "Have you called your embassy yet?"

When I replied in the negative Johann summoned a jail guard, who listened to Johann's order almost deferentially. Not too many minutes later, the same guard appeared with two mugs of coffee and told Johann that he had phoned the Canadian embassy in Paris to report my arrest. Then a mattress and pillow arrived and were placed on a bunk next to Johann's, the previous Algerian occupant having been quickly dislodged. Johann and I must have talked for a couple of hours before I fell asleep.

When I awoke my watch said it was 9:00 a.m., though the cell was in near darkness. It seemed no one rose very early in this jail. An hour or so later, doors started clanging, my name was called, and I was taken to a small room where a smart blue-blazered man introduced himself as the British consul in Lyon. He said that he had received a call from the Canadian embassy in Paris, adding, "I'm always happy to help chaps from any of our dominions."

After I explained the incident, the consul ventured, "Well, if it's like you say, and you never even gave that obnoxious taxi driver a black eye, let alone broke his jaw, I can't imagine you will be in here for long. I will return after lunch."

The consul was actually back an hour later. "I have been in touch with the chief of police, who is a member of my golf club. He has looked into this matter and says that you can go home at once. Just be careful not to rough up any more taxi drivers, because they have a strong trade union," he said, laughing.

Elated, I asked the consul how I could thank him. "Oh," he said, "there is one thing you can do, and that's come to church on Sundays. I presume that you are Anglican? If we don't keep our attendance up, the bishop will take away our vicar."

I went back later that day to repay my debt to Johann and, during the remainder of my stay in Lyon, he became a good friend, one with a great many useful connections. And, yes, on Sunday mornings I did attend the little Holy Trinity Church on one of the Rhône's quays, where the service was in English.

CHAPTER 26

"Lock This Commie Away"

Police chief, Jackson, 1961

MY ROOM IN THE Memphis, Tennessee, YMCA was a sparse one. It contained a wash basin, at least, though the showers and toilets were down the corridor.

That morning I shaved a little more carefully than usual with my Gillette razor. In the mirror I stared at the image of my face and eyes, wondering if I would have the fortitude to carry out my plan of travelling south by bus that day from Memphis to New Orleans, using only facilities available to "coloured people," as African-Americans were called down south in those days.

It was June 1961. Although the US Supreme Court had ordered the desegregation of interstate travel facilities, certain southern states were stubbornly resisting, which attracted the support of students and church ministers from the North. These people became known as the Freedom Riders and were intent on testing the application of the law. The activity had already resulted in a riot in Montgomery, Alabama, with the torching of a bus, and a White mob beating the Freedom Rider passengers, Black and White alike.

And now the target was Jackson, capital of Mississippi, then considered the most racist state in the Union, where the Freedom Riders were being arrested as they arrived, under Governor Ross Barnett's orders.

Mid-morning, I strolled with my battered suitcase over to the Greyhound bus terminal and bought a one-way ticket to New Orleans, with a meal stop in Jackson. The terminal had both "White" and "Coloured" sections, so I boldly took a seat in the Coloured section, to the curious stares of the early lunch crowd. An attractive young waitress came up and, smiling, said, "Well, sir, you must be from out of town. I'm sorry but we have two sections to our café and you don't look like you belong in this one."

"I'm absolutely fine here," I responded. "Would you mind getting me a tuna sandwich and a vanilla milkshake?"

Shaking her head, she said with a giggle, "Well, I think you are a bit lost, but I will see what I can do."

After my meal, I boarded the bus, taking care not to sit in the front, but close to the back, surrounded by a number of Black people, who looked puzzled.

"There's still lots of room at the front," the stocky driver said, punching my ticket.

"Thanks, but I am quite comfortable here," I replied.

And then we were off, taking only ten minutes to exit Memphis's built-up areas before getting onto a tree-lined highway heading due south among the cotton and corn fields. As the afternoon wore on and the shadows lengthened, we encountered more and more farm workers walking home towards the weathered clapboard cabins that were strung along the highway.

It was around 6:00 p.m. when we pulled into Jackson's Greyhound terminal, where the passengers disembarked after being told there was a forty-minute meal stop. Inside the terminal the restaurant was split down the middle with prominent "White" and "Coloured" signage. So I ambled up to the counter on the "Coloured" side. The Black waitress had a horrified look on her face as she came up to me and asked, "Sir, have you made a mistake?"

"No, there is no mistake. Just kindly bring me an order of your fried chicken and an ice tea."

Saying, "Oh sweet Jesus," the waitress stalked away and consulted a White female supervisor at the cash desk, who immediately picked up the telephone.

It took only three or four minutes for a city policeman to arrive. Without introducing himself, he said, "Get out of here right away or I am going to arrest you."

I countered, "Are you aware that the Supreme Court has ordered that interstate transportation facilities be desegregated? Your signage is outdated."

"You are under arrest. Let's go," he said, then escorted me to the back seat of his police car, into which the bus driver stowed my suitcase.

At the police station my arrival seemed to spark considerable interest. First, I was closeted with a young detective who had a whole series of questions, starting with asking me which group I belonged to, the Congress of Racial Equality or the Catholic Worker Movement. When I told him that I didn't belong to either of those groups, he said, "Then you must be a member of the Communist Party. Am I right?"

"No, I actually voted Progressive Conservative in the last Canadian election because I wanted to support John Diefenbaker," I responded with a smile.

"You're talking nonsense. How can someone be one of those fucking progressives and be conservative at the same time? You're a commie—don't try and make a fool of me," he said menacingly.

He left me alone in the interview room, and twenty minutes later I was ushered into the chief of police's office, where a battery of men were grouped, including one who told me he was the city prosecutor.

The chief finally said to me, "Son, it seems that you are a foreigner in our country and don't understand our laws. Maybe your queen has entirely different laws up in Canada, but we have been doing fine the way we have chosen to live for a couple of hundred years."

"What about the United States Supreme Court desegregating interstate transit," I asked.

"Well, those Yankee rules thankfully don't apply down in the state of Mississippi, and that's the lesson you have learned today. So I have got a patrolman who is going to catch up with that bus and put you on it so you can continue your sightseeing trip down to Louisiana, where they may do things a little different. Would that suit you?"

"Absolutely," I said, "but first I have to go back and finish the fried chicken I ordered in the Greyhound bus terminal."

"Oh my God, lock this commie away," the chief ordered, "and put him with the rest of them."

I was photographed and fingerprinted and taken down to a cell occupied by two young fellows. One introduced himself as Abraham Basford III. They were both apparently divinity students from Yale University.

After a not uncomfortable night, the next morning I met Jack Young, a lawyer provided by the Congress of Racial Equality, who said he would represent me in court that morning if I wished. The court session didn't take long. About twenty of us were ushered in together to occupy the front row of seats. After we pleaded not guilty it took less than five minutes for Judge Spencer to find us guilty of a breach of the peace. He sentenced us all to four months definite in jail and four months indefinite, plus a $250 fine.

CHAPTER 27

“The Screws Are Looking for a Chance to Hurt You Real Bad”

African-American trustee, Parchman, 1961

I AM SOMETIMES ASKED what it was like to be a prison inmate in Mississippi back in the early 1960s. Well, books have been written on the Freedom Rider experiences, but I suppose that each of us had individual reactions to events as they unfolded.

Life in the Jackson city jail wasn’t really that uncomfortable, though I believe there were twenty-six of us lodged in a cell designed for less than half that number. When I arrived, I was fortunate to be allocated a mattress on the floor some distance away from the sink and toilet, and I slept quite well, despite one or two friendly mice scampering around.

A few nights later we were woken at 2:00 a.m. and told that all the Freedom Riders were being moved to the Mississippi State Penitentiary located at Parchman, 130 miles north of Jackson, in delta country. Some White Freedom Riders decided it was their duty to resist the move and were gently carried by the trustee inmate down to the waiting paddy wagons as our jailers bid us not too unfriendly goodbyes.

When we arrived at the long, squat penitentiary building in the daylight hours, our reception was rather different, with a welcoming committee of burly guards wielding clubs and electric cattle prods. They ordered us to run into the building, strip and line up, which most of us did as if we were army recruits arriving at a boot camp.

The short-statured warden then addressed us: "Well, you Yankee boys are now going to do some hard time. We'll see how you like chopping cotton. We have 16,000 acres of it down here."

After showering, we were issued boxer underpants with the big initials "MSU" stamped on them. Someone whispered that they must have gotten them from the Mississippi State University, but a guard said, "Hell no, they are from our maximum security unit."

We were then assigned in groups of two to small cells that contained bunks and a toilet.

As soon as we entered our cells we heard screaming as the non-violent resisters were shocked with cattle prods to make them move, and finally dragged naked along the concrete floors by Black trustees clad in regulation black-and-white-striped uniforms.

We didn't actually get into the cotton-chopping business, for which I was grateful, because I didn't know how long I would last in the blistering hot sun. Instead we were confined to our cells, except for five minutes twice a week to take a shower. Our meals were slipped under the cell doors on steel trays three times daily by the trustees. I found the food novel, with plenty of grits and black-eyed peas, but not unpalatable, though subsequently I have never been able to eat corn bread. I was mainly distressed that my cellmate, John, a member of the Catholic Worker Movement from Chicago, refused to eat as part of his non-violent resistance. I felt somewhat guilty wolfing down my meal on the top bunk, making sure he couldn't see me eating. I told him that Gandhi had counselled that a non-violent resister should enter prison like a bridegroom entering the bridal chamber, full of anticipation and respect for what was to come. In other words, one should co-operate with the prison authorities.

In response John asked, "Then why did Gandhi go on long fasts while in prison as a way to incite support for Indian independence?"

"The difference is that Gandhi had a whole press corps following what he was doing, but no one here but me is aware of your fasting."

It tended to be a little boring day after day, lying in our bunks with only a Bible to read between the two of us. Fortunately, it was my favourite, the King James version, many chapters of which I still never tire of reading. We were not allowed visitors, except when John started to feel weak and he asked for a Catholic priest to administer the last rites. After a day or so a sallow-looking young priest turned up and, talking to John through the bars, explained that he would be expelled from his parish if he was caught giving mass to a Freedom Rider—his bishop labelled them as simply troublemakers.

When things were quiet, we tried to entertain ourselves by telling stories or singing the odd song loud enough that it could be heard by those in the surrounding cells. One evening we decided to protest our imprisonment by singing loudly as a group. We belted out "We Shall Overcome" and other protest songs, even a few hymns, with the choruses being taken up in the different tiers all around the maximum security unit. This brought the guards stomping in. We were told that if we didn't stop immediately the regular prisoners in other buildings at the penitentiary would believe there was a riot going on. When the singing persisted they came and, one cell at a time, stripped us of our bedding and the skimpy shorts we wore, saying, "Now you will really experience some hard time."

So for several days, while the lights shone day and night, we laid uncomfortably on the cold steel bunks. On one occasion we were even sprayed with a foul-smelling mosquito repellant. This resulted in one or two of my colleagues breaking down and crying, begging to be freed. Fortunately, our bedding was eventually restored—apparently just before a visit from a couple of northern state attorneys general, who had come down to Mississippi to investigate allegations of Freedom Rider mistreatment.

It was a bit surprising how delicate some of the White Freedom Riders were. They complained about nudity in the shower rooms, which they found demeaning because it revealed who was circumcised and who wasn't—a strange concern. Some even confided to me that their greatest fear was catching athlete's foot! Others complained bitterly about the food we were provided, saying that it wasn't a balanced diet or that it bothered their allergies. I must confess, I thought to myself that if these kids had experienced the spartan British boarding schools that I had, they wouldn't have felt that they were suffering so badly.

One thing I should mention is that right down at the end of our tier were Death Row and the electric chair. That's what the building we were housed in is still used for today in Mississippi.

As my roommate's fast progressed he wanted to talk more and more about food, telling me about his love for Cajun cuisine, even going to great lengths planning the menus he was going to consume when he was finally released from prison. John's reveries about Cajun cooking didn't really bother me, as I had never experienced it, but at the same time my stomach juices had been thinking that I would really enjoy a hamburger from White Spot, a Vancouver-based restaurant chain.

Eventually, on the twenty-third day of his hunger strike, John was taken out of our cell to be force-fed, along with two or three other prisoners. I never saw him again.

The reaction of the guards and trustees were interesting to us. I heard one burly guard, with a comic book stuck in his hip pocket, say to the residents of the cell next to mine, "With only a sixth-grade education, I am a lot smarter than you Yankee college kids."

When asked why, the guard referred to the chapter in the Bible about Cain and Abel, saying it was clearly God's will that "White folk and n——s shouldn't mix."

The Black trustees were another matter. They grovelled, saying, "Yes, boss" frequently to the White guards. But when unobserved, one said to us, smiling, "All the brothers in the pen here can't believe what you guys are doing for us, especially since you have church ministers and priests here with you. Just be careful, because the screws are looking for a chance to hurt you real bad. Just don't blame us if they make us do it, because we are all hoping to be released someday soon."

CHAPTER 28

"You Could Become a Habitual Criminal"

Warden, Mississippi State Penitentiary, 1961

As I WAS CHECKING out of the Mississippi State Penitentiary at Parchman, discarding my black-and-white-striped garb for my own clothing, the squat warden of the facility thought he should give me some friendly advice. He said, "You need to watch it. The way you are going, son, you could become a habitual criminal. I hear that you come from good stock, so it's too bad that you got involved with this group of commies."

"Thank you for your hospitality," I replied, "but I don't believe they will take much notice of this conviction back where I live, in British Columbia."

The warden asked a nearby guard, who was holding a cattle prod, "What's this boy saying? I can't understand his English accent."

My reply was repeated to him by the guard.

"Hell no, son, all them western states will send you away for life if you get four convictions."

Once dressed, I was hustled into a mesh cage on the back of the truck that was to transport me 130 miles south to Jackson, where a $500 appeal bond was being posted to allow me to exit the state. We drove in a convoy, with two state police cars in front and one following the truck I was in. Later I was told that Mississippi governor Ross Barnett had ordered the security because of Ku Klux Klan threats to capture and lynch some of the Freedom Riders.

After an hour or so, we pulled into a shady clearing in front of a run-down motel and restaurant. The state troopers drifted in to presumably have an early evening meal, while I sat on a bench in the wire-mesh cage.

"Look, they've got one of those Jew Freedom Riders," said a carrot-headed youth wearing a baseball hat.

"Yeah," said his friend, carrying a pitcher's glove. "We should show him how much we appreciate him coming down from up north to teach us how to look after our n——s."

They went off and returned a few minutes later with eggs and tomatoes, which they pitched at me. Fortunately, the objects didn't penetrate through the wire mesh, I just moved to the other side of the cage to avoid any splatter. By now, the crowd had grown to about a couple dozen young teenagers, and I could see the state troopers checking out the situation by peeking out from behind the curtains in the restaurant. All of a sudden my shirt and pants were splashed with a liquid that had come out of an apple juice can.

"That's my piss," said the youth who had first spotted me.

"And some of mine too," added his friend. "That's what we think of you Yankee Jews."

The crowd grew larger and now included some dungaree-clad adults who had stopped by in their pickup trucks, perhaps on their way home from the fields, including women with kerchiefs around the curlers in their hair.

"Okay, you have had your fun. Why won't you let us eat our dinner in peace?" shouted one of the state troopers as he emerged from the restaurant door, placing his hand on a holstered revolver.

When we finally reached the Jackson police station my clothes had dried but stank of urine. The bail procedure for me and a young Black woman who had come in the same convoy was swift, and ten minutes later I found myself at the home of Jack Young, the attorney provided by the Congress of Racial Equality. When the woman recounted what she had seen happen to me, from the comparative safety of a highway patrol car, the attorney's wife, Aurelia, quickly made me strip off my clothes and don one of her husband's bathrobes before we sat down to a wonderful fried-chicken dinner—the best meal I had had in weeks.

African-American men and women kept dropping by the home to say hello and to thank the young woman and me for what we had done for civil liberties in the American South. Among them was Medgar Evers, the local representative of the NAACP. Apparently the terms of my appeal were that I had to be out of the state by midnight, so before long my freshly laundered clothes were returned to me and I was driven to the airport, where I boarded a late-night flight to Chicago.

A few months later I read in the *New York Times* that the warden of the Parchman penitentiary had been indicted for embezzling funds from the sale of cotton. Two years later I read about the murder of Medgar Evers. Forty years later I returned to Jackson with my daughter Kyra and visited Medgar Evers's home, which is now a national heritage site.

I chose not to return to Mississippi in the summer of 2011, for the fiftieth anniversary of the Freedom Rides, but was surprised by the citations that I received from President Barack Obama, the governor of Mississippi and other officials.

CHAPTER 29

"Get Rid of That Castro Photo"

Sergeant-at-arms, Ottawa, 1961

I HAD ONLY BEEN back in Victoria for a week after leaving Mississippi when I received a surprising call inviting me to become a delegate to the founding convention of the New Democratic Party, which was to be held later that month in Ottawa.

I say "surprising" because I had never been a member of the old CCF party, which I considered too much of an adjunct of the trade union movement, but I had read with interest a book titled *The New Party,* edited by veteran Member of Parliament Stanley Knowles. The author had made a persuasive case that there was a need for a new political grouping of progressive forces in the country, which though based on the CCF would include left-wing liberal academics and small-business people.

I was attracted to much that was in the Knowles book, particularly an essay by a Montreal academic, Pierre Elliott Trudeau, on what he called "co-operative federalism." Trudeau made the case that more attention should be given to achieving left-wing governments at the provincial rather than the federal level, because of Canada's decentralized division of powers.

Such a strange thesis for someone who later became committed to building a stronger federal government than Canada had ever before experienced!

By the end of the telephone call I had accepted the invitation with the proviso that I needed some financial resources to get to Ottawa. That was remedied a few days later when the Esquimalt–Saanich Constituency Association elected me as one of their delegates to the convention, found me transportation and gave me seventy-five dollars for my expenses.

The transportation turned out to be a very old Volkswagen Beetle owned by a young CCFer named Gary Watkins. Four of us were to squeeze inside it for the 2,500-mile journey, with our luggage riding on the roof. It was an extraordinary trip in such a small car, particularly as in those days one had to drive part of the way through the United States. None of us had any money to spend on motels, so the idea was to drive in shifts twenty-four hours a day until we reached our destination. We did catch a few hours of sleep by the side of the road near the summit of Washington State's Stevens Pass, but the cold soon drove us back into the vehicle. We tried again at a picnic ground in northern Ontario, but the mosquitoes were too intense for us to rest long. And we certainly needed to keep rolling, hour after hour, because our old vehicle couldn't exceed fifty miles per hour except going downhill. And even that speed was hard to attain with our heavily laden roof rack in the face of prairie winds.

When we reached Ottawa we were thankful to be billeted at a Quaker's house on Grove Avenue, near the site of the convention. Francis Star, whose family was staying at their summer cottage, turned his whole house over to us. The first day after arriving, I believe we slept almost around the clock. I recall coming downstairs the next day and having a tall, pretty Vancouver girl named Tunya ask what she could cook us for breakfast.

I had never attended a political convention before, and I was fascinated with the whole scene, particularly the leadership race between Saskatchewan premier Tommy Douglas and the CCF leader, a Saskatchewan farmer named Hazen Argue. Many of the younger delegates, despite having enormous respect for Douglas, seemed to favour Argue because he pledged to take Canada out of NATO. It made sense to me at the time that Canada should play a more independent role in the world as a peacemaker rather than belong to a military alliance dominated by the United States.

One evening I was invited by Tunya to attend a so-called "secret" late-night meeting in Hazen Argue's House of Commons office, where strategy was plotted on how to attract rank-and-file union members away from the Canadian Labour Congress leadership. Because of my French, I was told by Argue that I would be particularly valuable in buttonholing Quebec delegates in the convention corridors and persuading them to support him on the grounds that he would be more sympathetic to a form of federalism that would give Quebec greater powers.

As the hot summer days went by, resolutions seemed to be passed one after the other, with the convention leadership referring anything contentious to a committee, which I was told was always an effective tactic for burying such issues. It actually became quite boring, as the trade-union juggernaut led by the Steelworkers and the United Auto Workers assertively pushed the agenda through.

One incident I do recall, though, was being tapped on the shoulder by a burly sergeant-at-arms who approached our table with his two deputies. “Get rid of that Castro photo,” he barked, pointing at the large picture of Fidel Castro that one of my Vancouver companions had propped up on our table. In fact, we had been pleased that it had more than once been featured on the television news during live CBC broadcasts from the convention centre.

I immediately stood up. “Well, you are going to have to deal with me first before we take that down. And how is that going to look on TV?” I demanded, standing a few inches away from the sergeant-at-arms. He stalked away and I got a little applause from those seated near our table.

Fifteen minutes later a pleasant young blond-haired woman appeared and said, “Mr. Audain, Tommy Douglas would like to meet with you,” to which I replied that I would be honoured to meet him, but that he should come and also meet my friends from Vancouver.

However, Tunya suggested, “Why don’t you at least give Tommy the courtesy of seeing what it’s about?”

So I went with the aide to a private room where Douglas seemed to be alone working on a speech. He apologized for meeting me on such short notice and said that he had read about my exploits in Mississippi and wanted to hear more. So I filled him in for a few minutes, and afterwards he said, “Michael, do you think we should equate Martin Luther King Jr. and Fidel Castro?”

I said, "No, they are very different men, though both are trying to do great things for their people."

Douglas agreed and told me that he would have no difficulty if we wanted to display a photo of Martin Luther King Jr. on our table, but he said the New Democratic Party (whose name had just been adopted) needed to appeal to a broad spectrum of Canadians.

He added, "If we were to become the government, some people might take umbrage at our displaying the photo of a foreign government leader, whether he be Fidel Castro or John Kennedy." I thanked Douglas for his advice and wished him well in the leadership race, then went back to my table on the convention floor.

After the next recess, we did remove the Castro photo, and in the leadership vote that shortly followed I cast my ballot for Tommy Douglas. He won by a landslide. Hazen Argue, who was supported by the left wing at the NDP convention, eventually became a Liberal cabinet minister, then a senator.

On the return trip, our old VW Beetle broke down in North Dakota. It became an object of curiosity when it was towed into a small town's farm machinery repair shop, where the mechanics were ingeniously able to wire together a repair that was good enough to get us back to Vancouver.

CHAPTER 30

"It's High Time We Don't Duck the Horrors of Hiroshima"

President Norman MacKenzie, UBC, 1961

As the year progressed, my courtship of Tunya Swetleshnoff, who I had met in Ottawa, got underway. Initially, I believe that we were attracted to each other because we shared the same aspirations for a left-wing government in Canada. We were not dogmatic socialists, but believed in a mixed economy similar to the Swedish model, in which co-operatives would play a major role, along with government and private corporations.

When I returned to the University of British Columbia in the fall, my priority continued to be the peace movement, with my new girlfriend helping to organize seminars and demonstrations. Over the course of the next few months, we fell in love and, wonder of wonders, through Tunya's patience and understanding, we achieved a satisfying sex life. After that occurred I was so elated I immediately proposed marriage. To my delight, Tunya enthusiastically accepted.

The following March we were married at Vancouver's Unitarian Church, with many leaders from political and trade union walks of life in attendance, as well as a large number of Tunya's Doukhobor relatives. My father and my new stepmother, Isobel (Marie had succumbed to cancer in 1956), were the only members of my family to attend, and I felt grateful to them for putting up with such socially uncomfortable surroundings for an hour or two.

Jimmy was not close to Tunya, who he referred to as a "bluestocking" for attempting to engage him in political discourse, but he seemed elated that I had finally found a compatible lady, thereby putting to rest his concerns about my masculinity.

Why was 1961 such a momentous one for me, a turning point in my life? Why was it the year in which I was transformed from a state of lonely unhappiness to one of positive elation, experiencing a sense of self-worth and recognition? Partly it had to do with my academic performance, which had become strong enough to win scholarships for my further education. It was, undoubtedly, related to the recognition and sense of "doing the right thing" I felt as a result of going to jail in Mississippi. But frankly it also had a lot to do with finding the girl who I believed would become my life partner.

I have on occasion been asked how my academic performance could have changed so remarkably in my university days. I believe it had more to do with deciding that the purpose of a university education was to get a piece of paper called a "degree" rather than just simply wanting to satisfy one's own sense of curiosity and thirst for knowledge.

I planned to approach each university course as if I was preparing for a battle. First, I did my best to achieve close and positive relationships with my professors, hiding any private misgivings I might have about them. I also made it my mission to attend each and every lecture, usually asking informed questions so that my commitment would be noticed. Term papers were meticulously typed, edited and always turned in on time. And when it came to exams, I crammed by using a folded piece of foolscap with all the salient facts about the content of the course. After memorizing them, I could dole the facts out in an impressive fashion. Anyway, the formula worked, and each year I reaped academic awards and scholarships, though I promptly forgot what I was supposed to have learned. For instance, even though I achieved high first-class honours in second-year German, when I visited the country a year or two later I found that I had forgotten ninety per cent of the vocabulary.

I started forming the Nuclear Disarmament Club at UBC in the fall of 1960, and in 1961 we became a fully recognized campus club. I was the first president. I had long been concerned with the horrors of Hiroshima and the threat of nuclear war, and believed that as a citizen the best thing to do was to campaign to keep nuclear weapons out of Canada.

The Nuclear Disarmament Club was controversial, with some people suggesting that we were a Communist Party front organization. I discovered later that we had certainly attracted the attention of the section of the RCMP concerned with national security.

At Club Day on campus we erected a booth in the armory to attract new members. On the walls we featured horrifying photos of Hiroshima victims, which even medical students said were tough to look at. After inspecting our booth, Professor Malcolm McGregor told us it was too controversial and should be dismantled immediately. When I refused, he said I was in danger of being expelled from the university. But thankfully, soon afterwards, UBC president Norman MacKenzie sauntered into the booth, and after carefully inspecting the photos asked me my name. He then said, "Well done, Audain, it's high time we don't duck the horrors of Hiroshima." The booth stayed!

CHAPTER 31

"You're the Strangest Screw"

Oakalla Prison inmate, 1962

I NEEDED A SUMMER job and had heard that the Oakalla Prison Farm near Vancouver recruited student guards in the summer so that the regular prison officers could go on vacation. I applied and was quickly issued a uniform and told to report at 7:00 a.m. a week later. When I did so, I found that I had been assigned to a series of cells called Death Row, in one of which an inmate named Eric Lifton awaited execution. At the end of the short tier was a disused elevator shaft that apparently would serve on the fatal day.

With his execution date about a month away there was a twenty-four-hour watch on the inmate to ensure that he didn't cheat the hangman. So I was given a chair in front of his cell and simply told to sit and watch. Given my personal opposition to capital punishment, something that I had determined some years prior, I was obviously rather bewildered by the situation.

Lifton had shot police detective Larry Short dead in February, at Vancouver's Bayshore Inn. I had some casual conversations with the prisoner, but during the few days that I was stationed there on the day shift, Lifton had a lot of visits from his lawyers, a chaplain and family members. For most of these he was escorted to a nearby meeting room. I often fetched meals for the man, but he was not too complimentary about them.

I had only been at Oakalla a few days when an item appeared in the *Vancouver Sun*'s Wasserman column, saying that Freedom Rider Michael Audain had been hired as a prison guard. This caused some consternation, with the head guard of the Death Row section saying, "I want the shit disturber off my turf!" I was immediately sent home and told to stay there until further notice.

Two days later I received a phone call telling me to report to Oakalla at 11:00 p.m., to an outlying building that housed several hundred prisoners in single cells of about sixteen on each tier, or "living units," as they were more euphemistically called. When I arrived, the inmates had already been locked up for the night and wouldn't be released from their cells until the 7:00 a.m. shift came on duty. There was just a supervisor and two of us summer student guards on duty throughout the night. Much of our time was preoccupied with counting the inmates, once when we came on shift, and again at 2:00 a.m. and 4:00 a.m.

The best part of those nights was when I could climb up in an outside watchtower and listen to a radio station broadcasting from the hungry i, a North Beach club that I had frequented in San Francisco. Then, at 6:00 a.m., it was my job to ride with a couple of trustees in the front of a truck that delivered food from the main kitchen to the outlying buildings. For this job, I was issued a .38 revolver with five bullets.

On my last shift at the end of the summer, one of the trustees said to me, "You are the strangest screw we have ever seen."

"In what way am I strange?" I enquired.

"Well, we notice you only pretend to load your gun. You never actually put the bullets in the chamber," the young Indigenous inmate said with a laugh. "What would you do if one of us made for the fence?"

"Well, I guess I would have to throw my gun at you," I replied, laughing with him.

Years later when I met Oakalla warden Hugh Christie in Ottawa, he told me that after the Wasserman column he had received express orders from Attorney General Robert Bonner to fire me on the spot, as a former inmate of the Mississippi State Penitentiary shouldn't be working as a prison guard. To his credit, Christie laid his job on the line by refusing to do so. In the end a compromise was reached whereby I was placed on the graveyard shift and was to have no direct contact with the inmates, until the end of the summer.

There were no attempted escapes for me to foil that summer, only an incident of one inmate cutting his wrist. When I noticed what was happening, I immediately reported it to the supervisor and asked him to give me a key to open the tier so that I could get the prisoner out of his cell.

"No," I was told. "That tier does not open until 7:00 a.m. and I don't care whether an inmate shits or hangs himself."

The need to defecate was a problem because the cells contained no toilets. Inmates had only an apple juice can to urinate in, so the smell was at times unbearable.

In the case of the wrist-cutter, an orderly came down from the prison hospital to bandage the inmate's wrist through the bars. I then placed my chair up against the cell and chatted with him, hoping to deter further damage. To my surprise, the first action of the day-shift supervisor was to have the inmate marched to the hole for solitary confinement as punishment for self-mutilation.

It's strange how circumstances change. Thirty years later, all the buildings in the Oakalla Prison Farm had been razed, and Polygon, our home-building company, was constructing townhomes on the site.

CHAPTER 32

"We Should Join Our Men in Prison"

Fanny Storgeoff, 1962

IT WAS A SUNNY September morning as my wife, Tunya, and I drove up the steep mountainside to the Doukhobor community of Krestova, perched high above the Slocan River in southeastern BC.

As we pulled into the village, people were emerging from the small makeshift huts they called homes and trudging towards the central gathering place, where a banner had been raised. Scattered along the road were the smoking hulks of cars and trucks that had been recently burnt.

By 10:00 a.m. several hundred people had congregated, mostly women, children and old men. I approached the stout leader, a woman in her late fifties who the press had nicknamed "Big Fanny." She wore what looked like several dresses flowing to her feet, and a folded scarf over her head. Using Tunya as an interpreter, I asked, "What's happening, where are you going?"

"Mary had a dream last night that said we should join our men in prison, so we are all going to march to the coast today," Big Fanny, whose name was actually Fenya Storgeoff, replied in Russian.

"But that's a long way to walk, how will you make it?" I enquired.

Instead of replying, Big Fanny started to sing in Russian, and soon the hymn was taken up by hundreds of voices. On that autumn day, as she stepped forward, the crowd surged behind her, some carrying babies, others holding the hands of little children. They had not gone far when

I noticed their huts starting to go up in flames, but not a single person looked back. They had a six-hundred-mile march in front of them, with no thought about how they were going to accomplish it.

The Sons of Freedom were a breakaway branch from the larger group of Russian immigrants called the Doukhobors. By the 1960s the Sons of Freedom had become notorious for their property destruction and nude demonstrations. They blew up hydro transmission lines, bridges and public buildings. Indeed, they were a thorn in the side of the government for decades, as well as an embarrassment to the majority of the Doukhobors' descendants in Canada, whose ancestors had arrived from Russia around 1908.

Members of a pacifist community that had long been persecuted by the Russian tsars, they gained the assistance of writer Leo Tolstoy to immigrate to Canada, first settling in Saskatchewan, then moving to southeastern BC between 1908 and 1912. But the BC government had used oppressive tactics to deal with the disruptive sect, including forcibly removing their children from their homes to educate them behind barbed wire in a government school at New Denver. The reason? The Sons of Freedom didn't believe in sending their children to public schools because they considered them to be militaristic.

Because my wife, Tunya, came from a Doukhobor family, I had a more than passing interest in this group. Familiar with my student activism on the UBC campus, sociology professor Werner Cohn contacted me to help organize the defence of seventy members of the Fraternal Council of the Sons of Freedom, who had been incarcerated and charged with conspiracy to intimidate the Parliament of Canada and the Legislature of British Columbia. Cohn was an expert on European ethnic organizations, such as the Romanis, and believed that if the Sons' charge was successfully prosecuted in court it could be used against any group the government found troublesome.

We quickly convened a group of university professors and lawyers, including veteran lawyer Harry Rankin, and applied to the court for *amicus curiae* (friend of the court) status, something which hadn't been granted before in Canada.

The presiding judge at the preliminary hearing was Magistrate William Evans, from Nelson, who had a long record of sentencing Doukhobors to lengthy prison terms. When he didn't grant our request, we began to mount a press campaign. For me, it was all rather odd, as that was the summer I was working on the night shift at the Oakalla Prison Farm, and I occasionally had to go to the evening meetings dressed in my guard uniform.

This would become known as one of the more colourful events in British Columbia's history, and Tunya and I were the only outsider witnesses to the start of the march. There was no media presence. We had received a tip that there might be something interesting happening that weekend, so we'd driven up to Nelson the previous day in our Volkswagen Beetle on the chance that we might be on hand for an event.

And it was certainly a strange day: at the base of the mountain, where the track up to Krestova joined Highway 24, we saw hundreds of people emerging. A banner was carried by a choir of middle-aged and elderly women, accompanied by a man with a long white beard who was stripped to the waist and pushing a baby buggy.

"I feel like I am back in the Middle Ages," I said to Tunya.

"Yes, it's hard to believe that we are in twentieth-century Canada," she agreed.

We stayed with the marchers for the rest of the day, then had to drive home to go to our jobs, leaving the Sons of Freedom behind us. But not entirely: weeks later, as they began to near Vancouver, we wondered where they would stay in the city, so Tunya and I took the initiative to establish a billeting service.

We obtained the co-operation of many Christian missions scattered around the Downtown Eastside, such as the Salvation Army, the Central City Mission and the Union Gospel Mission, each agreeing to take so many people—some just men, others just women and children. We broadcasted the need for accommodation over radio and television and received many offers from people of Doukhobor descent but who had no connection to the Sons of Freedom. We assured them that they had nothing to fear.

Tunya and I actually took seven teenage girls into our one-bedroom apartment for a week or two. They had a wonderful time taking off their kerchiefs and trying out Tunya's makeup. Each day they would go to Victory Square to sing and then return home in the evening to the large pot of borscht that Tunya kept warm on the stove. Fortunately, we had a lot of old mattresses covered with Indian bedspreads for furniture, so our apartment was much more comfortable for the girls than the leaking tents that had been their home for weeks.

After a month or two passed, the small group of women around Big Fanny who were deemed to be the leaders decided that their singing and presence in downtown Vancouver wasn't going to get them any sympathy, so they moved ninety miles east and camped by the roadside outside the Agassiz prison, where members of the Fraternal Council were housed as their case dragged on through the courts.

On weekends, we would occasionally drive out to Agassiz to maintain contact. On one occasion, I acted as liaison for a film made by the French division of the National Film Board. Another time, we took Canadian poet Al Purdy for a visit. Later, he sent us an autographed copy of his book titled *The Cariboo Horses*. In it you will find the poem "In the Wilderness," which in part reads:

> On the road to Agassiz in winter
> of 1962
> grandfathers
>   young wives
>   old children
> marching in the savage demolitions of hunger
> for their own people
> to the mountain prison at Agassiz
> where incendiarist husbands and
> incandescent nephews and
> sons of that pale yellow soap-like stuff
>   which is dynamite
> are locked away near a town named

for the gentle naturalist
                    Louis Agassiz
In a way unrealized
these are the Children of Israel
with a Pillar of Fire by day
and a Pillar of Fire by night
standing over them in the mountains
In this wilderness
of 1962

And there was another legacy. When eventually our first child arrived, Tunya and I decided to call her Fenya as a reminder of that singular event in our lives.

CHAPTER 33

"It Can Be Boring Earning a Living at a Typewriter"

Ian Fleming, 1963

I WASN'T PREPARED FOR the strong smell of excrement in the daycare centre situated in the middle of Kingston's huge Foreshore slum.

Tiny children seemed to be running around everywhere with only T-shirts on. Occasionally, one would squat in the corner to defecate. "We find it easier to leave their pants off and let them go anywhere, rather than have to wash nappies," my mother, Madeleine, said. She volunteered half a day weekly at the Red Cross-operated facility for slum-dwellers' children. Her husband, George Carmichael, had been posted to Kingston to manage the Jamaican assets of the British company Eagle Star Insurance.

When I arrived in Jamaica, George told me that since he knew of my social work interest, a tour of the Foreshore area had been set up, with Peter Fletcher, the son of Senator Douglas Fletcher, to accompany me.

Peter, a tall man of about my age, confessed that it was the first time that he had ever entered the Foreshore, which was an area rife with crime. But he said that he had some connections in the Rastafarian community and asked if I would be interested in meeting them, or if I'd prefer to go to a private club for tennis or a swim. I said that anything would be better than the stink of the daycare centre, but added that I had certainly heard of the Rastafarians and would be fascinated to meet them.

It didn't take long to arrange. When we arrived at our destination it seemed there was already a crowd of raggedly dressed men wearing beards and long matted hair waiting for us at the door. They hustled us down the narrow slum street into what appeared to be a beer hall—at least there was a lot of beer being drunk in that hot, dank room, which included a thoroughly trashed pool table and some dartboards.

We sat around a battered table. It was difficult to hear because of the incessant chatter, but I was able to ask a chap who seemed to be a leader some questions, particularly about when he expected Emperor Haile Selassie to arrive out of the sky to transport him back to Africa. When I enquired whether it was true that Rastas mostly earned their living cultivating and selling ganja, he beamed in the affirmative and promptly offered me some plump cigars rolled in newspaper. I was on the verge of trying one when Fletcher, with a gasp of horror, grabbed my wrist and cautioned me that if I took a few puffs of what they were offering I would be completely stoned for the rest of the day.

Looking anxiously at his watch, Fletcher suggested it was time that we be off to his Liguanea Country Club. But our exit wasn't so easy. Apparently I was considered a VIP visitor of the Rastas' clubhouse and as such had a job to do. We had to wait while one of the older men laboriously wrote out a letter to Dag Hammarskjöld, secretary-general of the United Nations, asking that the Rastas be repatriated to Africa. Another, learning that I was a Canadian, wrote much the same thing addressed to Prime Minister Lester Pearson.

I had to promise to deliver these letters in order to escape from the twenty or thirty Rastas who seemed to have the idea that I had planned to spend the rest of the day, if not the night, with them. "Stay here while you are in Jamaica. We will entertain you with the world's best music, all the girls you could ever want, and the highest-quality ganja," one of the Rasta leaders implored me eloquently in Jamaican patois.

Holding the folded letters they gave me in my hand, I politely declined, and after another half hour Fletcher and I were able to finally exit the beer hall and retreat to the air-conditioned comfort of his father's chauffeured Mercedes, which was waiting for us outside. As we departed the Foreshore area en route to the country club, I was amazed to see at least half a dozen Rastas on motorcycles escorting us until we entered the gated country club grounds.

CHAPTER 33

That evening at dinner, when I recounted to my mother and her husband the happenings of the morning, George said, "Well, I hope you didn't tell them where you are staying while in Jamaica."

"I simply told them that I was staying with you in Constant Spring, as I had forgotten the exact address."

"Oh my God," George said. "They are likely trying to descend on this house already now that you have given them some encouragement. Didn't you know that they are all dangerous criminals?"

After dinner George phoned the chief of police, who was apparently a friend, and demanded that some constables be sent immediately to beef up his security, which normally just consisted of a night-watchman. Sure enough, half an hour later a police car came and parked itself at the end of the driveway. Before retiring, George left a handgun by my bed, saying, "Be careful, as it's loaded with the safety off. All you need to do is point and fire it."

Apparently, George had complained to the commissioner of the Jamaica constabulary a couple of weeks prior about a hand coming in through the bars of his bedroom window, searching for something to steal, and it had taken forty-five minutes for the police to arrive. The commissioner responded, "We will always come when you call, George, but we would prefer that you have a body for us to take away."

The following morning George felt that for security reasons he should take my mother and I to Ocho Rios, on the north coast. There, Eagle Star Insurance owned a small luxury hotel called the Beach Club. My stay there, with its idyllic swimming and sailing, was considerably less interesting than my introduction to Kingston. But I did have an opportunity to dine with both Charlie Chaplin and Ian Fleming, the author of the James Bond books.

Chaplin told me that he knew my grandfather Rudolph Stulik, as he used to frequent his Eiffel Tower Restaurant when visiting London in the 1920s. At the table, I noticed that he was at times sullen, perhaps because he had been seated separately from his wife, Oona O'Neill, but then cheered up when my mother skillfully drew him out about his youth in London's East End before he embarked on a career in Hollywood.

On the other hand, Ian Fleming seemed totally relaxed and ended up inviting us to his house for a before-dinner drink the following day. Visiting his small seaside home was a fascinating experience. He showed me the portable Olivetti typewriter on which he banged out a James Bond novel every season, explaining that he could only sit at his desk three hours or so in the morning—he took the rest of the day off to swim and think about what he was going to write the following day.

"It can be boring earning a living at a typewriter, but like any other job there has to be a method to it," Fleming explained.

That evening, to my mother's amazement, I asked if I could return to Canada the following day. "But you have only been here for four nights. I thought you were staying for ten days — don't you enjoy these idyllic surroundings, where everything is paid for by the company?" she pleaded.

"Yes," I explained, "but unfortunately I have things to do in Vancouver that are on my mind."

I didn't say that when I was with my mother I felt like she was a complete stranger and longed to be home again with my new wife.

Rather than personally deliver the Rastafarians' letters, I must confess that I put them in the mail with a covering letter. There was no acknowledgment from Secretary-General Dag Hammarskjöld, but an Ottawa mandarin did eventually write back to me on behalf of Pearson, saying that he was unclear why Canada should have any responsibility for repatriating people who had lived for years in Jamaica back to Africa.

When a couple of years later Haile Selassie did actually visit Jamaica, the emperor wanted nothing to do with the Rastafarians, though they reportedly attempted to block the Kingston airport's runway to force him to repatriate them on board his airplane.

As to my mother, Madeleine, I made an effort to keep in touch by bringing her out to the West Coast for a short holiday every summer until 1994, when I was called to her sick bed in Hove, England, where she and George had retired. I was alone at her bedside until the end, and after scattering her ashes, I returned to Vancouver. I had loved her, I suppose, when I was very little, and was greatly relieved when she made a good second marriage and got her life sorted out, but as we had so little to do with each other for the greater part of my life, I confess her death affected me less than I might have expected.

CHAPTER 34

"We Always Appreciate Constructive Criticism"

Walter Shogan, 1964

ONE OF MY MOST disagreeable duties when I was a juvenile probation officer was escorting boys sentenced by the Vancouver Family and Children's Court over to Brannan Lake School, an institution established near Nanaimo for the confinement of so-called juvenile delinquents. I had taken the position after finishing my studies at UBC. The boys would be bundled into the rear of my Volkswagen Beetle while the other probation officer and I sat in the front. On the ferry from Horseshoe Bay, we would always give the kids a good breakfast, paid for out of our own pockets, while being sure to keep an eye on them—once a lad had hidden himself in the back of a truck on the car deck, and he wasn't caught until a month later. But what should have been a pleasant day away from the office on the beautiful British Columbia coast was actually always a sad experience for me.

After we signed the boys into the custody of the school, we were offered lunch at a special table in the dining room. It was so distressing for me to watch the boys, dressed in khaki work pants and matching shirts, lining up silently for their meal—small children as young as nine or eleven together with hulking lads as old as seventeen.

The school's authorities maintained that its purpose was to rehabilitate juvenile offenders so that they would become useful members of the community, but education was only available to grade nine, and there was no psychiatric consultation despite some of the children having mental health issues. The fact that the school was located far away from the Vancouver metropolitan area made parental visits difficult, particularly for those children who came from First Nations communities in northern British Columbia.

The dormitories and schoolrooms were spartan, but no worse than some of the boarding schools that I had attended in England. However, what I found appalling were the cells, with wire-mesh doors, used to confine children for up to two weeks of detention, on bare concrete floors, clad only in light pyjamas.

According to my research, the Brannan Lake School did not conform to widely accepted North American standards for the custodial treatment of youngsters. Corporal punishment had been abolished by the National Association of Training Schools in the United States some years earlier.

Shortly after starting the job I sent a memo to my boss, Chief Probation Officer Stevens, at the Juvenile and Family Courts in Vancouver, outlining my concerns. He subsequently called me into his office, where, with his deputy present, he warned me to mind my own business: "Any more bitching and you are out the door!"

Several of my probation officer colleagues said that they agreed with me that it was deplorable that we were having to commit kids to such an antiquated and overcrowded institution, effectively a school for crime. But they cautioned me that it was not up to us to try to change the system.

I pondered for a few weeks about what I could do to bring my concerns to the attention of the provincial government and the public. Deciding that a single letter to the minister responsible wouldn't achieve anything, instead I wrote long and detailed open letters to all members of the Legislative Assembly, and the day after I slipped them in the postbox I resigned from my job to save the government the task of firing me. I then sent copies of my letter to the media, after which all hell broke loose, with stories in newspapers throughout the province reporting my charges in considerable detail.

The reaction of the authorities was not unexpectedly swift, with School Superintendent F.G. Hassard in denial, explaining that children in the detention cells were given floorboards and a mattress to sleep on at 9:00 p.m., and claiming that one boy liked the school so much that he stole a watch just so that he could get sent back.

There seemed to be some confusion about the extent of the corporal punishment used, with Deputy Minister Ray Rickinson claiming that children were only strapped on the hand as in the public schools, whereas Deputy School Superintendent Walter Shogan said that the whippings were always given on the buttocks, with rarely more than six strokes administered. The government also denied that the children were secured and detained in wire cages, saying that the cells were more like bedrooms, though a photo was published clearly showing the wire screens on the cell doors.

A long *Globe and Mail* story titled "Shades of Dickens at Brannan Lake," by Douglas Collins, presented my charges in some detail, whereas in the *Victoria Times*, reporter Michael Valpy claimed that my description of the school was irresponsible, reflecting the outrage from Deputy Superintendent Shogan, who stated, "This is absolutely ridiculous. We always appreciate constructive criticism, but not irresponsible criticism."

A couple of weeks later, New Democratic Party MLA Dave Barrett invited me to lunch at the legislative dining room in Victoria's parliament buildings, with Opposition leader Tom Berger, where I was eyed malevolently by a number of Social Credit ministers, including Wesley Black, Minister of Social Welfare, and Attorney General Robert Bonner. Bonner had for some years been a family friend.

Barrett, a former social worker, commended me for playing the role of whistle-blower and promised that if and when he ever became premier, the first thing he would like to do is to close Brannan Lake School and adopt a more enlightened way of dealing with youngsters who get into trouble with the law.

Although I was in Ottawa in 1972 when Barrett was elected as premier of British Columbia, he phoned me a week after he had taken power to say that he'd kept this promise.

CHAPTER 35

"You Must Take That Baby Home"

Vancouver General Hospital nurse, 1966

When our first daughter was born, on April 20, 1966, I was working in community liaison with the United Way in Vancouver and had been accepted to start PhD studies at the London School of Economics and Political Science in the fall.

Tunya was a very confident expectant mother. I recall her saying that she didn't need to go into prenatal classes because everything she needed to know was in Dr. Spock's book. Also, she decided that she didn't want her baby in a hospital nursery but in her room at the Vancouver General Hospital. Our obstetrician, Dr. Gaiman, gained permission for this, so our daughter Fenya became the first child at VGH to have this "lying-in" experience, as it was called.

The birth was difficult and painful because Fenya was a big baby. Nevertheless, once it was over, mother and daughter did fine together, until three days later, when it was time to go home. I took the day off from work and drove Tunya and our baby back to the furnished home we had rented for the summer in West Vancouver. All went well for two or three hours, with Fenya sleeping and feeding normally. Then I suddenly heard a yell from Tunya, who was sitting on the toilet in the bathroom. She said, "I have been sitting here for ten minutes and the bleeding won't stop."

"Is there much coming out?" I asked.

"Yes, I am losing a lot of blood," she replied.

"Well, I am not going to wait for an ambulance. Get in the car and I'll drive you straight back to the hospital, and the baby will come with us."

I put Fenya, still sleeping, in a bassinet on the back seat of our Volkswagen Beetle. Tunya climbed in the front, wrapped in a housecoat with a whole bunch of towels around her middle. Without stopping to lock the house, I sped over the Lions Gate Bridge with my warning lights flashing. I went through the bus lane, using my horn to force my way onto the bridge, and proceeded with great dispatch back to VGH. Red lights were only respected to the extent of avoiding any obvious collisions.

By the time we reached the hospital the towels between Tunya's legs were sodden with blood. I rushed inside the door of the emergency department, saying, "I need help, quick!"

"What seems to be the matter?" asked an admissions clerk. "Everyone has to take their turn."

I grabbed a wheelchair and put Tunya in it, with more towels around her midriff, and wheeled her in the door, right past the admissions desk.

A nurse intercepted us and said, "You cannot force yourself in here like that! Is that woman your wife? What's wrong with her?"

I parted the bottom of her housecoat and said, "Take a look."

"Oh my God! You can't reveal your wife like that in a public area. Stretcher!" the nurse cried.

I left Tunya there and dashed out to the car to grab Fenya in her bassinet. A few minutes later, a young male doctor came out and said, "Your wife's hemorrhaging and it won't stop until we remove some placenta that's adhered inside the womb. She needs immediate attention, so she's already been transferred back into the maternity ward."

"Good, and I've got this baby here who needs to follow," I said.

"I don't know if they'll take the baby," the intern said. "There is nothing wrong with it, is there?"

"No, but I've got no one at home and don't have a clue how to look after a baby," I replied.

When we got to the admissions section for the maternity ward, they were adamant that the baby could not re-enter the nursery as it wasn't sterile.

"She doesn't need to be sterile, because she's going back into the room with my wife, where's she been the last three days," I replied.

"That's not our policy, it's absolutely impossible. You must take that baby home or find someone to look after it," an older nurse told me.

So I used a payphone to contact one of our friends who lived in North Vancouver. A former nurse, she responded immediately, "Come on over to the house, and on the way go to a drugstore and buy some baby formula and some diapers. I will show you what to do."

Amazingly, all this occurred while Fenya was sleeping contentedly in her bassinet, so I drove back towards the North Shore at a more sedate pace. I wasn't worried about Tunya now, as she was back in the hospital's care, but I was terrified of looking after our baby.

Tekla, the wife of author Bill Deverell, was marvellous. She showed me how to fold and arrange a diaper without sticking a pin through my daughter's stomach, and how to heat a bottle of formula and test its warmth against my wrist. We did a practice feeding and diaper change together, then I drove home to our silent house.

I phoned Tunya's mother in Saskatchewan, who said that she would be on a plane to us the next day. I phoned Dr. Gaiman, the obstetrician, who said that he was going to give the hospital a piece of his mind for refusing to let Fenya stay with Tunya.

I got a modest amount of sleep between diaper changes and feedings, and then an early call from the hospital administrator saying that they were indeed prepared to take the baby back into Tunya's room. So I returned to the hospital at 8:00 a.m. the next morning. The elevator operator refused to take me up to the maternity ward with the baby with me, saying it was against the rules, so I found the staircase and climbed the four floors with the bassinet.

Despite all the things I have seen happen in the world, I must confess that I was more frightened by this experience than on any other occasion in my life. My nails all went white and grey hair started forming on my temples even though I hadn't yet turned thirty.

CHAPTER 36

"Our Revolution Will Live on in the Hearts of the French People"

Daniel Cohn-Bendit, 1968

I HAD BEEN STANDING outside Professor Donnison's small office at the London School of Economics and Political Science (LSE) for twenty-five minutes before he turned up and curtly told me to take a seat.

"I know I'm late, but I have been reading your thesis draft on the top deck of a bus. It seems quite good, but I detest your American spelling," he said while slipping off his Harris Tweed jacket. The interview with my PhD thesis supervisor was the first that I had had in five months, but it only lasted half an hour, with the admonition to go off and do some more "digging."

After completing a Master of Social Work degree at UBC, I worked for a year at the United Way in Vancouver doing something called local-area social planning, for which the agency had obtained a federal government grant. My turf, so to speak, was an area called Strathcona, which included Chinatown and some public-housing projects.

I enjoyed meeting people in the area and in no time got a local-area planning council going, the chair of which was a realtor named Faye Leung. This colourful lady, famous for her numerous hats, many years later became instrumental in the resignation of BC's premier Bill Vander Zalm, who was alleged to have accepted $20,000 cash in a brown paper envelope during a transaction to sell his Fantasy Gardens amusement park, with its Dutch windmill—a deal being brokered by Faye Leung.

CHAPTER 36

Not exactly sure of my career direction, I decided it was time to broaden my horizons and prepare myself for possibly teaching at the UBC School of Social Work. I applied to both Columbia University and the London School of Economics for doctoral studies, and to support me in this endeavour I also applied for fellowships from both the Canada Council and the Canada Mortgage and Housing Corporation, telling the latter that I intended to study Canadian housing policy. I had developed an interest in housing as a result of my experiences in East Vancouver, where much of the older housing was deteriorated and families lived in either overcrowded conditions or paid an exorbitant amount of their income for rent.

Actually, my fieldwork placement for my social work master's program had been in the McLean Park public-housing development, where the objective was to form a tenant organization to develop community spirit, to overcome some of the sterility of the brand-new housing project, with its institutional look. It had been designed by Ottawa's CMHC for the neighbourhood's poorer families and senior citizens.

At that time, I'd started to wonder whether there weren't better solutions to the "housing problem" than grouping poor families together in government-owned residences with fairly strict rules. Such projects were managed by an entity called the BC Housing Management Commission, run by an austere man named Sutherland, who was once overheard referring to my involvement in his little housing empire as "an unfortunate but temporary burden."

To my surprise, my applications were accepted at Columbia as well as LSE, and I was also offered fellowships by both the Canada Council and CMHC. After a week's reflection with Tunya, we decided that London was more attractive, because the Canadian dollar would go further there and because of the excellent reputation of LSE's Social Administration Department, headed by Richard Titmuss. He was considered the intellectual guru of the modern welfare state that then pertained in the UK under Prime Minister Harold Wilson's Labour government.

My first challenge in London was to find accommodation that I could afford for a young family, our daughter Fenya being four months old.

That was a struggle due to the many "No blacks, no children" notices. "No smokers" notations were not so common those days, though somewhat to my amusement I often came across "No Australians" in the rental agency listings. After getting to know a young woman who worked in an "accommodation bureau," I finally located an upper floor of a semi-detached house in Wimbledon Park that suited us.

To my surprise, in those days LSE doctoral students had no lectures to attend, though it was considered good form to show up for the occasional seminar. You were just there to do a competent piece of original research, for which you were awarded a doctorate when your supervisor felt that you were ready to defend your thesis. Despite this, I made an effort to attend many of the weekly lectures by senior social administration professors, including of course those of David Donnison, my thesis supervisor. His main theme seemed to be that all government programs for people should be universal in scope rather than selective programs that focused just on poor people. His favourite model was the postwar Labour government's National Health Service.

The LSE professors argued that the main reason for this approach was that if social services just targeted those who couldn't afford to purchase services in the market, then they would inevitably be inferior programs. Also, the poor would refrain from participating in "selective programs" for fear of being stigmatized. This was an interesting concept, though I had a little difficulty squaring it with my supervisor's own education at Harrow, the boarding school of many of Britain's princes and prime ministers.

When it came to housing, Donnison at the time seemed to favour it mostly being provided by the state or non-profit housing associations. He did not rule out a limited amount of home ownership, which was perhaps understandable as he owned a home in the gentrifying Islington neighbourhood, but made the case that home ownership had always been one way or another subsidized by government at the expense of tenants.

I had been assigned to Donnison because, having spent a year at the University of Toronto, he was somewhat familiar with Canada, and he was very knowledgeable about housing policy in general, being the author of a survey of European urban policies. In the beginning, I got along well with my supervisor, as he appeared to be anything other than a stuffy university don, but as time went on we became irritated with each other. I particularly had difficulties obtaining appointments with him. Like many LSE professors, Donnison seemed to have a full calendar, having been appointed to a number of government commissions and advisory bodies, including the Plowden Royal Commission on Education. I got the feeling that what he expected PhD students to do was just to get on with their thesis, with only very minimal advice from their advisors.

With rather crowded conditions at home, including a boisterous young baby, I did most of my research in the LSE library, which was open to graduate students from 9:30 a.m. on, then I would return home on the London Underground around 6:30 p.m. After a few months, I found the conditions at the magnificent blue-domed British Museum reading room better, where I had access to many early Canadian government documents in the State Papers room. When I took lunch breaks there, it was fascinating to wander through the Babylonian and Egyptian sculpture galleries, which in winter were usually quite deserted.

I didn't form any close friendships at LSE—evenings and weekends I tended to spend with my family when I wasn't travelling to housing tours and conferences. My closest relationships were with sociologists John and Beth Hutman from San Francisco, who were both enrolled in doctoral studies. I recall visiting their flat and being amazed at how they had things organized, with three IBM typewriters and a full-time secretary banging out manuscript drafts from Dictaphone tapes, whereas my own draft was laboriously typed by Tunya on a portable manual typewriter while the baby took her afternoon nap.

However, Tunya and I lived well in London. With my two fellowships and no income tax liability, my net income was higher than I had ever experienced, giving us sufficient funds to attend museums and plays and become frequent attendees at the Royal Ballet at Covent Garden. We also took trips to France, and one Easter toured Eastern Europe, including the Baltic States.

That European trip was absolutely thrilling, travelling by train to East Berlin, Warsaw and then Vilnius, the capital of Lithuania. As we crossed the border from Poland into Lithuania, which was then part of the USSR, and beheld a huge railway steam engine with a red star on its front, I remember Tunya exclaiming, "Oh, they've obviously seen *Dr. Zhivago*!"

Once on the train, the Russian border guards started to hassle some members of our group, so Tunya remonstrated their captain for them to desist. Glad to meet someone from the West who could speak Russian, the captain in no time was amicably showing us pictures of his children and told his soldiers to stop rifling through our luggage for forbidden literature.

We generally had a great time in the cities we visited, until I had to call a doctor to our St. Petersburg hotel to examine Tunya, whose legs had been swelling daily during the latter portion of the trip. A female women's trauma doctor arrived with an assistant and an ambulance crew. From what Tunya told me, the doctor considered her situation dangerous and said that she needed to go to a sanitarium for at least a month, where she would get free treatment. We were both somewhat horrified at this, thinking about our need to get back to London, where our baby was temporarily in the care of a neighbourly family from Mauritius who happened to live next door. I immediately decided that we would fly to London and consult doctors there, to which the doctor said, "Well, that is your right. But if your wife were a Soviet citizen I would order her immediately into hospital."

That evening we flew back to London via Helsinki. The next day Tunya was hospitalized in London with a case of sarcoidosis, a condition which does seem to benefit from extensive bed rest, though not nearly as long as what had been prescribed in Russia.

As things turned out I was becoming increasingly bored with my doctoral thesis, so when I returned for a final term of residence at the London School of Economics I found the time to become involved in the student movement on campus. The main issue was opposition to the appointment to LSE of Dr. Walter Adams, formerly the principal of the College of Rhodesia and Nyasaland, who it was believed had been sympathetic to Prime Minister Ian Smith's secessionist regime in the country now called Zimbabwe.

Adams had been selected to become the new principal of LSE, as the head of the school was called in those days. Although considerably older than most of the undergraduates who were agitating against this appointment, I joined in because I felt that a major mistake was being made by appointing an academic we were told had been comfortable with South Africa's apartheid policy.

On one occasion, an anti-appointment rally sponsored by the Socialist Society was scheduled to be held in LSE's Old Theatre. When the use of this room was banned by the administration, the students stormed the doors and, in the process, an elderly porter, who was trying valiantly to block their passage, suffered a heart attack and died. Fortunately, I wasn't involved in the melee, but when Professor Donnison was appointed to chair a three-person disciplinary committee to punish the student perpetrators I got dragged in to the controversy. Unavoidably, Donnison took notice of my support of the rally and our relationship, while never close, definitely became strained.

The decision of the discipinary committee was that David Adelstein, president of the LSE Students' Union, and another student were to be "sent down," meaning they were suspended for a specified period. There were no charges laid in respect to the unfortunate death of the porter.

In the spring of 1968, when France erupted in a general strike, I became very interested, because though strikes were not uncommon in France, it was the first time that the students and all the trade unions had decided to work together to bring down the government. Here was an opportunity, I thought, for the youth of our generation to take over and create a better world, unencumbered by an entrenched coterie of old men who lacked the understanding that the young of the world wanted a more just society, in which all nations could live together in peace.

The leader of the student movement in France was a German named Daniel Cohn-Bendit, known by the British tabloid press as "Danny the Red," and the LSE Students' Union decided that the way to get a revolution of the young going in Britain would be to bring Cohn-Bendit to

London. The question was how to get to Paris to invite him. All types of transport, including air and rail, had been shut down in the general strike. Some suggested going to the Netherlands or Germany and driving in from there. I happened to find that there was one cross-channel ferry to France that was still working, so I volunteered to try that route. A French student named Francine offered to go with me, so I hired a Ford Anglia in Wimbledon and filled the trunk up with three jerry cans of gasoline, because we had been told that the fuel stations were all closed in France.

After landing on the French coast, we made Paris the same day, as there was hardly any traffic on the roads. Paris itself had an almost surreal air about it with no public transport and few cars—the main vehicles to be seen were military or police ones. Though we were stopped at roadblocks, we were just waved through with our GB plates. In the Latin Quarter there was a real air of excitement, with the black flag of anarchy hanging from the Odeon on the Boulevard Saint-Michel.

After trying that evening to contact student leaders at the Sorbonne, we were told that all the action was at the University of Nanterre, a campus in suburban Paris. So the next morning we rose early and quickly located what seemed to be a control centre for the whole student movement in the Nanterre's administration building, from which all the regular staff had been evicted. Messengers on motorcycles were continually coming and going, and we were told that the telephone lines had been tapped by the government.

While Cohn-Bendit welcomed Francine and I warmly, he said that he had already been inundated with invitations to go to Rome, Madrid and even America.

"Don't people understand that I have my hands full? I could spend all day talking to journalists, but nothing would be accomplished. The comrades and I must spread the revolution to every corner of France so that when the parachutists come to take me away, as they surely will, our revolution will live on in the hearts of French people everywhere who cherish the ideals upon which this republic was founded."

Cohn-Bendit did, however, promise to send a delegate to London as soon as he could spare someone. And that afternoon, we met with student leader Alain Krivine, who told us that he would come to LSE as soon as he could.

A day or two later, Cohn-Bendit fled Paris for the west coast of France, where he was soon arrested and deported to Germany. After that the communist-led French trade-union movement made an accord with the government and a general election was soon held. The Gaullist Party was returned with almost three-quarters of the seats in the National Assembly, obviously a tremendous defeat for those of us with roots in the student movement.

The resurgence of what one might call the Ancien Régime in France was a great letdown for me. Up to that time I had thought that the movement of history was towards the establishment of a new society unfettered by the ideologies of the past. Wherever rebellions of the young had emerged, on university campuses in North America and Europe, I had identified with them, believing that we were in the vanguard of the struggle against nuclear war and for a more just world.

I became so depressed that I decided it was time to move on from being a professional student. Fortunately, just at this time, I was contacted by Dr. Albert Rose, head of the School of Social Work at the University of Toronto, who told me that he was on the board of the Ontario Housing Corporation, which was building thousands of public housing units across that province. He said he was keen for their endeavours to have a social side and asked if I would come to Toronto to head up their new community relations branch.

My preference would have been to return to British Columbia, but after a quick trip to Toronto I said yes, and within a few weeks I was at work there and living in suburban Don Mills with Tunya and our growing family—a second daughter, Kyra, having being born in Ottawa while I was doing fieldwork earlier that year.

My PhD thesis remained unfinished, something that I have always been rather ashamed about. Not because it would have enabled me to put "Dr." in front of my name, but because it was a waste of many hundreds of hours of research into dusty government documents, as well as scores of interviews.

Ironically, in the early 1970s I retained David Donnison to give a paper at a symposium on housing policy in Toronto. Driving him in from the airport, I expressed my regret about my failure to submit my PhD thesis. He responded kindly, "Well, Michael, some people are destined to write about history and others to make it. I suspect that you are one of the latter."

CHAPTER 37

"This Is as Close to Nirvana as You Can Get!"

Yvette, Woodstock, 1969

AFTER A YEAR AT the London School of Economics, I obtained permission to go to Ottawa for six months of research in the library of the Central Mortgage and Housing Corporation. I also spent a short time doing research in Toronto, where I rented a room in the Rochdale College Housing Co-operative. This was a rather unpredictable experience, because when I came home in the evening, I never knew who I might be sharing my two-bedroom apartment, or so-called "gnostic chamber," with. For me, Rochdale College, on Bloor Street, wasn't an educational institution, but just cheap lodging while I did research on my doctoral thesis in the University of Toronto library

Financed by the Canada Mortgage and Housing Corporation as an experiment in urban living, Rochdale was billed as a new form of high-rise housing, and it was fast attracting an unusual set of occupants. I signed a three-month lease, feeling quite fortunate, but the first evening, when I came home at 10:00 p.m., I found that my locked room had been robbed of my typewriter, radio and, most importantly, the only two suits that I owned.

The next morning I called the Toronto police, as procedure for making an insurance claim, and waited for them to arrive. An hour later I got a call on the intercom from the Hells Angels, who had apparently been retained to look after front-door security. They told me it was not their policy to admit the police to the building unless they had a search warrant. So I went downstairs to the front door. The bearded security fellow, in a tight black T-shirt and with bulging muscles, told me, "If you have been ripped off you should report it to us. We will get your stuff returned quick." I had never heard the term "ripped off" before, so that had to be patiently explained.

I met with the young Toronto police constable in a nearby coffee shop and explained what had happened. He said it was very strange that I was living at Rochdale, because I didn't look like a hippie. "Didn't you realize that the place is a hotbed of crime?" he asked.

I explained that, while I had noticed a lot of young people who seemed to be into the music scene, for me Rochdale was just an inexpensive place to live close to the campus. But I accepted the constable's advice and got a locksmith to put two large locks on the door of my bedroom, after which I had no more thefts.

The building was admittedly a little unusual, as every evening people came to my door offering various forms of pills. I was told that I could buy LSD for my head and/or MDA for my body. I never availed myself of these pills, but there were often certain smokable products that one could buy at a good price.

Another unpredictable aspect of my residential arrangements was that I never knew who I was going to find in my kitchen/bathroom area when I came home for the evening. One night there were two nice American ladies in their seventies, who were very enthusiastic about Rochdale being home to a great many Vietnam War deserters.

Rochdale purported to have an academic program, which consisted of a series of lectures or seminars on a wide variety of subjects. Most were not to my interest, though I did attend one on interplanetary space travel, an appropriate subject because this was the summer that Apollo 11 landed on the moon, an event I watched while staring through the window of a television shop on Bloor Street.

One evening when I came home, I found two pretty sisters from Drummondville, Quebec. They seemed quite lost in Toronto, because neither of them spoke a word of English beyond "Yes" and "No." I soon struck up a close relationship with Yvette, the older girl, who seemed a bit more sensible than her younger sister. She told me they had come to Toronto to see if the English Canadians were really as bad as they had been told, but not having any English language skills, she had been unable to draw any conclusions.

After a couple of days, the sisters told me that they were on their way to Woodstock, New York, where there was to be a large rock music festival. Without giving it much thought, I said that I would be happy to drive them there. So we set out the next morning, and when we arrived we found that New York State troopers had blocked off access to the town, but we were directed around some country roads to a series of fields where tents and other temporary residences had been erected far from the large stage and audience area. We walked about twenty-five minutes before arriving at the gate.

Originally there had been an admission charge, but the number of attendees was wildly beyond what the promoters had estimated, and by the time we arrived at the gate people were just crashing through for free. The music seemed to go on all night, yet after listening to the Grateful Dead and Janis Joplin, and having become separated from my lady companions, I was done and somehow managed to stagger back in the dark and the rain to my car. I slept underneath it in a sleeping bag on a ground sheet while water gurgled down the hillside around me.

Early the next morning, after consuming tofu and beans kindly offered by some neighbours, I finally rediscovered the Drummondville sisters huddled together near the stage. When I explained that it was time for me to return to Toronto and resume my research, Yvette asked me, "Why would anyone want to leave? This is as close to Nirvana as you can get!"

Well, that may have been true for the many thousands of young people who attended and camped in those soggy fields, as Woodstock became symbolic of the 1960s generation, but by this time I was mainly a fan of folk, jazz and classical music, not rock. Later I was told that Arlo Guthrie and Joan Baez had also performed at Woodstock, but I missed them.

CHAPTER 38

"Thank You for Saving My Bacon"

Charles Hendry, 1970

I WAS SITTING AT the rear of the stage, waiting to give a talk on housing policy in front of an audience of 1,200 people at the Skyline Hotel in Toronto. At the podium, attempting to give a keynote address, was a short, white-haired individual, Dr. Charles ("Chick") Hendry, director of the University of Toronto School of Social Work. He was in difficulty: a group of anti-poverty activists in the back of the room was hurling abuse at him.

As was the custom in the late 1960s, the conference organizers had gone into depressed areas of Canadian cities, such as the Petite-Bourgogne in Montreal and Vancouver's Downtown Eastside, to recruit participants. The theory was that by helping the poor organize, they would be able to improve their community and social conditions—something to which I was most sympathetic, and experienced in, having done such organizing in the Strathcona area of Vancouver as a social-work student.

The organizers of the Canadian Welfare Conference, which was usually a gathering of social workers, had on this occasion convinced the Trudeau government to fund the travel of members of anti-poverty organizations to the national meeting so that their voices might be heard. But the more radical among them believed that it wasn't just a matter of being heard, they wanted to take over the conference and direct the agenda.

The noise of two- to three-hundred activists, who even on the first morning of the conference were bored with the speeches, became so loud that Dr. Hendry's voice was drowned out. He halted briefly, looked around bewildered, and then attempted to stumble on. The half-dozen people on the stage, me among them, just sat there with eyes averted, wondering whether we would receive the same treatment when it was our turn at the microphone.

I decided to make a pre-emptive strike. I strode up to the microphone, took Dr. Hendry's arm and moved him aside. All of a sudden the room grew silent at the intervention by this tall figure with moustache and long sideburns, and clad in an army surplus jacket. "Okay," I said. "It sounds like someone has something to say. I'll tell you what I'll do. I'll give you ten minutes at the microphone out of my time to tell us what's on your mind, after which I expect you to be more polite to a man with such a distinguished record as Dr. Hendry. So who is it going to be?"

A huge man built like a butcher moved to a microphone at the back of the room and started to speak in French. He said that he and his colleagues had come to Toronto, not to listen to social workers, but to tell the Canadian people that conditions needed to be changed in the neighbourhoods in which they lived. I let him go on for about ten minutes then signalled for the microphone to be cut off, saying, "You have my word that there will be many opportunities for activists from across the country to speak, and now we will complete our agenda." There was thunderous applause.

Dr. Hendry went back to finish his remarks, and then it was my turn. Unfortunately, I spoke too fast and thus didn't do a great job giving my speech on the need for a new Canadian housing policy. Nevertheless, it was well received. At the end of the morning Dr. Hendry came to me and said quietly, "Thank you for saving my bacon, Michael."

Later that year I was on a visit to Vancouver when I received word that my father had died in Victoria. After kicking his drinking habit in 1948 Jimmy had lived a life of outward respectability, serving as a civil defence official, organizing boxing clubs for underprivileged youth, counselling alcoholics through the local AA chapter and writing books. In 1962 he was even nominated by the Social Credit Party to run to become a Member of Parliament for Victoria. In 1956 he lost his loyal and long-suffering wife, Marie, to cancer, but was fortunate enough to find a new partner in Isobel Temple, an Englishwoman from a well-off Lancashire family. They married in 1958, and she brought him the first real financial comfort he'd ever known.

They were happy together, at least at first, and I am tempted to stop there and leave his story with a fairy-tale ending. Alas, the devil that drove him through his early years was slumbering within and reasserted itself towards the end. Jimmy was always an addict of the track, and in Ireland his third wife made the mistake of buying him a racehorse named Supreme Verdict. The horse turned out to be just good enough to eat up a small fortune. A small fortune was about all Isobel had, and after a few years of increasingly costly horseplay—including entering Supreme Verdict in the Epsom Derby, buying a breeding farm near Victoria, and much jet-setting to and fro across the Atlantic, with stops in Paris and Monte Carlo—Isobel was pretty thoroughly cleaned out.

At this point Jimmy started entertaining a new mistress, and it was in her Victoria apartment building that he breathed his last breath.

Poor Isobel, who was recovering from a brain tumour, was particularly horrified of having anything to do with the mistress. I went over to Victoria on the first plane and found myself engaged in a macabre contest of wills between my late father's final two lovers. The mistress, let's call her Rose, was making a piteous attempt to be with her man to the end, but I felt I owed my first loyalty to Isobel, who I knew was a decent person and ill-used in the circumstances. At her insistence I ended up putting security guards in Hager's Funeral Home to prevent the very determined mistress from visiting. The same thing happened when the funeral cortège reached the cemetery. But there was no keeping the grieving Rose from taking a seat in the back row of the service at the jam-packed Christ Church Cathedral, whose dean had declined to allow guards to be stationed on the doors.

Such was the dramatic passing of Jimmy Audain, cavalry officer, sportsman, author, rake, and my father. When I say he was one of the people who influenced me most profoundly, I don't mean to downplay any of his many faults, which I suffered as sorely as anyone. But he did accept responsibility for raising me and applied himself to the task to the best of his abilities, according to the code passed down to him by his military forebears. He had many virtues, which I have probably not given as much attention to as I should have. Like many sons and fathers, we had a love-hate relationship. But mostly love.

CHAPTER 39

"How Much Did You Really Want?"

Premier Dave Barrett, 1973

IN THE FALL OF 1973 I was asked to prepare a budget submission for British Columbia's newly established Ministry of Housing. After twenty-one straight years in power, the Social Credit government of W.A.C. Bennett had been defeated by the NDP and I had been appointed as special advisor to the Minister of Housing to help get the new ministry going. Originally I had been offered the job of deputy minister by Premier Dave Barrett, the former social worker and political organizer who had once tried to persuade me to run for the CCF, and who'd made good on his promise to close the Brannan Lake School upon taking office. But after looking around Victoria for a place for my family to live, I soon came to the conclusion that I didn't want to move them to BC's capital.

When I told the premier, he said, "Well, deputy ministers have to live in Victoria, but I will appoint you as a special advisor at the same salary," which was $26,000 in those days.

So I spent about four days every week in Victoria, usually finding business to do in Vancouver on Fridays because flying the thirty-minute route by seaplane every day was tiring, particularly in the choppy winter months.

When I was told to prepare draft estimates for review by the Treasury Board for the new ministry, I consulted with Assistant Deputy Minister George Chatterton and the ministry's research director, Larry Bell, as to what I should ask for.

In the previous year, under the former Social Credit government, $6 million had been allocated to housing, which I felt was totally inadequate considering the government's desire to build a large number of social-housing units and co-operative homes for low-income families and the elderly.

At the end of the day, I gave the young minister, Lorne Nicolson, a set of draft estimates that totalled $46 million and sent him into the cabinet room to have the program endorsed by his colleagues. I told him that if he had any trouble explaining I would be right outside the door and he should, if necessary, secure permission for me to come in and make a presentation. Nicolson said that would not be needed, but sure enough, after about ten minutes, the premier came to the door and said, "Michael, could you come in and explain these numbers. Your minister doesn't seem to know what he's talking about." So I went in and faced the half-dozen ministers who comprised the Treasury Board, plus Deputy Finance Minister Gerald Bryson.

My presentation was not well received by Minister of Lands and Forests Bob Williams, a professional planner. He accused me of being a CMHC lackey and someone who didn't know how to get housing built. I assured him that I knew from my Ontario Housing Corporation experience how to lever huge amounts of money out of Ottawa for investment in social housing, saying that all the province needed to do was put up ten per cent of the capital required and underwrite a portion of the ongoing subsidies. There seemed to be no resolution of the issue at the meeting, so I was simply told that we would hear in due course about the housing funds that we would have available for the following year.

Well, we didn't hear anything for some weeks and Nicolson said that he was loath to stir the pot by pestering his colleagues for some resolution.

In the interval between Christmas and New Year's, the Parliament Buildings in Victoria were almost deserted, with just about all the politicians and most of the civil servants taking a Christmas break. I happened to be up in the minister's office catching up on some correspondence when the telephone rang. An administrative voice said, "Mr. Audain, the premier would like to see you in his office immediately."

I went downstairs and was invited to share a cup of coffee with the premier and Gerald Bryson. Premier Barrett, who was also the Minister of Finance, said, "You know, we never did resolve the housing estimates that are going to be in my budget."

"I have a list of the programs you proposed, but we seem to have misplaced the figures you needed to accomplish them," said Bryson.

"How much did you really want?" Barrett added.

"Well, I could go back upstairs and look for the draft estimates we presented to the Treasury Board," I suggested.

"No, we don't have time for that," Barrett replied. "Let's settle this now. Let me see, how much do you need for social housing? And what's the figure for this program for front-ending trunk sewer installations for municipalities?"

Off the top of my head, I threw out some numbers as they went down the list, and at the end Bryson said, "Well, if my arithmetic is right that comes to $108 million."

"Yes, I seem to recall that's the number, or close to it," I agreed, recalling quite clearly the actual number had been $46 million but knowing the higher figure could be very well put to use.

They thanked me and I went back up to the office, wondering about the curious budgetary process of the NDP government.

Sure enough the budget was tabled in the legislature a few weeks later. The vote for housing came to $108 million—eighteen times more than the previous year. Minister Nicolson was surprised but the senior officials in his department were ecstatic as they proceeded to plan how they could spend all those funds in the coming fiscal year.

CHAPTER 40

"We Will Never End Up in Front of a Firing Squad"

Scott, Burma, 1974

WE SET OUT TRAVELLING NORTH on a narrow country road while it was still dark. With me in the back of the dilapidated pickup truck was Hans, a blond-haired Austrian backpacker.

The two of us had shared some noodles and bottles of Singha beer the night before in one of the dingy Chinese restaurants in Mae Sot, Thailand, where I was taking a break from government and family responsibilities. He told me that he was buying hill-tribe silver for a friend's shop in Vienna. As we were winding up our evening, a lanky American dropped by our table and said to Hans, "Do you still want to see a bit of the country tomorrow morning?"

Hans introduced me to Ryan, who apparently had developed a bit of a reputation for trading with the hill tribes across the river in neighbouring Burma, or Myanmar, as the government there preferred to call it.

Ryan told me that the drive involved a trip down the Moei River, which separates the two countries. He promised we would be back by late afternoon, as I had plans to return to Hong Kong the following day.

"Just bring your passport and wrap it in a waterproof covering in case we run into the wrong people across the river," said Ryan with a wink. He went on to explain that while the Free Karen Army, or Karen National Liberation Army, controlled much of the territory immediately across from Mae Sot, occasionally there were clashes with Myanmar government forces. The Karens are an ethnic minority that at the time represented some seven per cent of the Myanmar population, and they were engaged in what since has been called the world's longest civil war. To the north was the Shan Army, representing another rebel group within the country. This devil's brew of warring factions even included remnants of a former Chinese Kuomintang Army, which had fought Mao Zedong's communists in the Chinese revolution.

"Being a Canadian, none of these groups will bother with you," Ryan assured me.

After a couple of excruciatingly bumpy hours along what amounted to little more than a dirt track, we arrived at a rickety pier where Ryan had a boat—a long, shallow-draft river craft with an inboard engine to power a long propeller shaft draped over the stern. A Thai man appeared out of the morning mist and helped Ryan transfer some heavy packages from the truck to the boat.

For the first time I noticed that Ryan had a holstered pistol strapped to his belt, while his Thai helper carried what looked like a rather old 12-gauge shotgun. Hans and I clambered into the boat's long tail, and we were soon off. Ryan sat in the bow, and the Thai assistant ran the noisy GM engine, which propelled the boat downriver at a fast clip. The Thai man steered around obstacles by swinging the whole shaking assembly back and forth on its pivot bearing. Though seen less often today, this was the most common type of powerboat used throughout Southeast Asia at the time.

The sun started to warm the riverbanks, and on both sides we could see families bathing and water buffalos drinking. Strange for Asia, there was no river traffic other than small canoes, whose occupants were busy fishing. The scenery was idyllic, with a low, jungle-clad mountain range beyond the Burmese side of the river and small rice paddies fringing the banks on both sides.

We had only been gone about half an hour when Ryan suddenly shouted, "Duck!" The boat went to starboard under some low-hanging trees and proceeded for a few minutes up a narrow creek, obviously a tributary to the main river. The engine was then cut, and Ryan and his Thai mate started to paddle. As the creek narrowed further we emerged into a large palm-fringed pond, around which were a number of thatch-roofed houses. It was a tranquil scene.

At the dock we were met by a skinny young American with shoulder-length hair. "Did you bring the tapes?" he asked Ryan, ignoring us, Ryan replied that he had brought some tapes, but whether they were the right ones, he didn't know. "Well, I would be happy to listen to anything if only we could get a generator to work," replied the man, who we later learned was named Scott.

Addressing us for the first time, Scott said, "Oh, by the way, I am Libertyville's immigration officer. Passports please." He quickly examined them, apologized for not having a stamp, and said that we were welcome to look around while Ryan transacted a little business. He added that he was confident that Ryan wouldn't have brought us along for the ride had we been Americans.

It was apparently a Paduang hill-tribe settlement, as the women wore long white cotton dresses and some had grotesquely elongated necks encircled with thick brass rings. Seeing both Hans and I reach for our camera cases, Scott said firmly, "Oh, by the way, no photos. These people are sensitive about tourists. Leave your cameras in the boat."

A troop of children followed us as we climbed up the bank to where a rather corpulent bearded White man was sharpening a spear. He greeted us and introduced himself as Louisiana Ed.

"Have you had breakfast?" he enquired, thrusting out a hand to shake. "After I've eaten I'm going to do some fishing." We took him up on his offer and were soon served a delicious meal of egg fried rice by the woman who appeared to be Louisiana Ed's housekeeper. When I asked how many Americans were in the village, Ed replied evasively, "Not many. But this morning they are mostly busy, as we work mornings and play the rest of the day."

When asked about the nature of the work, Louisiana Ed replied, "Oh, a little bit of this and that. The local men appreciate our teaching them military tactics, and we even try to teach them English. In fact you will find most of the kids in Libertyville, as we call it, speak a reasonable brand of English, though the adults don't."

As we ambled around the little settlement of half a dozen houses, I remarked to Louisiana Ed about the verdant poppy field growing behind the homes. "Oh yes, but if we don't keep an eye on the crop, it has a habit of disappearing. God knows why, because the stuff grows like a weed all over these hills. Would you like to try some?" he offered, still carrying his fish spear.

Hans responded that he had already had a pipe in the hills north of Chiang Mai but suggested that I might want to take a few puffs as a souvenir of Burma.

So Louisiana Ed invited me to the upper floor of one of the houses, apparently his own, and sat me down on a rug. Within a minute or two he had an ornate pipe going. He thrust into my hand. "Take it very slowly," he cautioned.

I took a couple of puffs, swirled it around in my mouth, and couldn't sense anything other than the pleasantly sweet taste of the opium tar. I relaxed and started to inhale. A little sensation crept up my spine. After a few more puffs I felt drowsy but still aware of what was going on around me. Ed and Hans were chatting away about music.

A few minutes later the colours circling the room became a predominantly blue haze. I started to feel cold. I closed my eyes. When I opened them, I panicked: the world was completely black.

"Oh my god, my sight! What the hell did that pipe do to me?"

I felt a small hand go over my mouth and heard a female voice say, "Shhh. You sleep daytime. You let people sleep now."

"Where am I," I asked, "in hospital?"

"You lie same place all day."

"I am so thirsty."

"Wait, I get water."

A candle was lit and a young woman clad in white slipped from under the mosquito net, returning a few minutes later with a plastic bottle of water.

As I gradually became more aware of my surroundings, I told the girl, whose name was Yumi, "I must go out to pee."

"Cannot," Yumi said. "Much danger."

"No danger if you give me the candle," I said.

"Tiger come sometime," Yumi advised.

That settled it. She offered me a large empty can and obliged by turning her back. Once I was lying back down again with the candle out, I asked Yumi—who seemed to be sleeping on a platform bed in the same room—who she was and how she had learned English. In a whisper, she explained that her older sister was "Lou's" wife, and that he and the four other Americans in the village had taught her English. "Lou" was apparently how they referred to Louisiana Ed,

When I asked what had happened to my boat and my passport, which was no longer in my pocket, she said, "You sleep again now. Lou say everything in morning."

I had no idea of the time because I couldn't see my watch, so I lay on the hard bed until sleep returned.

It didn't seem long before there was a huge ruckus of cock-calling, both outside and right under the house. Not long after that a dog started howling and I heard some stirrings. My shoulder was shaken by Lou, who stood naked above me holding a towel, which he handed to me.

"It's bath time. The women around here are shy, so we bathe separately."

We descended the ladder to the lower floor, then he led me up a short trail to what he called the "male side" of the pond. Scott and a couple of other White men appeared to be bathing and doing their ablutions, surrounded by noisy kids. Handing me a bar of soap, Scott said, "Too bad you missed your ride home. I guess we'll have to feed you for the next month or two."

"Oh my God," I said. "I have to be in Hong Kong this week and then get back to Vancouver."

Scott replied that he was just kidding and that Ryan and his long-tailed boat would likely be back in a week. "How else would we get our mail and newspapers? To say nothing of gas for the generator."

When I got back to the huts, I had a hearty breakfast of rice porridge, prepared again by Lou's wife, "My Doris." I was surprised to see half a dozen green-uniformed soldiers talking nonchalantly to Scott. He introduced me, saying that his friends in the Free Karen Army had decided to drop by the village to see who the new visitor was.

"That's why I kept your passport," Scott said, returning it to me. "They have never heard of Canada, so I simply told them that it was next to America, which seems good enough for them. You see, their bosses have contacts with the CIA. In fact, the Agency knows all about Libertyville and won't bother us. A raiding party staged by US military police from across the river would be quite another matter. They are probably aware of us, but a raid over here would annoy the FKA, who are anti-communist. In fact many of them are Christian, having attended church schools."

Thus I spent an idyllic week up a creek somewhere in Burma and felt I got to know the five Americans living there well: Leon and Grey, both from New York; Louisiana (Lou) Ed; California Dave; and Scott, obviously the leader, who never let on which state he hailed from. They each recounted horrific stories about Vietnam. Apparently they had decided together to set up Libertyville and ride out the war years there.

When the sun started to fade and the evening meal was eaten, cribbage, chess and card games ensued—none of which I play—and we would gather around and sip the sweet local whisky while sharing life's experiences. The guys must have heard their own stories too many times, as they were content to be regaled with my anecdotes about cricket matches while England was under Nazi siege, salmon and trout fishing on Vancouver Island, and my clumsy attempts at amateur boxing.

All my tales were considered strange by the young Americans, who seemed so average except that they had chosen to desert their country's armed forces in time of war, for which the ultimate penalty was death. By contrast, they had taken up a peaceful Robinson Crusoe lifestyle, fortified by a generous lifeline of supplies from the other side of the river and by the ministrations of their Karen girlfriends—a couple had already borne children.

In a sense, I was sad when Ryan's long-tailed boat suddenly shot once again into the pond. As I boarded, Yumi and her sister My Doris tearfully bade me goodbye. The guys all came to shake my hand and I wished them good luck. I recall Scott saying, "Don't worry about us, Michael. One thing is for sure, we will never end up in front of a firing squad."

CHAPTER 40

When I got back to my hotel late that afternoon, I found that pursuant to Ryan's instructions the owner had packed my clothing into my suitcase and put it in safe storage. I spent another night there before leaving on a flight to Bangkok early the next morning. By evening I was in Hong Kong, and a day later I was in Vancouver.

I never heard what happened to Libertyville, nor have I until now recounted this experience. But as the years have slipped by, I have sometimes wondered if I didn't just stumble into a CIA-sponsored project. Perhaps those guys were not actual Vietnam deserters?

A decade later, while my wife, Yoshi, and I were travelling in Thailand, I signed us up for a hill-tribe tour in the Mae Sot area, but it was cancelled at the last minute by the Thai tour company on account of military activity in the border area.

CHAPTER 41

"We Can Do Anything to People Who Don't Believe in Allah"

Philippine Navy marine, 1975

As the golden globe of the sun faded into the murky sea at almost precisely 6:00 p.m., it served as a signal to order my first Johnnie Walker Black of the evening. The seaside bar at the Lantaka Hotel started to fill with guests who didn't seem to mind having to listen to terrible renditions of "Feelings" and "L.A. International Airport" from the aging male singer the manager had retained to lend some character to the place.

"I came near to murdering him the other evening," a tall middle-aged White man muttered, jerking his thumb towards the singer. My bar mate, Rudy, spoke Tagalog, as well as good French and German, those being the languages of his native Switzerland. He was an interesting fellow and told me that he managed a large coconut plantation on Basilan, the big island to the south, but that he didn't feel secure enough to spend more than the odd night there.

Like me, Rudy had a couple of Philippine Navy marines who tailed him everywhere. I had picked mine up at the airport, paying a fee in advance for their protection, as that was part of the cost of visiting the province of Mindanao in those martial-law days with President Ferdinand Marcos in power. My marines tagged along wherever I went, even sleeping outside my hotel room with their AK-47s close by. Being very young, they were often hungry, and apparently it was also my job to pay the kitchen to keep them fed, a not-inexpensive proposition.

CHAPTER 41

I have been to a few places in the world where violence was in the air. I can remember the stares that Yoshi and I earned when we walked boldly through the main market of Sanaa, Yemen's capital, where turbaned tribesmen muttered away, their ancient rifles slung on their backs, and fingering their *jambiyas,* the long daggers that seemed to be a *de rigueur* part of their baggy costumes. Then there was the Ashura festival in Srinagar's back streets, where crazed zealots flogged themselves red with razor-studded whips while crying "Allahu akbar!" When my guide Ali determined things were threatening to get out of hand, he shoved me into a doorway and yanked my cap over my face to shield my identity.

But here in the Philippines I had been told on arrival at the local airport that security couldn't be guaranteed for anyone on the island of Mindanao, given the activities of the Moro Islamic Liberation Front, who had killed thousands of people and particularly liked kidnapping foreigners for ransom money.

The violence wasn't perpetrated only by those dubbed "terrorists." When I turned in my first night and heard shooting going on outside the hotel, I phoned the front desk and was reassured that it was only members of the army and marines taking potshots at each other, apparently a common weekend occurrence, since there was no love lost between the two armed services.

I had come to the southern Philippines to learn about the water gypsies, the Bajau-speaking people, who were reputed to have moved from island to island throughout the southern Philippines, Indonesia and eastern Malaysia. I wouldn't have to go very far to meet them because a Bajau family's canoe was already moored at the Lantaka Hotel's small beach. On my first morning I searched for a guide who could speak both English and Bajau. This wasn't too difficult because near the hotel was a sizable community of houses perched on piles and occupied by Sama-speaking people. It had been explained to me that Bajau was really a dialect of the Sama language. That afternoon I was invited aboard the canoe, or *vinta* as the locals called it, a vessel that was less than three feet wide and twelve feet long, supported by outriggers on each side.

The father explained that he and his wife had lived their entire lives on the *vinta*. Their two children, with hair bleached blond by the sun, were even born there. He said that to go ashore would make him feel sick, and the only times in his life that it would be necessary was to either repair the canoe or to bury their dead. The man made a living primarily by diving for colourful seashells, which he sold to hotel guests. In former days he would dive for pearls, but that had become too risky as he aged. The guide told me that Bajau men could free-dive holding their breath longer than any other human beings, often over ten minutes.

I learned that another surprising trait of the Bajau was their ability to forecast changes in the weather. For example, when threatened by a typhoon while in open water, the Bajau were able to read the elements in time to get themselves into a sheltered lagoon before the storm struck.

The next day I filled my camera with film and ventured out for a sail with the Bajau family—on my own, as with my bulky frame there was no room for the guide. Once the sail was raised I was shocked at how fast the little vessel could skip over the waves, with just a gentle breeze filling the multi-patched triangular cotton sail.

Back at the hotel, I used the services of my guide to ply the Bajau family with questions concerning their diet, which was obviously fish but also cassava, tapioca and rice. I also did my best to find out if they had any system of government. I learned that while they generally just existed in independent family groupings, at certain times of the year hundreds of Bajau would gather in the lagoon for marriage and religious festivals, on which occasions they would don the colourful clothing that was tucked away safely under the canoe's floorboards.

From talking to a number of families about religion, I gathered that they had no interest in the prevailing Muslim religion of the Sama shore people, but practised a type of animism in which the power of the sun and the moon seemed to predominate. But they also mentioned spirits of the east wind and of the lagoon, as well as those of sea creatures, such as whales that they encountered far from shore.

While in Zamboanga City, I was invited by my Swiss friend to take advantage of the marvellous diving around the area's coral reefs, as he had a launch to take us over to Grande Santa Cruz Island, replete with his two and my two marine guards, who said they would keep watch for terrorists while we went underwater. Fortunately, the launch had some diving equipment aboard, and based on some diving instruction I had had in Thailand, it didn't take me long to get down to a nearby reef.

Once there I was so mesmerized by the hundreds of fish in dazzling colours that I just wanted to float motionless, willing them to come right up to my mask. Unfortunately, Rudy wanted to find something bigger for his spear gun, so I had to swim along with him, even though I didn't care to go as deep as he chose to go. Before an hour was up, I indicated that I had had enough, to the disappointment of my partner.

When we got back to the beach, I was absolutely furious to see that a couple of the marines had been systemically destroying Bajau tombs on the shore. As I mentioned earlier, one of the few times that the Bajau come onshore is to be buried in the shallow sand. Above the grave the Bajau would often leave a beautifully carved model outrigger canoe representing what I surmised to be transportation for the deceased to an afterlife. When I strongly remonstrated the marines for their vandalism, one explained, "We can do anything to people who don't believe in Allah."

I was seething with anger and threatened to report them to their officers. But Rudy told me that would be to no avail, because the Bajau were despised for being so poor, illiterate and having neither Islam nor Christianity as their religion.

On a subsequent day, I travelled with Rudy to his coconut plantation on the large island of Basilan. This time, when we landed, we were met by the plantation security corps of six guards, who would accompany us, in addition to our own four marines. When I mentioned that surely this amount of security was unnecessary, I was admonished and informed that the jungles on the island were full of Muslim separatists who had already launched a couple of deadly attacks on the plantation.

"Because they know I am Swiss, there is apparently some rumour that I am worth way over $1 million as a target. The only comfort that I get from that is knowing that perhaps I am worth more alive than dead," Rudy explained.

What I didn't mention is that my own insurance was sewn into the lining of my shorts, in the form of a letter from a Victoria friend, Ben Pieres, addressed to Nur Misuari, leader of the Moro Islamic Liberation Front, then based in Libya. Pieres, a former college student of Professor Misuari, advised in his letter that I was a nice guy but worthless as a kidnapping target.

We proceeded to tour the plantation and its factory, which husked the coconuts, preserving the meat for food processors, while at the same time grating the husks for coconut-fibre production. Fortunately, all went well and by sunset we were back at the bar of the Lantaka Hotel drinking Scotch and listening to the evening's first rendition of "Feelings."

My brief visit to the Philippines finished with Rudy and I sharing a pleasant Christmas dinner together at a restaurant in downtown Zamboanga City called the Woody Woodpecker, adorned throughout with Disney characters. As we walked back to the hotel with our marines in tow, I was surprised by the number of people on the street who greeted us with a friendly, "Merry Christmas, Joe," a holdover from World War II, when the area was liberated from the Japanese occupation by GI Joes.

CHAPTER 42

"You Gentlemen Better Do Some Nursing"

Mother Teresa, 1976

AT 1:00 A.M. THE Calcutta airport seemed deserted. I was with John, a tall American civil engineer in his mid-thirties who I had met on the Pan American flight from Bangkok. We appeared to be the only foreigners around. The few Indian passengers who had disembarked had quickly melted away. Outside the airport doors was a single old Ambassador taxi. I had the presence of mind to negotiate a five-dollar fee to the Oberoi Grand Hotel, then we climbed into the back seat, the driver having ensconced an assistant in the front seat beside him. This was the first time I had ever experienced double staffing in a taxi.

Ten minutes later, it was evident that we were no longer on the road to downtown Calcutta (now Kalkota), but appeared to have entered the bush-strewn private drive of someone's house. In the almost complete darkness, I immediately brandished the long dagger that I carried on airplanes in those pre 9/11 days, and demanded that the burly turban-clad driver get back on the road to Calcutta.

"I cannot, Sahib, because we have no petrol," the driver claimed. "That's why we have stopped here to see my friend." Sure enough, a few minutes later someone emerged in the darkness carrying a flashlight and what looked like a couple of pop bottles full of petrol.

"Please pay us the fare now, Sahib, so we can buy petrol to get you to your hotel."

I indignantly refused, but John, perhaps wiser in the ways of India, gave the driver two dollars and said that would have to do for the petrol. Sure enough, the petrol was poured and the car restarted. We reached our hotel half an hour later, at which time the driver claimed to be totally dissatisfied with the three dollars that I gave him, crying, "Sahib, you have forgotten the baksheesh!"

After stepping gingerly over the people who seemed to be sleeping under the hotel's portico, I quickly retired to my room, promising to meet John downstairs for breakfast. At 9:30 the next morning we were just finishing a leisurely breakfast by the hotel's pool when a man in a doorman's uniform appeared, announcing that our driver was ready for us. Puzzled, John said, "We haven't requested any driver."

"But this driver says that he brought you from the airport last night and you instructed him to wait for orders," the doorman said.

As it turned out, John had a free day before going up-country to take a look at a World Bank-sponsored water project, so he said, "Maybe we should do a little sightseeing and I can charge it to the bank. I will take responsibility for the car."

An hour later I had another one of those culture shocks that India seems famous for. I became separated from John and the priest who was guiding us around a temple devoted to Kali, the four-armed Hindu goddess. It was apparently one of Kali's festival days, and hundreds of men, women and children were attempting to squeeze through one of the temple's doors from the small courtyard I was in, while I was attempting to go in the opposite direction, back to the street. The pilgrims bore a huge variety of gifts for Kali: baskets full of fruit and vegetables plus, more alarmingly, animal parts, including more than one freshly cut water buffalo head. It was obvious from the cries that children and old people were being squashed and perhaps even trampled in the crowd. After taking ten minutes to extract myself, I noticed that my white safari suit had become grubby and smeared with a variety of stains.

At my request, our next stop was almost across the street, at an abandoned Hindu temple that had been converted into the Refuge House, a hospice operated by the Missionaries of Charity. A portly white-sari-clad nun greeted us when we arrived and offered us chairs. She then asked if we had an appointment with "Mother." I explained that we didn't want to bother Mother Teresa, but would appreciate a short tour of the facility.

"But you can't come here and not meet Mother," the sister told us. "Do you bring an offering to help our work?"

"Oh dear, I have left my passport and traveller's cheques in the hotel, which I believe was rather wise given the ordeal I just went through over at the Temple of Kali," I told the sister.

"Well, then you gentlemen better do some nursing," a sharp female voice behind me said. I jumped up from my chair, and there stood the diminutive Mother Teresa with a smile on her face.

After we introduced ourselves, Mother Teresa pointedly told me how much she admired the work Canadians had been doing in India. She then led us to a large dormitory that housed the sick and dying men the sisters had rescued from the Calcutta streets.

"Thank you for volunteering today. Sister Rachel will show you what to do."

It was a relief that we weren't asked to change bed linen, because with the smell in the ward and my experience at the Temple of Kali I was wondering how to keep my substantial Grand Hotel breakfast down. Instead, we were given bowls of what looked like chicken-and-rice soup and asked to offer it to the men on the ward.

"If someone doesn't take it from you, it doesn't mean they don't want the soup," the sister explained. "You just have to feed them." And that's what we did for the next hour or so, after which we made our excuses and climbed exhaustedly back into our car, having great difficulty closing the windows given the hands of the little street children who were reaching through them.

John, once again proving to be an old India hand, told me that it was always wise to get the car moving before closing any windows. "If you catch one of the kids' hands or arms, you will end up having to pay a lot of money to their parents," he said.

Within half an hour, we were relaxing by the pool in the landscaped hotel courtyard, guiltily eating our fill of lamb samosas.

CHAPTER 43

"You Are Our First Guest to Sleep in the Street"

Oberoi Grand Hotel doorman, 1976

I SPENT FOUR DAYS in Calcutta visiting all sorts of sites, including dusty museums full not of statues of Hindu gods, but rather the debris of the Raj: large overstuffed furniture, dirty chandeliers and mildew-clad paintings of men in regimental uniforms, whose descendants were probably unaware of their long-lost ancestors. I went to schools and universities and even a model farm outside the city, and toured the docks on the Ganges River where traders had moored for centuries. What fascinated me the most, though, were the nightly encampments of people sleeping in the street and the parks, which had been completely taken over with tents housing Bangladeshi refugees.

The concierge at the hotel was unhelpful concerning how I could get more information about the street-dwellers. "They have always lived that way, Sahib," he just said with a smile.

I wore a pair of scruffy hiking boots so I'd never be bothered by the scores of lads seeking to give me a shoeshine. But one evening I wore a white shirt to a neighbourhood restaurant, and en route something made me nod affirmatively to a bright-eyed young teenager, who accosted me with a smile, saying, "How can you walk about with such dirty shoes when your clothes are clean?"

"I don't shine my hiking books with polish," I replied. "Anyway, I am on my way to dinner."

"Have a good dinner, Sahib. I will see you later," the lad cried.

CHAPTER 43

It was two hours later when I sauntered back to the hotel. All the other shoe-cleaners except for my "lad" seemed to have disappeared for the night. "Please sit down now," the boy said, pointing to some stone stairs in a shop-front near my hotel's entrance.

Having enjoyed a couple of chotapegs of Indian Scotch from the hotel bar, and a beer or two from the restaurant, I obliged him. Before I knew what was happening, my trouser bottoms had been rolled up and my boots had been removed in the dim light.

"Where are my boots?" I yelled in alarm.

"Sahib, please don't be upset. My assistant is looking after them."

Puzzled, as I hadn't seen any assistant around, I had no option but to chat for a few minutes with the boy, who told me his name was Baru, which I believe he said meant "noble." I asked him if it wasn't rather late for him to be out, and how long it took him to get to his house. "Oh, I can be home in less than an hour," he said, adding that he lived with his mother and two sisters, who he had to support through his shoe-cleaning business, his father having died two years back.

"Do you ride the tram home?" I asked Baru. He said that he could only hitch a ride sometimes for a short distance, as he couldn't afford to pay the fare. "Well, then, why don't you live closer to where you work?" I asked.

"Well, Sahib, it would be far too expensive to live in front of this hotel," he told me.

Taken aback, I enquired if the boy lived in the street. Yes, he had always lived in the street, since coming to Calcutta from his village. Suddenly I had an idea: would he allow me to meet his family? Baru's eyes widened and he said with a smile, "It would be an honour, Sahib, to introduce my mother to you this evening."

All of a sudden my boots reappeared, delivered by a different urchin, younger and smaller than Baru. They indeed looked like they had been thoroughly cleaned, with the insides stuffed with old newspapers. "Sahib, I have had your boots reconditioned," Baru told me.

"Shall I give something to the youngster who brought them back?" I asked.

"No, he is only my assistant, and anyway there is no charge because tonight you are my guest."

A bit mystified but excited to learn about life on the streets, I dashed up to my room to get a sweater to ward off the cold night air plus my small tape recorder. When I got back, Baru told me he had already negotiated with a bicycle rickshaw friend to take us to his home. The hotel's Sikh doorman shook his head, saying, "Sahib, it's very dangerous going out alone at night in Calcutta, let alone with street people."

It seemed like we had only been riding for fifteen minutes when we arrived in the commercial quarter, where hundreds of people were already bedding down on the sidewalk. Baru's mother was still awake and we exchanged namastes. Baru apologized that the family had already finished their dinner, so didn't have anything to offer me, but if I would care to sit with his mother, he would come back soon with something to eat. I protested that it was quite unnecessary, as I had already had a large dinner.

There I was, sitting on the sidewalk, under a shop canopy, hardly able to say more than a word or two in Bengali. But not many minutes later Baru re-emerged from the darkness with a large cardboard box full of chapatis and various kinds of sweets.

"How could you afford to buy all that food?" I asked.

"The shopkeeper gave me credit because I told him I had a sahib visiting my family," Baru said, laughing.

"The only thing we need now is a fire, but I can't get credit for the wood," he added. I thrust a bunch of rupees at him, and he soon came scampering back with two or three men carrying bundles of wood, which looked like broken-down wooden shipping crates. These were hastily made into a roaring fire right in the street. As soon as it got going, the fire started to attract scores of neighbours, who huddled around enjoying the warmth of the bright fire on that cold January night with the temperature about 13 degrees Celsius.

By now, Baru's younger sisters had been woken up to introduce themselves to me. A gnarled old man with a staff emerged from the shop's front door. "This is our landlord," said Baru, introducing me. When I asked how he was the landlord, Baru explained that to sleep in front of the shops, the family had to pay rent to the shopkeeper under whose canopy they lived.

Word had gone up and down the street that a "European" had arrived to spend the night with them, and more and more people drifted by to take a look, with quite a number of them bringing me gifts of what looked like various kinds of Indian bread. I graciously accepted the offerings, but declined to eat them, instead passing them on to Baru's mother.

Other than Baru, the only other English-speaking person turned out to be an unemployed schoolmaster wearing a tattered tweed jacket with a large silver pocket watch in his waistcoat. When I asked how he could be unemployed, the schoolmaster claimed that he had lost his job because he wasn't a member of the local Communist Party. Since then he had been living with his family on the streets.

"How do you survive? Do you give lessons to children?" I asked.

"No, sir, it would certainly not be professional to do that outside a properly licensed school. Rather, I have chosen to temporarily enter the communications industry," he replied, apparently not wishing to elaborate further. Later, Baru told me that the former teacher wrote letters and filled out government forms for the street people.

After a while longer, as our fire continued to burn, some musicians appeared and we listened to an impromptu performance of a pipe band, who were rewarded with a few rupees. Eventually, I was offered a mat to lie upon and, exhausted, I actually got an hour or two of sleep.

Baru returned me to my hotel in the cool early morning mist, and the doorman, who seemed to be just coming on shift, caught me rewarding the boy with a US twenty-dollar bill.

"That street boy makes far more money than anyone in this hotel, except perhaps the manager," the doorman said. "And did he tell you that he's got an Englishman who is getting him a university scholarship, and a California dentist who wants to get him into that profession?"

I told him that while Baru had not, he had shown me a fine evening.

"You are our first guest to sleep in the street when you have a room in the best hotel in India," he exclaimed, shaking his turbaned head.

CHAPTER 44

"We Thought We Could Improve Your System"

Linda, 1977

AFTER THE ELECTION IN late 1975, the Social Credit Party formed the provincial government in British Columbia and I was out of a job. I had actually seen the election loss coming because the government was undermining confidence in the provincial economy. I wasn't fired by the new administration, though. In fact, they implemented a great many recommendations of the commission of inquiry on mobile homes that I had chaired in 1975. I just decided to make some changes in my life and left my position. My government work hadn't left much time for family life and our marriage had suffered.

I found myself without a regular salary for the first time since I had been a student. Since the age of eighteen, when not studying at university, I had always had a full-time job. I felt uneasy about being unemployed. It wasn't only about the loss of a regular paycheque, most of my social life had always revolved around my job. Even today I look forward to going to the office on Monday mornings to greet my colleagues. I decided to take advantage of the interregnum in my life by trying out some different ways of making a living.

One of the ideas I came up with was trading in commodity futures. In the early 1970s I had accumulated about $200,000 in free capital, mostly by trading in junk bonds, and I decided to place half of it into the futures market. I studied futures trading systems at a weekend conference at a nondescript New York hotel and came away convinced that if I used a mechanical trading system based on moving averages, I would prosper over time.

For quite a number of months, things went well, very well in fact, as the prices of grains, precious metals and foreign currencies soared. I was trading as many as eighteen different futures indices at any one time.

To manage my system, in those pre-computer days, I used a calculator and reams of paper for recording the closing prices that were telephoned to me at the end of each day. Three moving averages were calculated, which meant over sixty separate calculations every afternoon. I rose at 4:30 a.m. and would phone in my orders to Merrill Lynch before the currency markets opened at 5:20 a.m. Pacific Time.

I became totally absorbed with the process and eventually sourced a sophisticated Hewlett Packard calculator that could work out the calculations I wanted, in conjunction with a long strip of thin cellophane on which the date for each futures contract was stored.

My initial capital investment had doubled by the first month-end. And at the end of another month I was up fivefold. Oh, this is fun, I thought. Why not get someone to manage the system while I do some travelling?

So I trained a part-time secretary named Linda on how to run the system and went off to a beach resort in Thailand, telling the broker to telex my net worth every Friday. Things continued to go quite well as my wealth swelled in my absence. It was a time of high inflation and a weak US dollar.

And then one Friday there was no telex. On Monday I phoned the futures broker from Thailand and asked, "Did you forget to send my net worth?"

He replied, "I didn't forget, Michael. The figure's gone down quite a bit, and I didn't want to ruin your holiday, because things are most likely to move in a more positive direction for you this week."

"Well, my system doesn't need a positive direction. I should be making money, and whether I am going short or long doesn't matter," I explained.

After a couple of sleepless nights, I got the feeling it was time to return to Canada. As I was flying home, I read in the *South China Morning Post* that Arthur Burns, the chairman of the Federal Reserve, had come out with a defend-the-dollar package that had sent metals, grains and just about all commodities spiralling downward while the US dollar regained its former power. When I reached Vancouver, I took a taxi immediately to Linda's apartment and asked, "Have you been sticking to the rules of my system?"

"Oh yes, we have," she said. "But my husband Larry and I decided that it wasn't a good idea to go short while there is still so much inflation in the world. We thought we could improve your system, so we have been only playing it from the long side."

"Do you realize what this has done to my net worth, Linda?"

"Oh no, Michael, we were not told that part of it. We just work your system and phone Merrill Lynch when it looks to us like it's time to make a trade," she said.

I called the broker at home that evening and said, "I want you to get me out of all my positions. Just get me out at any price."

"We can't necessarily do that, Michael," he replied. "Commodity prices like gold and grains are collapsing, and you are locked into many of your long positions because the market opening limits have been down every day, even though the exchanges are now increasing the limits."

I felt so stupid for putting so much faith in untrained and unsupervised people, and I now found myself locked into commodity markets where I had absolutely no liquidity. I knew that I could lose a great deal more money than simply the margin that I had initially put up. If prices continued to move against me, I would continue to be personally liable to the brokerage firm for the losses. I was still struggling to come to terms with our failing marriage, and financial ruin on top of that was too much to bear.

Later that evening, feeling extremely depressed, I got in my car and drove south into the United States, thinking that if I was to end my life it would be better not to do it in my hometown. I took with me in the car a section of cord that would be useful in hanging myself. Eventually, after driving for several hours, I checked into a small motel off the I-5, somewhere between Seattle and Olympia, Washington. I lay down on the bed and tried to figure out how best to hang myself.

CHAPTER 44

Once again, as at a previous time when I had come to the absolute end of my mental resources, my dozing mind was suffused with the sound of heavenly choir music:

> Bring me my Bow of burning gold:
> Bring me my Arrows of desire:
> Bring me my Spear: O clouds unfold!
> Bring me my Chariot of fire!

Slowly it occurred to me that killing myself that evening would be a great burden on my family; being unemployed I even lacked life insurance. How would my family survive with a large mortgage to pay?

I came to the conclusion that the best plan was to take my lumps and sell whatever assets I had in order to support my family for a period of two years. I chose a two-year time horizon because I had been told that most life insurance company policies would pay off, when the cause of death was suicide, if the policy had been purchased at least two years prior.

In the morning, I turned around and drove home. I never mentioned to Tunya and my children what had happened. By the end of the month, when I received the figures, I found that I had lost all the winnings that I had made through commodity trading and a good deal more. My original capital of $200,000 had been reduced to $25,000, from which I took $10,000 and bought two term life policies, making sure to read the fine print related to suicide.

I never traded commodity futures again. Nor did I mention the shame of my loss to anyone other than my accountant, Robin Elliott.

CHAPTER 45

"Don't You Know Your Nematodes?"

Lord Iveagh, 1979

THE LATE 1970S WAS a turbulent time for me. I seemed to be trying to work quite a number of schemes at the same time. For five years I didn't have a settled direction, and the number of things I tried in my desperation to get back on my feet makes a curious list. For instance, I had the idea of opening a shop on Robson Street. I pursued that to the point of incorporating a company called Famous Sweaters Ltd. I also did a feasibility study for a Vancouver-based trust company. I spent Christmas 1975 in the southern Philippines on a round-the-world research trip for an intended book on people who live on the water in all different countries. I was making frequent trips to Asia in these years, and I became seriously interested in trading in antique Chinese snuff bottles, small objects made from a variety of materials—porcelain, precious metal, glass, and jade—that were collected in large numbers by members of the Imperial Court. I was also considering writing a novel about Siamese court intrigue in the seventeenth century.

On a more pragmatic level, I signed up as a sessional lecturer at the University of British Columbia School of Community and Regional Planning, where my star pupil was a cocky youngster named Glen Clark, later known as the thirty-first premier of British Columbia, and later yet as president of the Jim Pattison Group. I also set up a company I called Audain Planning Ltd. to take on some short-term research contracts in the housing-policy field and to promote the growth of co-operative housing by linking BC co-op groups with private developers prepared to build townhome projects.

I think it's fair to say, though, that despite a myriad of different business schemes and adventures happening concurrently, the one that absorbed most of my time, and indeed the one that I thought had the most potential, was my foray into the agricultural sector.

I had never lived on a farm or been vaguely interested in farming. I became involved through my acquaintance with Vern Paulus, with whom I had negotiated the purchase of the home-building company Dunhill Development for the provincial government in 1973. Vern told me that he was interested in putting some serious money into farming somewhere in the United States. Knowing that I was at loose ends, he wondered if I would like to give him a hand by locating some suitable opportunities. I was intrigued, and having nothing better to do at the time I quickly volunteered, after negotiating a modest retainer.

Wondering how I should proceed when I could barely tell the difference between a sheaf of wheat and one of oats, I signed up for a six-week course at the University of California Davis, at the end of which I was awarded an impressive-looking certificate in farm management and rural appraisal.

The course provided opportunities to spend practical time in almond plantations, strawberry fields, avocado groves and even fields solely devoted to the manufacture of Heinz tomato ketchup, all of which I found quite interesting. Armed with that crash course, I decided to check out as many varieties of agriculture as possible in order to determine which combination of location, crops and weather would provide the best investment opportunities. Realizing that this was an exercise I couldn't simply figure out from books, I decided that I needed to "burn rubber" and visit as much of the country as possible to view the crops and figure out where the best place might be for my client to invest.

Paulus told me that he would prefer to put his money into land in the western United States, so that at least somewhat circumscribed my travel. There are twenty-two states west of the Mississippi (not counting Hawaii and Alaska), and I felt it necessary to visit each and every one. My modus operandi was to fly into a major airport, such as Denver, on Sunday evening, pick up my Hertz rental car, then start at dawn on Monday visiting farming centres of the region, while looking at crops and farming operations as I drove along. When I came to a small town, the chief people I wanted to interview were the state agricultural agent, a real-estate agent and the local banker. Presidents of small-town banks always seemed pleased to bid me welcome and usually turned out to be very knowledgeable about the financial conditions of their farmer clients.

During this period I became a self-appointed inspector of Holiday Inns, as I found it most convenient to use their telex reservation service as I moved from one town to another, from one indistinguishable room to another, with the same plastic glasses, the same dark-green window coverings and restaurant with the same grilled-cheese sandwich as the place I had slept the previous night.

My travels were not without the occasional hazard, including a burst radiator in the back hills of Arizona; an order over the radio to seek cover from late-afternoon tornadoes as I drove into the outskirts of Wichita, Kansas; and a late-spring hailstorm that shut down the highway for a few hours in western Wyoming. And I did "burn rubber," so much so that when I turned in my car keys to Hertz on a Friday evening, the agent usually gasped at the mileage I had recorded. Fortunately I was always on an unlimited mileage plan!

After staying in three dozen Holiday Inns, my report for Paulus recommended that the two best places to invest in US agriculture were in northern Missouri and central Washington. I found Missouri attractive because you could buy farms in the northern part of the state where the soils were similar to the productive black loams of Iowa, yet with a Missouri address they commanded half the price per acre of those located in northern states. The climate was so good that you could grow almost any type of grain or soybean crops without worrying about irrigation.

The sandy soils of central Washington also had a lot going for them, as long as you had good water access for irrigation. Central Washington boasted great yields of potatoes, grains, tree fruits and, more recently, wine grapes. Paulus became keenly interested in the central Washington idea, as the region was located closer to his home base on the coast, where he had already assembled some farmland.

However, before I zeroed in on central Washington, I thought it might be worth checking out a cattle ranch that I had stumbled across in southern Nevada. It boasted just over a million acres: 1,007,500 to be precise. On a per-acre basis, it was the cheapest vacant land that I had encountered, with a list price of less than $4 million, plus terms available to pay over fifteen years.

Why was it so cheap? Well, basically, two reasons: the mineral rights were not part of the sale, and actually, except for around 2,500 deeded acres surrounding the ranch headquarters, the rest of the land comprised federal leases from the US Forest Service and the US Bureau of Land Management—not an unusual situation in the western US.

I had already learned that it was impossible to buy a cattle ranch as an investor and make money off it. The only ranchers who made a living from their land were those who had inherited it. Americans generally buy ranches, particularly large ones, for recreation and ego satisfaction. I imagine nothing would impress the boys at the golf or yacht club more than the news that one had a little place out west of over a million acres!

To my surprise Paulus was intrigued, so I started digging into the history of the property, with the help of Luke, an old real-estate broker (sporting seven turquoise rings) whom I had met in Reno. After I put together a basic brochure, I made a date with Luke to fly me over to the ranch at 8:00 on a Tuesday morning in his Cessna 172. Paulus told me that he and his wife, Paula, would fly in directly and meet me at the ranch headquarters. Upon our arrival from Reno I was astonished to see Paulus's plane already parked on the small airstrip, along with four others. Once everyone had gathered around the coffee table in the quaint but serviceable ranch house, it became apparent that the second and third planes belonged to the listing agent from Idaho and a couple of clients he had invited up from Texas to view the property. The ranch manager also had an aircraft.

The manager gave us a brief pep talk, saying that the best way to see the place was to fly around it, unless you wanted to spend days driving in a dirty pickup truck, which he didn't think would appeal to our ladies. The ranch only supported a couple thousand cattle at the time, though we were told that could be expanded if some capital could be invested into hay production. When I asked why more hay wasn't being grown, the manager replied, "Actually, there is not much level land to irrigate. Also, we don't have enough guys on the place to move irrigation equipment around."

He went on to say, "Anyway, the cattle in these parts don't need hay. There are sixteen varieties of sagebrush on this ranch and the cattle can do well on thirteen of them." That was news to me. The course at UC Davis had never mentioned farming sagebrush.

Finally, after coffee and cinnamon buns, it was time to view the ranch. A debate ensued about how best to accomplish this, because no one seemed to want to ride in anyone else's airplane. Or perhaps there weren't enough seats. My broker, Luke, decided it was time for him to scoot back to Reno, so the ranch manager and I were each offered a seat in the Pauluses' spacious Beechcraft Bonanza, while the Texans would follow us, and the listing agent behind them, in their own aircraft.

With the ranch manager sitting up front telling our pilot where to go, I tried to follow along on the extensive topographical maps we had been provided with, but frankly one hill in that outback country looked like another, with just the occasional glimpse of a couple of cows. It was a monotonous landscape, with only a few patches of green on the hilltops. When we suddenly came across a herd of a dozen wild horses, the ranch manager told us it was too bad he hadn't brought a gun along as what he called "mystiques" competed with the cattle for the feed, a comment that didn't impress the rest of the passengers. Eventually, though, we landed in a valley where some branding operations were going on, and we were able to join a bunch of cowboys for lunch. Fortunately, I ate beef back in those days.

Over dinner at the MGM Grand in Reno that evening, Paulus decided to leave the opportunity to own a million-acre ranch to someone who needed that kind of trophy more than he did, particularly because with so little private land it seemed he would really only serve as a caretaker for the US government.

However, it wasn't long after the Nevada adventure that I came across what I considered to be an outstanding agricultural opportunity in central Washington. I found a huge irrigated farm near Pasco, Washington, with ninety circular pivot-irrigation systems on about 40 to 80 acres of land, which had been cultivated in rotations of potatoes and corn. It was owned by Donald Worley, a Moses Lake businessman with a lot of bank debt that Worley and his partners seemed unable to service. What made the Ice Harbor Farm especially attractive is that it had a large pumping station on the Snake River with very long-term water rights as well as an ideal microclimate. It also seemed suitable for a range of crops.

In talking to some of the smaller farmers in the area, I found that one or two of them were experimenting with asparagus, which grew easily in the sandy soil providing it was adequately irrigated. Although I didn't know much about asparagus except that it was typically eaten green in North America and white in France due to the soil being humped up around the plants as they grew, I thought it might be worth doing some research in Asia, as many other Washington State crops, such as apples and cherries, were exported there.

To my surprise, I found that green asparagus would be quite a novelty in China and Japan. Several importers told me they were happy to place orders as long as the crop could be shipped fresh, which I assured them could be possible, with the spears being cut the morning before they would arrive at Tokyo or Shanghai airport by chartered air freight. Moses Lake Airport, with its 13,500-foot runway, could easily handle 747s and, in fact, was used by Japan Airlines as a training base.

Paulus was excited by this idea but said he would need to bring in a partner to take care of most of the down payment required to buy the land, and that a lease arrangement would be preferable to take the risk out of the deal. Fortunately, I had heard that the Green Giant Company was looking around for land on which to grow asparagus in Washington State, so a few days later Paulus and I found ourselves in their Le Sueur, Minnesota, head office. In less than a morning, we were able to initial a deal to lease out the land and improvements on the property for twenty years. Green Giant was interested in my Asian market research, though they told me that their plan was that most of their asparagus crop would be frozen or sent to one of their canning plants. They also showed us a fascinating machine, recently invented to harvest asparagus, that incorporated cameras to determine the length of each spear to be cut, leaving the rest of the plant intact—obviously a huge saving over the cost of scores of field-hands that would otherwise be required every couple of days during the harvest season.

The partner came by way of one of Paulus's fishing connections, in the form of the 3rd Earl of Iveagh, from Ireland, whom I was told was the current head of the Guinness brewing family. Lord Iveagh turned out to be a friendly fellow only two months my senior. When I confessed to him that his family's legendary dark stout wasn't quite my cup of tea, having only tried it once, Iveagh admitted that he also wasn't keen on it, but suggested since he was chairman of the company, I should keep that a secret.

Travelling from Vancouver on the flight to Pasco, I was told to sit with Lord Iveagh ("Call me Ben") and brief him on asparagus, which I did, telling him that the barriers to many farmers getting into the game was that it took asparagus two or three years to get a decent crop, and also that the plants would have to be replaced after twenty years, with the land then needing to revert to other crops. "Why not replace those plants with younger ones?" Lord Iveagh asked me.

"Apparently there are nematodes that will eventually thrive on the roots," I replied.

"Yes, but what type of nematodes?" Lord Iveagh persisted. "Don't you know your nematodes?"

When I confessed my ignorance, with a twinkle in his eye, Lord Iveagh mentioned a couple of Latin names, adding with a smile, "Don't worry, you have been doing well. I just happened to study agronomy at university and by chance took a special interest in asparagus."

I felt a bit deflated, but nevertheless the farm inspection went well, with the deal completed two months later, after which I was paid a handsome bonus.

I continued to make use of what knowledge I had picked up about US agriculture and spent another year devising a plan for European investors to acquire irrigated US land, which would be managed by a Paulus company. I even had a handsome brochure printed, with which I made the rounds of prospective investors in France and England who had responded to advertisements inserted in the *Economist*. But for one reason or another, having a role in creating what the Green Giant Company told us was the largest asparagus farm in the world turned out to be the greatest—and only—highlight of my career in agriculture.

CHAPTER 46

"I Will Sell You Half of My Company"

Vern Paulus, 1980

PERHAPS THE MOST CHALLENGING aspect of this story to write about is my business career. Nowadays, people are surprised to hear that in my earlier life I made my living from engaging in livelihoods other than business. In fact, if you add up my career paths, I think there were five main ones: 1) airline employee on the road to a flying career; 2) juvenile probation officer; 3) housing-policy consultant; 4) agricultural investment advisor; and finally 5) home-builder.

When I have time for a yarn, which isn't often, people seem taken aback, sometimes to the point of disbelief, learning that I went to jail for civil rights, that I was a delegate to the founding convention of Canada's left-wing New Democratic Party, or, indeed, that when the CBC back in the early 1960s wanted to do a film about a radical on a Canadian university campus, I was the subject.

When I'm asked how I made the transition to becoming a residential developer, I tell people that I have never really understood it myself, but perhaps it had something to do with a change in focus from ideas to people. My socialist friends might call it a change from ideas to money! Let me have a go at explaining.

When I was in my twenties, I was consumed with ideas and was prepared to make personal sacrifices for them: ideas about racial equality, religious freedom, peace among nations, and income redistribution.

The interest in racial equality came naturally to me. I am not sure why, especially when as a child I was brought up very much in the ethos of the British Empire and told at school that somehow it was "The White Man's Burden" to rule the other races—something that never did make much sense, as early on I had read about the man called Kublai Khan who ruled all the lands from the Oxus River to the China Sea, from the Himalayas to the Arctic wastes. I had also read about Ozymandias, king of kings; Rameses II, whose lands stretched from the Mediterranean to Lake Victoria; to say nothing of Mughal emperor Shah Jahan, who built what is still the world's most beautiful building, the Taj Mahal. Were they all White men? I think not.

My interest in racial equality eventually took me to the American South and also to becoming one of the founders of the BC Civil Liberties Association.

Religious freedom and tolerance is something that I may have inherited from my Huguenot ancestors, who had to flee from France in the late seventeenth century to escape persecution or even being burned as heretics. As a boy I attended both the Catholic and Anglican churches and read widely about religion, including readings from the Holy Bible, the Koran, the Talmud, and the Hindu Book of Prayer. An involvement with the Sons of Freedom Doukhobor sect was motivated by both my interest in religious tolerance and family ties, Tunya being a Doukhobor.

The other big idea that I was seized with was income redistribution. Crudely put, that means taking money from the rich and giving it to the poor, though my professors in the social administration department of the London School of Economics and Political Science described it more elegantly. What they advocated for was more generous family allowances and old-age pensions, better teachers in the public school system and, yes, much more publicly owned rental housing for those who couldn't afford to buy their own homes. Their ideal, which became mine for a period, was not a communist society in which the government would own all property and industries; rather, it was a welfare state in which wealthy individuals and companies would be highly taxed to create a society with much less income disparity.

These were the ideals I fervently believed in, so I identified with people who espoused similar ones and tended to despise individuals or governments who stood in the way of their realization. Real-estate developers were a special target of my scorn because I believed that it was immoral to profit off windfall capital gains on the value of urban land and houses, something that was simply a result of demographic forces. For instance, Ephraim Diamond, the chief executive officer of Cadillac Fairview Corporation, came in for particular attention when I organized a picket of that developer's offices for allegedly trying to blockbust a Toronto neighbourhood—that is, assembling a number of the houses and filling them with rowdy tenants to encourage the remaining owners to sell so that the property could be redeveloped at a higher density.

I so strictly adhered to my principles about profiteering from raising real-estate values that I refused to accept a profit when I resold our first two family homes—in Toronto and Ottawa—thereby probably passing on the capital gain to the new owners. No wonder each house sold within a day of our putting up a lawn sign!

I used to spout off arrogant rhetoric about being more interested in ideas than people, expressing the Marxist view that there are inherent contradictions in the capitalist system that would lead to its downfall. In other words, a just society would come about inevitably regardless of the political personalities involved.

Mind you, I wasn't just living in an academic dream world during this period. I became involved with people to start new non-profit organizations, to plan demonstrations, and most importantly to solicit the government for funds to further my broad social-development and housing-policy objectives. Prime Minister Pierre Trudeau's federal government was very helpful in this enterprise, as they considered it expedient to maintain relationships with left-wingers such as myself.

What changed my orientation was when I moved from the position of merely advocating social-development objectives, particularly in the housing field, to one in which I was actually given the responsibility for achieving something—that is, to build a lot of public and co-operative housing in BC in the early 1970s under the NDP government of Dave Barrett.

I quickly discovered that to get something done I needed people. I lacked an organization, and there wouldn't be time to build up a big bureaucracy like the Ontario Housing Corporation, where I had worked some years previously.

I immediately phoned Jack Poole, chief executive officer of Daon Development, the biggest development company in the province, and told him I needed help. He sent his executive vice-president, Norm Cressey, over to Victoria the following day. I also strongly supported an idea hatched by Bob Williams, one of Barrett's ministers, about acquiring a private development company called Dunhill Development Ltd. and having it develop land on the government's behalf. That's when I initially connected with Vern Paulus, as he was Dunhill's chief executive officer at the time; he would also become influential in helping the government develop thousands of homes. Once purchased by the government, Dunhill Development changed its name to the Housing Corporation of British Columbia .

As time went on, I learnt that harnessing the private housing industry to achieve the ends of expanding government and non-profit housing stock was an effective way to go. In the process I met many industry executives who did not seem to fit in with my previous image of them as immoral and slippery business operators whose objective in life was to simply exploit the public and make a profit any way they could. No, for the most part, they were ethical and civically minded. They were also people with strong family connections, generous to their employees and committed to their communities—far from the image that I had earlier held.

By the late 1970s, I was helping co-operative housing groups take advantage of the generous support programs that the federal government had at that time to develop co-operative housing. My role was to link these groups with developers who had suitable sites and were willing to build the accommodation. I was a consultant and troubleshooter, facilitating all sizes of projects, from small to large. It was a line of work I had trained for and had by now acquired quite a lot of experience in, after my various posts in government. I was comfortable in my role and had no reason to expect any big changes in my life unless I decided to make one myself.

Then, one day in mid-1980, at an otherwise inauspicious lunch with Vern Paulus, after our forays into agricultural investing had wound down, my settled life pivoted 180 degrees and brought about pretty much everything that has happened since.

Vern said to me, "Why don't you do for me what you are doing for other developers, and I will sell you half of my company."

CHAPTER 47

"You Could Always Write Your Book Later"

Ajahn Khan, 1980

WHEN VERN PAULUS FIRST invited me to go into the home-building industry, I was really torn over whether I should embark on a new business career or return to the dream I had harboured of writing a novel set in seventeenth-century Thailand.

I had first visited Thailand in 1970 en route from Hong Kong, where I was exploring the possibility of dealing in antique Chinese snuff bottles. Where I developed that particular interest, I don't recall. In any case, it was the time of the Vietnam War and I had heard that Bangkok had a torrid nightlife. I thought that the town might be interesting to visit for a weekend, which I did with a Canadian friend.

Bangkok in those days was a picturesque low-rise city complete with many functioning canals. We spent a weekend seeing the sights, including the Royal Palace and the Floating Market, as well as the GI go-go bars in the Patpong area. Then it was time to go home.

It was only at the airport before the return flight that I realized that Thailand was the country originally called Siam, made famous by Rodgers and Hammerstein's hit musical *The King and I.*

A year later I was drawn back to Thailand and started to explore the country, from Songkhla in the deep south to Chiang Rai in the north. The Buddhist culture suited me, and I found the language captivating, so I endeavoured to learn to speak it and studied the country's history.

Over time I became intrigued with the life of a Greek figure who became chief minister of the kingdom when the court of King Narai was based at Ayutthaya in the late seventeenth century. During periodic visits to the country I became convinced that I would write a historical novel based on this colourful individual's life, which unfortunately ended when he was unceremoniously trampled by a bull elephant, a rather unique form of execution. I learned that in 1673 Louis XIV of France sent an emissary accompanied by scholars to try to convert King Narai to Christianity. When the doctors of jurisprudence—botanists, zoologists, physicians and trade commissioners—went home, they all wrote extensive reports, most of which were published and lodged in various French archives. Through the good offices of the UBC library I was able to obtain many of these reports through interlibrary loans.

I had done a number of plot outlines, and I was actually on the verge of taking a year off to write the manuscript, when Vern Paulus made his offer to bring me into the residential development business. I recall giving him a tentative "Yes," but asked if I could spend the month of August in Thailand, as I had some obligations to clean up in that country. I knew that my life had to change course but was confused whether to take the risk of becoming an author or to try my hand at becoming a developer among a business crowd that I had been hostile to in prior years.

In discussing my dilemma one evening with Dolf Riks, the proprietor of a well-known restaurant in what was then the small seaside resort of Pattaya, I learned that when Thai people need advice they usually go to see a monk. So that's what I did. I asked Mr. Tin, who was the staff supervisor at the Nipa Lodge, where I was staying, if he knew a good monk I could consult.

The next day Tin took me on the back of his motorcycle to a very small temple called Wat Huay Yai, located in the rice paddies near the town of Sattahip. When we got there Tin reminded me that the protocol was to always keep my head lower than the monk's and point my feet away, towards the wall.

We climbed up a set of stairs to a little thatched-roof platform, near what looked like the ruins of a small temple. There, clad in a saffron robe, sitting cross-legged in the front of numerous statues of Buddha, and attended by a number of novices, was the small figure of Abbot Ajahn Khan. Seated around him were numerous villagers, all making small offerings and wishing to receive his advice.

My Thai was very rudimentary at that time, so when my turn came Tin did the translation. He told the abbot that I was a government worker, but I needed to know whether I should become a writer or a businessman. I interrupted and told Tin, "Please make sure you tell him I want to be a bestselling novelist, not just any writer."

Tin did his best to explain, and the monk smiled broadly, showing his impressive rows of gold-capped teeth. He then read my hand and drew my horoscope using Chinese astrology. For some reason he also examined the shape of my ears.

The monk then picked up a ballpoint pen and began to write. Without saying anything, he gave the piece of paper to Tin, who thanked Ajahn Khan profusely and suggested that I make an offering, which I did by placing 100 baht (equal to about $2.50 in those days) in a silver bowl.

Later, back at the hotel, Tin translated the note for me. Ajahn Khan believed that I would be successful either as a writer or a businessman, but it was probably best to do business first, because once I made some money, "You could always write your book later." That evening my mind was at peace and I sent a telex to Vern Paulus asking him if my employment start date could be brought forward.

CHAPTER 48

"You Will Marry an Asian Lady"

Ajahn Khan, 1981

AFTER RECEIVING THE ADVICE from Abbot Ajahn Khan about entering business, I thought it might be useful to visit him once more and ask him about my remarriage prospects. Tunya and I had separated circa 1973 for a long list of reasons, which can be summarized as two very independent people discovering they couldn't or didn't want to compromise their diverging interests. The parting was fairly amicable and became more so over time, to the extent that Tunya today lives quite nearby, in West Vancouver, and we both attend all family occasions. But after nearly a decade apart I was feeling the weight of bachelorhood and was determined to do something about it. During a holiday in Thailand, I once again went to Wat Huay Yai to see Abbot Khan with Mr. Tin from Nipa Lodge.

This time, I waited an hour or so to see him, as he was taking his midday meal. The Thai Buddhist monks go out in the early morning to beg for their food and bring it home to the temple to eat. After midday they do not eat again until the following morning so that full stomachs do not interfere with their prayers.

When at last I did see Ajahn Khan, he said, "I gave you the advice that you needed last year. Why have you come back so soon?"

With Tin translating for me once again, I replied, "Well, I forgot to ask you when I am going to meet a new wife. I have been separated from my former wife for about seven years. While I have had girlfriends, none of them have appealed to me from the point of view of setting up housekeeping." Ajahn Khan didn't write anything this time. He said, "I remember your horoscope from your visit last year. You will marry an Asian lady."

"Oh," I said. "When am I going to meet her?"

The monk said, "Well, you have already had a lot of opportunity. Foreign men seem to find our Thai girls very beautiful. I can tell you one thing. You will bring a lady to see me within the next year, and I will tell you whether she is suitable or not."

I went away encouraged but perplexed, because while I did indeed consider Thai women attractive, I had heard that most of them were not happy living in the West, separated from their families, their culture and their traditional food. And I had read that over 90 per cent of the marriages American GIs made in Thailand had failed.

Back home in Vancouver, I dated one or two Chinese-Canadian women, and every time I did I thought about that monk way off in the Thai rice paddies and wondered if he would find this or that one suitable for me, or me suitable for her.

Then it happened. One day I was having my hair cut in a shop on Vancouver's Seymour Street when I saw in the mirror a small Asian woman in purple velvet hot pants running energetically around the shop floor talking to herself and joking with the customers. On the way out I asked the manager whether my next appointment could be with the Asian lady. "Oh, you mean Yoshi," he said. "And, by the way, she's Japanese."

After I had a couple of haircuts with Yoshi I mustered up enough courage to ask her out for a drink.

"Sorry, but I don't go out for drinks with the customers, both because it's not professional and because it's usually a good way of losing a customer," Yoshi said in heavily accented English.

"But I am not your customer. I am your future husband," I insisted.

"Well, that's news to me," she replied. "Anyway, I am having dinner with my girlfriend tomorrow, and how do you know I don't have a husband already?"

"I have a gift for reading minds," I replied.

Fortunately, Yoshi did agree to have a drink with me at the Four Seasons Hotel the next evening, which was followed by dinner at Trader Vic's at the Bayshore Inn. When she told me that the week after next she was going to visit her parents in Japan, I said, "That's wonderful, because after that you will be coming to Thailand to meet my monk."

Yoshi was incredulous at my audacity, but ten days later she met me in Tokyo, on a flight that I had originally boarded in Seattle, and we arrived in Bangkok in the early hours of the morning.

We had quite an adventure getting to Pattaya, because the road was badly flooded, causing our taxi to stall with the water up to the door of the passenger compartment. The driver tried to flag down some trucks that were driving by in the night, but no one would risk stopping at three in the morning.

Finally, I waded out into the snake-infested water. I took a shirt out of my suitcase, opened the engine compartment and felt my way in the dark to the spark plugs, each of which I dried thoroughly. That done, the driver turned over the engine, and lo and behold the taxi started. The driver ended up depositing us in Pattaya just as the sun was coming up.

Despite the long trip in economy seats and the harrowing night, after breakfast and a shower we were off to Wat Huay Yai with Mr. Tin as our translator.

When Yoshi, crouching on the floor, bowed down before Ajahn Khan, he beamed from ear to ear. He then quickly cast her horoscope and wrote a long page of notes, which explained that a rat would be a very suitable mate for an ox like me.

Yoshi has often asked me what would have happened if Ajahn Khan had not approved of our relationship. Frankly, I don't know, but the story does not end there.

A few years later, after we were married in Canada and my business was going fairly well, we went back to Ajahn Khan and said that we would like to thank him for the good advice and luck he had bestowed upon us. I took a chance and said to him in Thai, "Your wish is my command."

In other words, we would be willing to give you whatever is in our power to give.

The monk thought for a minute, then explained that for many years he had been trying to get a larger temple built, but though he made good money from fortune-telling, his practice had been to recycle all of it into the village that had grown up around his temple, in the form of wells, a health clinic and a house for homeless old people, to say nothing of looking after the dozens of dogs, cats and monkeys that seemed to inhabit the temple grounds—all castaway pets.

Ajahn Khan added that what he really needed were two sets of teak double doors for his temple. He had one of his monks bring some plans so that I could see the door designs. The doors were about four metres high. Without even asking the price, I said that Yoshi and I would be honoured to provide the doors.

In due course, four long slabs of teak were ordered and two families came down from Chiang Mai to undertake the intricate carvings. Several months later, when finished, the exteriors of the doors were covered in gold leaf carvings, and to our great surprise each set of double doors contained the words "Michael Audain" carved on the right side and "Yoshiko Karasawa" on the left.

Many years later, when we returned to Pattaya, dense urban development had replaced the rice paddies around Wat Huay Yai, and Ajahn Khan had moved on to his next existence in the Buddhist cycle of life. The little temple looked somewhat forlorn, but those huge doors with their strange foreign names were still there.

CHAPTER 49

"What's a Welfare Officer Doing Running a House-builder?"

Lord Sterling, 1991

WHEN VERN PAULUS AND I got down to discussing details of how I would buy into his development business, I asked him how much money he was prepared to commit to the enterprise, since I understood that it cost a lot to acquire land, get it zoned, then have it constructed upon. Paulus replied with a smile, "It really doesn't take any bucks to make dough."

Paulus told me that he had a dormant company, Polygon Properties Ltd., that had about $4 million tied up in a couple of apartment buildings, and that he would sell me 25 per cent of it right away for $1 million.

"How do I finance that?" I asked.

"Well, how much money do you have?" he enquired. I told him that I had about $50,000 in the bank, but there were mortgages on my wife's house and my own condo that came to more than that.

"Okay," Paulus said. "I will take your $50,000 as a down payment and I will get the Bank of British Columbia to finance the rest if you are willing to pledge the titles to your homes."

"What's my salary going to be?" I asked.

"How much do you need to live on?" When I told him $40,000 a year because I was supporting my family, Paulus quickly agreed. I wasn't particularly smart in making the deal, as I never questioned the value of the properties Polygon owned, but I did insist on getting fees equal to what other developers had been paying me for consulting on social-housing deals.

CHAPTER 49

For the first three years of my tenure at Polygon, we just built social-housing units, which were profitable and risk-free projects since we did them on a turnkey basis, with the co-operative groups providing cash flow from their CMHC-insured loans as the construction progressed. But as time went on I realized that such government programs were not likely to continue forever, and I had to move into market housing.

In terms of getting into business without any capital, Paulus taught me that there were two ways this could be possible. The first was to find a deal and then find a partner to put up the equity in return for a share of the profits. The second way was to find a guarantor for a bank loan. The latter was essentially how Paulus operated in the days when I did business with him.

I was happy to be able to learn the residential-development game, with Paulus making frequent trips to Vancouver from his Washington State home to advise me on land acquisitions. But I was not getting any wealthier, even though I was gradually paying down my bank loans through the incentive fees I earned. The profits that the company made were expertly drained south to support Paulus's operations in Washington and California, through a series of management fees that I seemed to have no say in.

Paulus also encouraged me to balance the residential sector of our business by developing commercial offices, as he had done successfully in the Seattle area. For example, in the mid-1980s, in Burnaby's Metrotown, we built the largest office complex outside of downtown Vancouver up to that time. However, this part of the business did not prove to be particularly profitable.

Then, one morning in 1988, Paulus called me into his office, sat me down and told me bluntly, "I am fed up and want to wind things up. I don't know whether you are just inept at running a development business or whether Canada is going down the drain, but I have things to do in the States. I want out of here. You have sixty days to buy me out or I will simply liquidate the company."

To say that I was stunned would be an understatement. We were operating profitably, while not at the level we had achieved in the early

1980s, largely because Vancouver was just starting to recover from a long real-estate recession. The next day I asked Paulus whether he would let Polygon pay him back over time, say a couple of years. "No, what I want is $4 million for my 75 per cent of the shares."

"What about all the cash that has flowed down to fund your operations in the States over the past few years? We would have had some very profitable years if it hadn't been for your huge management charges."

"That's all water under the bridge. I gave you the opportunity to get into business," Paulus replied with a smile.

I wasn't just concerned about getting funds to buy out Paulus, but both his and my personal guarantees were behind all our bank loans. Paulus's net worth statement looked a great deal more solid than my own. Fortunately, a mutual friend of ours, George Stekl, came to the rescue a week later. Stekl was a chartered accountant with an incredible mind for figures. "If I can find a substantial British company as your partner, would you be interested?" he asked. I naturally replied, "Yes," because with my limited knowledge about business finance, I had no idea how I was going to deal with buying Paulus out and I didn't want to lose the company for which I had spent almost eight years building a reputation and a brand.

After negotiating an additional thirty days from Paulus, Stekl got me together with Robin Cordwell, the president of Laing Properties Ltd., a wholly owned Canadian subsidiary of a British public company with a solid reputation in the British construction and housing industry. Fortunately, Stekl fostered the building of a personal relationship between Cordwell and myself, which resulted in Polygon being recapitalized with a $6-million debenture, to the point that my personal guarantee would no longer be required for loans. Laing also loaned me sufficient funds to acquire another 25 per cent of Polygon, though I later arranged to sell off a portion of my shares to our executive vice-president, Rick Genest, who thereby became a junior partner in the new enterprise.

The Polygon officer who was invaluable to the transactions was our vice-president finance, Ralf Schmidtke, who Stekl assured me was capable of running a back office with the strong financial controls that befitted a well-managed company.

CHAPTER 49

It made a big difference that Laing brought a Bank of Nova Scotia relationship to our company. For the first time we had a line of credit that we could write cheques on without having to get prior approval from the bank. This was a real revelation to us.

Another good thing that the relationship with Laing brought was the introduction of a new level of corporate governance and financial planning to Polygon, with quarterly board meetings and detailed financial projections. It's hard to believe today, but for eight years we ran a substantial business that lacked board meetings—at least I wasn't invited to attend any, though I was supposedly a director and a 25-per-cent shareholder. Once a year a bunch of legal papers were put in front of me and I was directed where to sign—which I dutifully did.

While Paulus had controlled Polygon, I had been content to go along with him, because he had given me that crucial break to get into the development industry, and because he had taught me a lot along the way. But we had fundamentally different styles and attitudes towards business. Whereas Paulus was self-admittedly a deal junkie, and a brilliant one at that, I believed in putting customers first to build a strong brand over the long term.

The new corporate board consisted of Robin Cordwell, Laing's chief financial officer Simon Russell, and myself. As the months went by and the financial results we reported looked better than our projections, we got along well with the Laing people, to the point that in early 1992 I was told that the Laing family was inviting Yoshi and me to their box at the Ascot Racecourse, as they were keen to meet us. This caused some sleepless nights for Yoshi, worrying about what sort of dress and hat she should wear for this important occasion; whereas I knew that all I had to do was rent a morning suit and top hat from London's Moss Bros.

In the end the worry was for nothing, because one night a few weeks later, while Yoshi and I were aboard the Swan Hellenic *Orpheus* (a small cruise vessel converted from an Irish night ferry) on the storm-tossed Mediterranean, I was urgently summoned to the radio office behind the bridge to take a call.

It was Robin Cordwell on the line, saying, "Something rather unbelievable has happened. Laing's parent company in the UK received a hostile takeover bid from the British conglomerate called P&O. The Laing family is going to fight it, but I think you should know."

Well, no one stands in the way of P&O chairman Lord Sterling, so the takeover did succeed, despite resistance from the Laing family. A few weeks later we were visited by a group of P&O representatives, curious about the half interest in the Vancouver home builder they had acquired. While Yoshi was relieved that the invitation to Ascot was off, I was more curious about how I was going to get along with a new partner that I had no role in securing.

Initially I didn't worry too much, because P&O executive Tim Harding said that, along with Robin Cordwell, he would represent P&O on our board and that we could continue with business as usual.

I met Lord Sterling, the chairman of the great British shipping firm, as he briskly stepped off a private jet on a crisp winter morning at Vancouver International Airport. As soon as I had settled the short balding man into the front seat of my car, he lobbed a question at me. "What's a welfare officer doing running a home builder?"

How do I reply to that, I thought, without recounting my life story or explaining that I had been involved one way or another in housing for over twenty years?

"To make money," I eventually replied.

"Oh, then we have something in common," said Sterling.

He had principally come to Vancouver because it was the head office of the Canadian branch of Laing Properties PLC, the company he had acquired the previous year. At a Vancouver Club dinner that evening, when I told Sterling how important P&O's Princess Cruises were to the Vancouver economy, he professed not to know that many of their ships were based here during the summer months. Instead, he mentioned that Margaret Thatcher had told him Canada had gone soft on socialism and therefore he was doubtful that there was much future for P&O in Canada. This conversation was useful in that I detected a receptiveness to winding down Laing's business in Canada and an eventual buyout of their interest in Polygon Homes Ltd.

CHAPTER 49

With the strengthening of the Vancouver housing market in the early 1990s, stimulated to some extent by people's fear of mainland China's takeover of Hong Kong, Polygon's business expanded, as did our profitability. At the same time, though, P&O's tentative stance regarding the Canadian assets that it had acquired was starting to hamper our growth. For instance, we were told to stick to building woodframe low-rise buildings. As a consequence we had to sell a wonderfully located high-rise apartment site on Burnaby's Central Park to one of our competitors. We realized that, with low-rise sites not being in abundance, if we were to expand it made sense to be in the high-rise apartment sector. P&O also indicated that they were not interested in us exploring other markets, such as Seattle or California, as they already had business relationships in those areas. I was therefore quite relieved when Tim Harding told me in 1992 that P&O had decided to dispose of its Canadian assets and we would be able to buy them out. Alternatively, they would offer their Polygon shares to another party. With this in mind I told Harding firmly that the shareholder agreement I had initially negotiated with Laing gave me the first right of refusal to buy their shares and that he should tell his investment bankers that these shares would not be for sale.

After a couple of months of skirmishing, and again with George Stekl's help, we were able to negotiate the purchase of P&O's shareholdings for $21 million. This was done with the help of the Bank of Nova Scotia's CEO, Peter Godsell, who told me in their Toronto head office that, despite his bank having lost more money in United States real estate in the last three years than it had made in its prior history, he liked what Polygon had achieved in the Vancouver market, and added rather alarmingly, "If you get into trouble, Michael, you are still young enough to come back."

And so, in the lawyer's office on December 1, 1992, after signing piles of documents, I became the 100-per-cent owner of Polygon. But I quickly realized that it would be prudent to take some partners, so I offered shares to executive vice-president Rick Genest and an equal portion to Milan Ilich, a Richmond, BC, land developer. Our financial vice-president, Ralf Schmidtke, who had by then been with the company for fourteen years, was later offered an allocation.

It was sad to say goodbye to Robin Cordwell from our board of directors, because he had helped Polygon through a crucial time in our history. However, it felt good that Polygon Homes Ltd. would now be a 100-per cent BC-owned-and-operated company, committed to building well-designed and constructed homes for the people of Greater Vancouver.

One thing I feel I should emphasize is that my transformation from a reform-minded social worker to a large-scale residential developer took place as a natural progression in my thinking. In my mid-twenties, the lack of decent housing for ordinary families was a social issue that stirred me. But once I became actively engaged in actually creating housing supply, I came to the realization that only private industry could do the job on the scale required to meet demand, so it was perhaps an easier step to become a private developer myself. Certainly in that role I have been able to create far more affordable homes for ordinary BC families than I ever could have had I remained in the government or non-profit sectors.

Many of my old colleagues on the left still seem to believe that government should provide housing and improve the market through various kinds of regulation, and while I agree there is much the government should do, it is not necessarily in the form of the increased intervention they envision. Of course, government should play a role in helping people with special needs to secure appropriate accommodation. I'm thinking of the frail elderly, and people with disabilities. Many single mothers often also need extra help. But if we rely solely on government to house the population, we might all end up in public housing or waiting ten years for a tiny subsidized flat, like they do in Hong Kong.

The distressing homeless situation is another story, though it's often not a housing problem but a mental health issue. Nevertheless, no one should have to sleep outside if that's not their choice, and this is clearly a place where the government and non-profit partners have a vital role to fill.

Housing has become a big subject in British Columbia due to the appalling cost of accommodation in Vancouver, which has a spillover effect on prices throughout much of southern BC, and those of us in the industry are as frustrated by the situation as everyone else. My editor has pressed me to provide some ringside insights, but the situation is complex and there are no quick fixes, at least not ones that would be universally welcomed. The bottom line is that Vancouver is a very desirable city, and demand for affordable housing tends to outstrip supply, pushing prices upward. This situation is not unique to Vancouver—many large cities have a similar problem. Nobody expects to find affordable family housing in downtown New York or London, especially of the detached single-family kind favoured in BC. One way these older cities have coped is by expanding into the surrounding countryside and using good public transit to move workers in and out of the core. But in Vancouver this option is limited by geography, with mountains on one side, the sea on another, and protected farmland on another. This has placed a premium on suitable development land, which drives up the price of any housing built on it.

One of the ironies of the situation is that in a market where governments are supposedly searching high and low for solutions to high housing costs, they are themselves one of the major contributors to that cost. Municipalities hate to be seen levelling new charges and taxes directly on their voters, so they do it indirectly by loading the charges onto developers, who then take the heat for the high cost of homes. A 2018 report by real-estate consultant Paul Sullivan found that combined government charges, levies and taxes add $220,000 to the price of a $620,000 condominium in Vancouver, a cost increase of 35 per cent. Comparable charges in Toronto are only $70,000, or 11 per cent.

Another contributor to Vancouver's unaffordability crisis is a general reluctance to increase density. If you can't spread out, you can always go up. If you visit other cities that are as popular as Vancouver, with similar land constraints, they all have very high housing prices and rents unless they have densified considerably, an example being, say, Athens. There, housing prices are so low the government has taken the opposite tack to Vancouver and offered incentives to foreign buyers to come in and stimulate the market. Our company is frequently in the position of being limited to fourteen to eighteen floors for apartment buildings on sites where we could easily build thirty-six or more floors without expanding the perimeter. If the building lot costs were, say, $10 million, this might mean each buyer would pay about $250,000 for the land cost per condominium apartment, compared to $700,000 if a lower building were built. Building costs would also be lower on a per-unit basis in the larger structure. Today, many of Greater Vancouver's two dozen municipalities allow relatively few apartment buildings higher than five or six floors, while of course vast parts of the region are still restricted to single-family-home neighbourhoods, there being a sad reluctance to rezone.

Vancouver's West End, which was created by clearing out single-family homes and replacing them with high-rise apartments in the 1960s, remains a crucial housing resource, especially for the young professional class and the elderly, but it is doubtful Vancouver's West End apartment zone could ever happen today. I appreciate the appeal of single-family neighbourhoods and live in one myself, but choices have consequences, and one of the consequences of resisting densification in the Vancouver region is our deplorably high housing costs.

CHAPTER 50

"How's Business?"

Queen Elizabeth, 2002

ALONG WITH A NUMBER of other Vancouver business people, I was asked to stand in line to meet Queen Elizabeth on her visit to Vancouver in 2002. I was ten years old when I fell in love with Princess Elizabeth, who I had hardly heard of up until that time. But the 1947 royal marriage was a tremendous postwar event for war-torn Britain, where food rationing, coal shortages and bombed-out buildings were still common. My mother kindly sent me British newspapers depicting the event, and I recall reading them over and over for many weeks.

Oh, I did stand by the roadside for a couple of hours to watch the Queen drive by in 1951, while she was still a princess. I also recall distinguishing myself at an Air Force Cadet parade in Port Hope, Ontario, on Coronation Day in 1953, when I fainted after standing for an hour or so at attention in the hot sun. My reward for that was to be one of only two boys at Trinity College School who were denied a Coronation Medal, which every schoolchild in the country was entitled to.

But, every year, no matter where I am in the world, I have endeavoured to hear the Queen's Christmas broadcast, because it is the only occasion all year when she is allowed to speak from her heart. And when I haven't had an opportunity to hear her message directly, I have made sure I was able to read an account of it. There is actually a website that you can visit to hear as many of those past Christmas broadcasts as you wish.

What I so admire about the Queen is that she is totally dedicated to doing her duty, despite the prime ministers who come and go, the strange foreign dignitaries she is obliged to entertain, and the antics of her three sons.

My love and respect for Queen Elizabeth has not been completely unreserved. For instance, I was greatly distressed that she did not do more to comfort and counsel Princess Diana when Diana had to put up with the adulterous behaviour of her wayward husband. Certainly Princess Diana was better off with the divorce, but it was callous of the Queen to strip Diana of her "Royal Highness" title and not to include her in family gatherings. And I say this because I feel a great love and respect for the Queen. But when history books are written a hundred years from now, Princess Diana will be a shining star, especially for her commitment to helping people with AIDS. Seeing Princess Diana warmly embracing an AIDS victim greatly affected the opinions of so many people worldwide, including mine.

Diana's exceptional leadership in the campaign to clear landmines from large areas of the world where they still continue to maim and kill people, including so many young children, will also be long remembered.

Waiting to greet the Queen, we were gathered in a restaurant area of Vancouver's hockey arena and formed into line by protocol people. At the front of the line were some hockey stars, including Wayne Gretzky and Gordie Howe. The Queen was introduced to them as television cameras lit the scene. She moved swiftly along, and when she came to me the television camera lights suddenly turned off.

Premier Gordon Campbell introduced me by saying, "Your Majesty, please meet Michael Audain, chairman of the Business Council of British Columbia." Out shot a hand wearing a purple glove, and quick as a whip the Queen asked, "How's business?"

"A lot better, Your Majesty, since we now have a free-enterprise government in British Columbia," I said.

"Oh, I am glad to hear that," she replied.

You are briefed not to ask the Queen questions—it's her job to do the asking if she wants to chat. Despite those protocol instructions, I perked up and said, "You know, it's a real pleasure to meet you in this fashion. I recall waiting out in the rain for two hours just to see you drive by on your first visit to British Columbia as princess back in 1949."

"Actually, it was 1951," the Queen corrected, smiling sweetly.

"Yes, ma'am. You obviously have a much better memory than I."

She replied, "Well, I'm pretty good on dates. But I do have trouble finding my glasses. I find it's best to have a number of pairs made, then I'm sure to come across one when poking around the house."

"Ma'am, I am so delighted that you have been able to come to spend part of your jubilee year with us in BC," I said.

"Do you think people really care anymore?" she enquired.

"Well, did you hear the crowd roar as you dropped the hockey puck at the start of the game tonight? We certainly do care."

"Puck? Oh, that's what that black thing is called. I mustn't forget it," she murmured with a twinkle in her eye.

"Yes, and I also appreciate you coming so soon after the loss of your mother, who was so widely respected throughout Canada."

"Oh, my mother said she always felt more at home in BC than in any other part of this country. She loved her visits here." said the Queen.

"Yes, I knew that because she was the colonel and chief of my father's regiment," I replied.

"Which one was that?" the Queen asked.

"Well, it was originally the 7th Hussars, and then it got merged into the Queen's Own Hussars, and now I don't quite know what's happened to it. I wonder if you have appointed a new colonel and chief yet."

"Well, I'm not sure about that. I'll have it checked for you when I get back to London if you want. By the way, do you still have any people over there?"

"Well, we have one nephew who has just graduated from Manchester University and a niece at Plymouth University," I replied.

"Well, Manchester is an excellent university, but Plymouth—can a small town like that have a university?" she asked.

"Well, I think it was probably a polytechnic that has changed into a university," I said.

"Oh, that's what's likely happened. There're so many universities these days I can't possibly keep track of them. What's your nephew doing now that he has finished his studies?"

"Well, I believe that he is working for a company near Reading," I said.

"Reading? Then he's very close to us at Windsor," said the Queen. "It's probably a high-tech company. There seem to be quite a lot of them these days."

Being keen to extend the chat, I said, "I have been told that it is not protocol to ask you questions, but ma'am, I wonder if I might bend the rule a bit."

"Shoot."

"Well, I admit to being curious whether it's true that you always start eating as soon as you are served."

"Well, actually, I do, because the kitchens at Buckingham Palace and Windsor are some distance from where we dine. But I am much better than my great-grandmother Queen Victoria, because when she put down her knife and fork everyone's plate was taken away whether they were finished or not," the Queen replied with a chuckle.

"Oh, what do you do at the end of the meal?" I enquired.

"Well, at home I just ring a little bell. But at state dinners I have a man who looks after that for me," she said. "Anyway, it's been lovely to chat. I'm afraid there are one or two other people that seem to want to meet me this evening." She smiled as she moved away.

When I went home that evening, I said to Yoshi, "Shake the hand that shook the purple glove."

But she had no interest. "I had a wonderful dinner down the street with Dr. David Suzuki. I really think we should try doing some composting," she said.

CHAPTER 51

"I Will Always Be Your Friend"

Rick Genest, 2002

TODAY, THE CORPORATE LEADERS who are consistently successful are those who establish a network of close personal relationships through industry associations, sports and recreational activities and, yes, consume innumerable social breakfasts, lunches and dinners.

As I made the transition into building market condominiums and townhomes in the mid-1980s, Polygon began to grow and I started to think about what business schools call "branding"—that is, how to distinguish our operations from those of our competitors. Having never attended a business school, I don't propose to teach all the wisdom I have built up by hook or by crook over the last four decades, but I don't mind mentioning a few things that seem to have worked for Polygon and contributed to our success in building and selling over $10-billion worth of homes.

First, I believe it's fair to say that much of our success has to do with the strong personal relationships that our team has established over the years. These come into play right from the start, specifically when acquiring land on which to build, a high-priced commodity in Vancouver. It's difficult, if not impossible, to just go out and pay cash for a piece of land. But because of the long-established relationships we have with non-governmental agencies, we are often able to "get the nod"—not because we pay a sub-market price, but rather because the vendor knows that Polygon will perform.

Any experienced banker will tell you that personal relationships matter, and certainly our banking friends are very important to us. In over four decades of operation, and after more than three hundred residential projects, we have never lost a single dollar for our banks. In fact, we have made them pots of money. But unlike in the old days, when my partner Vern Paulus preferred to deal simply with a single bank, we have spread our business among more than half a dozen. We never play them off against each other by inviting bids to finance a single project; rather, we try to gauge their respective appetites for the type of homes we plan to build.

Secondly, our management structure focuses on a platform of teamwork, or what some people would call "horizontal management." Instead of giving all the responsibility to a single project manager, we tend to move projects through different groups. Obviously the land-acquisition group takes the first responsibility, and then the development team, which is responsible for design and municipal entitlement, after which the site becomes the responsibility of the construction group, and ultimately the sales and marketing teams take over. So there is a lot of overlap in the process, which may be why our company is famous for so many meetings.

The next distinguishing feature of Polygon is our focus. We only build multi-family housing within Greater Vancouver—no office buildings, industrial warehouses or shopping malls, and no projects in other locations around North America—which means our staff can comfortably drive everywhere we build. It's true that we do have an involvement in the single-family home market, but that is structured through Morningstar Homes Ltd., a company that has a separate head office and management.

We are told by our auditors that Polygon maintains about the most rigorous financial control and reporting procedures in our industry. This is something that I learned to do early in the operation, because I am only comfortable when I am on top of what is going on—not on a quarterly or monthly basis, but on a daily basis. One of the benefits of this is never experiencing any unpleasant financial surprises. This practice also facilitates joint ventures with various educational and health institutions, as well as with private investors.

We are a market-driven company, which means we want to be as close to the consumer as possible, understanding what they want for accommodation and designing our products to make them as affordable as possible.

People matter in all our business dealings, but the relationships we value the most are within our own company. No firm can do well if morale is poor and there is a lot of staff turnover. At Polygon, we have been most fortunate in this respect and have a large number of staff with over twenty or even thirty years of service. At a recent Christmas party, we recognized controller Lance Mitamura, who had been with our company for all but three of the forty years we have been in business.

Every corporate executive will have their own recipe for managing people, and for our president, Neil Chrystal, I think his model is the successful hockey coach. He sees it at his job to teach, encourage and cheer for a job well done. Neil is a natural leader who instinctively knows that the company's success is entirely dependent on how much his team is determined to win. Neil has now successfully led Polygon for over seventeen years. He has not only built far more homes than were built in the years I served as CEO, but he has earned wide respect, not only from our staff, but throughout our industry.

Certainly, over the years, some people have joined our company then left a year or two later because they didn't find a sufficient fit between what they wanted to achieve in life and what we could offer. That's inevitable, but the important thing is that over the long term, we all remain friends.

Perhaps I should also say a word about relationships with the building trades: the carpenters, electricians, drywallers, plumbers and the many other skilled people who work on our construction sites. I actually found this to be the most challenging part of my role as a home builder, as I had absolutely no background in construction. It's true I had some brief school lessons in carpentry when I was about eight years old in school, but I recall the crusty old tradesman who was our teacher being annoyed with me because I couldn't hammer a nail straight or cut a piece of wood without jamming the saw. When I first went onto a construction site, in the early 1980s, I didn't know my way around and had absolutely no credibility.

My construction inexperience was not helped by Vern Paulus suggesting that I keep out of this area and leave it to a former employee of his, a huge, tough fellow who, though originally from Denmark, had flown fighter planes for the Luftwaffe in World War II. While seemingly knowledgeable about construction, Chris Ronnenkamp enjoyed taking many shortcuts to have the satisfaction of bringing his projects in way under budget. He also had a habit of beating weak trades into submission, even bankruptcy, by starving them for cash. It took three or four years before I felt strong enough to move him out of the picture. His replacement, a young engineer named Ivan Campbell, was considered fair by the building trades and developed a series of loyal relationships that remain today, even though we now sometimes deal with the second or third generation of family members in the trades.

I do believe that it is fair to say, as I mentioned earlier, that the key aspect of my transition from being a left-wing social worker to becoming a real-estate developer was my making the shift from dealing primarily with ideas to dealing with people. As a social worker, I worked directly with families and children, and sometimes with citizens groups and communities, but I was always motivated by putting big ideas into operation. As soon as I started in business, I became aware that no matter how smart an idea you may have about making money, unless you are a hermit locked up in a cell with a laptop, you need to relate to people. It's the quality of those relationships that will usually determine the degree of your success.

Few relationships were more critical to the success of Polygon than the one I formed with Rick Genest. Rick and I had an unusual relationship ever since I hired him in 1982. He was then a young real-estate agent with just two years of experience under his belt. He soon became responsible for all our land acquisitions, a vital role in a housing company, because without land on which to build, no business can be done. With his strong relationship and negotiation skills, Rick was ideally suited for this part of our activity. Six years later, he became Polygon's executive vice-president and a partner in the company.

I believe that Rick and I hit it off well because we were so different. I had my broader education and experience in dealing with public officials and cultural interests, whereas Rick tended to be more competitive, a sharper negotiator, and someone with a strong sports bent. Some might say that Rick was more entrepreneurial than I am, and I certainly would not argue with that. On the other hand, he granted that with my purview of the world economy I probably had a better feeling for the housing market. Anyway, we were good for each other. Although we disagreed quite strongly at times, an argument never survived into the following day. That would have been troubling for both of us.

The last time I saw Rick we had dinner together at Bishop's restaurant on Vancouver's West Side. Being a wiry man of modest stature and simple tastes, I suspect that the upscale Bishop's was not Rick's favourite kind of restaurant. He might rather have been at the Keg, where he could be sure of something hearty and filling, but he'd agreed to humour me. Before Rick arrived, I quietly asked proprietor John Bishop to ensure that Rick had a double portion of whichever main course he chose.

We dined together only very occasionally and, as on other occasions, we didn't talk business. Mostly we chatted about family matters, such as Rick telling me about his aspirations for his children's water-skiing—he was leaving the next day for his Bridge Lake resort in the northern Cariboo country. Afterwards, we stood outside the restaurant chatting on the sidewalk for another fifteen minutes—neither of us seemingly anxious to head home. I mentioned that I valued our relationship and I wondered how it would work after my retirement, something that I was contemplating at the time. I recall Rick calling out, just before slipping into the driver's seat of his Mercedes coupe, "I will always be your friend, Michael."

I still recall the shock I felt the following day when I got the call from Rick's wife, Marie, saying that he was dead. On the highway north of Kamloops a huge boulder had fallen down the mountainside, crashing through the windshield of the car and hitting him squarely. Rick's nineteen-year-old daughter, Natalie, seated in the passenger seat beside him, miraculously survived, physically unscathed.

I felt devastated, more than I had for anyone I had personally lost, including my parents. I'd not only lost an important business partner, but I'd lost a friend. Some nights I still dream about two men: my father, born in 1903, and Rick, a man born over sixty years later. It just goes to show how deep a business friendship can grow over the years.

As well as having good relationships with your own team, I believe that there are advantages in having warm and personal relationships with competitors. That's why I was so surprised that, in the late 1990s, when we entered the residential construction industry in Seattle and I went around and introduced myself to the leading home builders, I discovered that many of them had never met each other.

In Vancouver, it's different. I recall how refreshing it was on fishing trips organized by Citibank in the mid-1980s, when I met some of my competitors. When you are tossing about on a boat chasing some salmon, you soon start to forge friendships, and those have remained to this day.

In fact, after one of those trips, builder Andre Molnar and I decided to launch an informal lunch club for a dozen of us, which still meets all these years later. The opportunity to sit and deal with major issues facing our industry at Urban Development Institute board meetings is also very useful for making friends of one's competitors. It doesn't mean we don't aggressively compete with one another, but it does engender respect and makes for a more comfortable business climate.

CHAPTER 52

"Don't Worry, Granddad, You Are Good at Making Money"

Cameron Cope, 2003

My ten-year-old grandson Cameron and I were drifting towards the rocks in my Monaro 27 powerboat when the line of the crab trap we were hauling in became tangled around the propeller. I tried to untangle it, to no avail. Then, glancing over my shoulder as the waves pushed us closer to the rocks, I instructed Cameron, "Get out of the way, I am going to cut the line."

"Let me have a go at it, Granddad," Cameron said and he leaned over the side with a boat hook, trying to grab the line. As we got ever closer to the rocks I had visions of my recently acquired boat being holed and us bobbing around in the water waiting to be rescued, so I unsheathed the long knife I always attach to my belt when boating and moved towards the line. Suddenly Cameron freed it. I lunged back into the wheelhouse and reversed in the nick of time.

"I'm sorry for panicking, Cameron. It's amazing what you did. I'm just not very good with boats," I told him. Despite having dinghies of my own since the age of seven, and subsequently a whole range of sailboats, the *Niju Maru*, which we were on that day, was actually my first powerboat.

"Don't worry, Granddad, you are good at making money," Cameron replied. I was quite stunned that my grandson actually thought that I was good at something.

Children are amazing. Not having had playmates of my own when small, I always enjoyed my children, even though I believe that I failed them at times. I recall tobogganing in Ottawa with Fenya and Kyra, as well as vacationing together at the lovely lakeside cabin we owned in Quebec's Gatineau region. Later, after Tunya and I had separated, it was a joy to visit them in Cuernavaca, Mexico, where Tunya had gone to study. There were the inevitable vacations within BC, but for me the trip of a lifetime was when I took them to Thailand for three weeks.

After a couple of days of Bangkok temples, we went to stay in a quiet resort in Pattaya. The children did their homework under coconut trees in the morning and played in the pool with the monkeys and on the beach with a young elephant in the afternoon.

For all that, I didn't spend enough time with my children. I lived nearby in West Vancouver after Tunya and I separated, but I was never there to take them to sports, dance, drama or whatever else young girls do. And as time went on, I lost track of them. I never went to see Kyra at university in Moscow or met her friends there. Fenya developed her own social group around her Salt Spring Island home, yet I had no involvement.

But you do get another chance with your grandchildren, so I try to be more deeply interested in their well-being, not just because I love them, but because the old have so much to learn from the young.

CHAPTER 53

"Can We Put the Bodies on Your Back Seat?"

Kamala resident, 2004

As I rode in the taxi to catch the 6:30 flight from Bangkok's Don Mueang Airport to Phuket on Boxing Day morning, I noticed red clouds hanging across the sky from east to west. I pointed it out to the driver, saying that in my country a red sky in the morning was a sailor's warning, but given the intensity of the sky today it could mean war or a catastrophe.

Once I was winging my way to Phuket, I didn't give this natural phenomenon any further thought. I would pick up a rented Honda CRV at the airport, stop at the Big C supermarket and be at our beach house for a late breakfast.

Leaving Phuket's main highway after stocking up on groceries and wine, I turned west towards the coast and was surprised to see trucks jammed with people, motorcycles with three or even four passengers, and people running towards the highway from the coastal road, which had been blocked off by police-van barriers.

Somewhat bewildered, I asked one of the officers, "What's happening?" He said that he didn't know, but they had received orders to block entry from the highway.

Nonetheless I navigated around the barrier and kept on driving west against the heavy traffic coming in my direction. I turned the radio on, but the stations that were on the air seemed to be in complete confusion, with people speaking Thai so fast that I couldn't follow what they were saying. Finally, I saw a family loading a pickup with what looked like the contents of their house. The teenage girl spoke some English and said, "Big wave come. Buddha says Phuket is finished. We must escape."

This was panic like I had only seen in a King Kong movie. People were so intent on fleeing from the coastal area that they drove on both sides of the road, often forcing me onto the verge. Ten minutes later I stopped at the small shopping mall of the Laguna hotel complex, thinking there would likely be some English-speaking people there who could give me more information. As I parked my car and walked to a shady area, I noticed that it was occupied with foreign tourists who were sitting or lying on the ground nursing plastic water bottles. "What the heck is going on?" I asked.

"We escaped drowning because we were on the second floor of the Sheraton, but what's going to happen to us now? Will we survive when the next wave comes?" a middle-aged man asked me.

I walked over to where two or three taxi drivers were gathered. "Is the road open to Kamala Beach?" I asked.

"No, Kamala is gone," one said. "I have lost my family there."

I got back in my car and continued to drive the winding coastal road past Surin Beach and up over the hill overlooking the northern end of Kamala Beach. The traffic had vanished, and I seemed to be the only car driving towards the ocean. At the top of the hill I stopped again when I saw what looked like hundreds of people standing or sitting quietly, looking out at the water. Usually wherever Thai people congregate, it is noisy, but this morning the silence was eerie.

"Would I be able to drive through Kamala to reach my house on the south side of the village?" I asked one young man.

"It's not safe down there. We have to wait for help," he replied.

Ignoring his advice, I drove on down the hill and entered the outskirts of the village. There was devastation everywhere. A few buildings were still standing, and the main road was covered with debris, but thankfully there was a bulldozer already at work clearing a path. I followed closely behind it as I made my way slowly south.

A grizzled middle-aged man held up his hand to stop me. "What shall we do with the bodies?" he asked, pointing to two bikini-clad blond women laid out on a plastic tarp by the road. They looked like mother and daughter, possibly Scandinavian.

"What's happening to the other bodies?" I asked.

"We are taking the Muslims to the mosque and the Buddhists we are sending south to the temple in Patong. But we don't know what to do with all the foreigners."

"Well, I believe relatives are going to want to have them sent home, so the bodies should go to the airport," I said.

"Can we put the bodies on your back seat?" he asked.

"Sorry, but first I have to find out what has happened to our house, and the staff, so I don't know what my plans are," I said.

I drove on, over debris and fallen wires, until I reached the Kamala Beach Estate. Jumping out of the car, I encountered Dominic Stroud, one of the homeowners. He said, "I saw the wave coming and was able to get everyone up to high ground by the pool, but the wave took out my house."

"What about mine?" I asked.

"Yours is okay, it just escaped. But we hear there's another wave coming at one o'clock, so everyone is going up into the hills. You better come because there is no knowing how big the next wave will be."

After taking my groceries to the house, one of the gardeners motioned me to the back of his pickup truck. I took as many water bottles as I could find, not knowing how long we were going to be in the hills. Ten minutes later we were back on the high ground south of Kamala.

All along the side of the road were people talking quietly about their experience, while the wounded moaned. I told people not to worry, that help would be there soon—the US Marines would undoubtedly land later in the day to set up a field hospital. Of course, that turned out to be totally incorrect because what I thought must be a local event was actually an Indian Ocean-wide tsunami caused by an undersea earthquake off Sumatra.

For an hour or two I was busy helping some of the wounded. Using the knife I carried, I was able to make a splint to bind what was obviously a broken arm. With the first-aid kit in my knapsack, I was able to disinfect and bandage some minor wounds. One o'clock went by and then another hour with no report of more waves. Growing impatient, I hitchhiked a ride back down the hillside to Kamala. I walked through the village, which seemed deserted, and picked up my car.

By now, my main thought was to get through to Yoshi to tell her I was fine, but my cellphone wasn't working because the tsunami had knocked out wireless aerials throughout the island. I didn't feel that I could do much until international help arrived, so I headed directly back to the airport, where I found long lines of tourists waiting for evacuation, some of them obviously wounded. Many told tales of how marvellous and hospitable the Thai people had been to them, though they were less complimentary about the European managers of their hotels, who had in some cases just fled to safety, leaving their guests to fend for themselves.

Thai Airways seemed to have everything well organized. They assured us that special 747 evacuation planes were being dispatched from their international routes to evacuate Phuket, and that accommodation was being arranged for foreign visitors without money or passports at a Bangkok university campus. I only had to wait a few minutes before boarding a plane, as no ticket was required, and later that same evening, in a Bangkok hotel, I was able to get through to Yoshi in Japan to tell her I was fine.

The following morning I conceived the idea of a Kamala Beach Disaster Fund to help members of our staff who had lost loved ones, as well as to help others in the Kamala village get back on their feet. Since I had the email addresses of all the owners of our estate, I sent out an immediate appeal, saying that I would personally match all donations. The response was a warm one. And thanks to the good offices of Dominic Stroud (who soon after became the estate's general manager), we were able in some small way to show our sympathy and appreciation for the people of Kamala, which was the hardest hit community on the island of Phuket.

When I recount the events of that day, people often ask me whether I wasn't personally shocked by the sight of bodies strewn around in the debris of the village and by the wounded on the hillside. I tell them that strangely I was not, because after all as a child I had been through some fairly tough experiences. In fact, walking with my father and our dogs on the beach in South Devon, we not infrequently came across the swollen, seaweed-strewn bodies of Germans and of our own forces. I have always found that the strong stench of death, whether of an animal or a human being, is more difficult to take than the visual sight of the remains.

Altogether, the tsunami reportedly caused nearly 230,000 deaths in the countries surrounding the Indian Ocean, including 5,400 in Thailand. Our village of Kamala was the hardest hit on Phuket, so I was glad I missed my customary early morning beach walk that day.

CHAPTER 54

"Michael Audain, One of BC's Most Notorious Leaky Condo Developers, Will Receive BC's Highest Honour for Outstanding Achievement"

James Balderson, 2006

AFTER FOUR DECADES IN the home-building business, I am sometimes asked what has been my greatest challenge. Well, there were some rocky years in our early days, times when I considered cancelling our Christmas party in order to make the payroll at the end of the month. We also once faced the shock of the former Bank of British Columbia demanding repayment of all our loans within sixty days, despite our loan payments having been kept current.

In the late 1980s I had to deal with Vern Paulus forcing me to quickly buy him out, under the threat of liquidating the company. And then there was the anti-business posture of Glen Clark's NDP government in the 1990s, which obliged us to shift the focus of our activities to Seattle, despite our strong Vancouver-based brand and relationships. These were all challenges, but with the support of senior staff and friends in the local business community, they were challenges that we were able to surmount and now look back on as learning experiences.

But it was the so-called "leaky condo crisis" that hit our industry in the late 1990s that provided far and away the greatest challenge, not only to Polygon Homes staying in business, but also to me personally.

Briefly, what happened was that our customer service group began to face a mounting series of demands regarding some of the three- and four-storey woodframe apartment buildings that we had built in the Vancouver area. There were problems caused by water penetration, especially around window assemblies. At first, we responded by sending a serviceman up a ladder with a caulking gun, and for some buildings we applied an elastomeric paint to the exterior stucco. But these conventional remedies didn't work, so strata councils sought help from a variety of engineering and remediation firms, who convinced them to open up the wall systems for full inspection.

I recall going out to inspect an apartment building we had built eight years earlier in Richmond, taking along the project architect as well as some construction managers. When we arrived at the site, we were amazed to see that not only was the plywood sheathing in the wall wet, it had started to decay, and the rot was already spreading to the two-by-four studs that provided the building's structural integrity.

"How could this happen?" I asked Ivan Campbell, our senior vice-president in charge of construction.

"The municipal building inspector said that we had to put a polyethylene vapour barrier in the wall and this had the effect of sealing in any moisture that was trapped inside, which of course ultimately caused the wood to rot," Campbell explained. "It's all a function of the changes made to the National Building Code back in the late 1980s to make the buildings more energy efficient. You see, before the addition of the vapour barrier and extra insulation, the heat escaping from the interior of the wall served to dry it out and prevent rot."

"Well, how can we prevent this from happening in the future?" I asked.

The response I received from the architect, as well as from our own construction managers, was that they didn't know, because they had to simply respect the current building code or our buildings wouldn't pass municipal inspections.

As the months went by, not only was Polygon faced with new building warranty claims every week, but stories arose in the press about condominiums all over Greater Vancouver facing immense remediation bills that were greater than the financial capacity of their owners to sustain.

On top of that, apartments in buildings with a leak record became difficult to sell.

Understandably, condominium owners began to organize, and the most active group was led by James Balderson, a former professor at UBC's Faculty of Education.

During this trying period, much of my time was devoted to dealing with litigation and claims on our course of construction insurance policies, even though the company took the official position that buildings that were in need of remediation were long out of their warranty periods. We knew that we had to defend the lawsuits if we were to continue in business. At times our sales offices were even picketed by aggrieved condominium owners.

It was about this time that the provincial government responded by appointing former premier Dave Barrett to head up a Commission of Inquiry to investigate, hold hearings and make recommendations to the government concerning what was rapidly becoming a crisis in coastal areas of British Columbia. I happened to be one of only two major developers who went before the commission to explain what we thought had occurred.

"Obviously the system under which we design and construct multifamily housing has failed these people," I told the commission in early 1998.

The leaky condo crisis caused great hardship for many thousands of people in British Columbia. Many owners lost their savings; others lost their homes, as in some cases they were forced to abandon them instead of face the remediation bills. Whole apartment buildings were abandoned to the mortgage holders. It was a great shock and difficult time for companies such as ours that strived to maintain a high standard of integrity and were proud of the buildings that we had designed and constructed throughout Greater Vancouver.

I recall a long conversation with Rick Genest one morning at my house in West Vancouver. We discussed the alternatives. Should we: 1) wind up our business and go into some other field of endeavour; 2) concentrate on building in the Seattle area, where we were already getting established and where due to building code differences there had been no leaky condo crisis to date; or 3) just soldier on, take the flak and hope that the crisis would pass? I knew colleagues in the building industry who were opting for one or more of those alternatives. And then we both thought of a fourth alternative: why not cease building until we could adopt a construction technology that would ensure the integrity of the homes we build in our moist West Coast environment?

With the support of our senior officers, we resolved to take this path. But first, Rick and I felt that we had to educate ourselves, so we invited a number of building-envelope engineers to our office to brief us on problems they had encountered and what the solutions might be. The most helpful among them was Pierre Gallant of Morrison Hershfield. On Rick's initiative we also decided to consult the wood-product scientists at UBC's Forintek laboratories. There we financed a project that consisted of testing an array of different building-envelope mock-ups by bombarding them with simulated rainstorms.

The outcome of all this activity was the development of a new protocol for designing and constructing woodframe residential buildings, which we called the "Polygon New Generation Weather Shield." This principally involved "umbrella architecture" with wide roof overhangs to shield the building envelope from the elements, as well as rainscreen technology, employing a protective barrier of drainage channels installed between the exterior and interior wall surfaces to allow the building to shed water. All this was accompanied by a set of standards for building material selection, site testing and inspections, to create a quality assurance protocol for building in our West Coast climate. To test the new technology, together with CMHC we put it into practice in our first New Generation building, the Greenwich, on West Fifth Avenue, in Vancouver's Kitsilano neighbourhood. Based on exhaustive testing, the new approach proved to be a great success and set a new industry benchmark for building woodframe apartments that last.

We were not alone in being moved at times to despair during the leaky condo crisis, as it affected many thousands of homeowners in coastal British Columbia. However, the Barrett Commission did not find the developers and contractors solely responsible for what had occurred. They also cast the blame on municipal building inspectors, the architectural profession, engineers, and even the building trades for shoddy workmanship. Interestingly, the commission avoided blaming the provincial building code itself for what had occurred, explaining that it was the interpretation of the code that was at fault, thus it claimed that the province had no responsibility in that regard.

In terms of the many lawsuits that were launched against our company in the 1990s, I am pleased to say that with the help of our insurance companies and the willingness of my partners to financially contribute their resources, all the lawsuits were settled by Polygon without any of the claims being tried in court.

The strong sales from Greenwich on Fifth and subsequent projects proved that the Polygon brand remained strong despite the travails of the leaky condo crisis. But of course angry consumer groups like to have a target and will never give credit to a company they've zeroed in on, even one that has always done its best to put the interest of its customers before making a profit. Therefore, it wasn't a huge surprise when in 2007 James Balderson's blog denounced my being awarded the Order of British Columbia, casting me as "one of BC's most notorious leaky condo developers."

There is no doubt that the leaky condo crisis was a stain on my career as a development industry executive, but at the same time I cannot but take some pride in the way that our company surmounted it and, of course, under the capable management of President Neil Chrystal, how Polygon has gone on to earn its profile as one of Canada's leading home builders.

There were many sleepless nights as I tossed and turned thinking of how the crisis could have happened. One day Dave Barrett, who I had known since the early 1960s, took me aside for a coffee and said, "Despite what the commission's report is going to say, I personally believe that much of the leaky condo syndrome is really the fault of you builders taking shortcuts to cheapen your product."

His statement shocked me: the suggestion that we would compromise the integrity of our buildings to save money had never arisen. Yes, I had always believed in optimizing profitability, but never at the expense of compromising the structure or durability of our buildings.

But I suppose that life isn't always fair in the worlds of business or politics, and one has to bear the blame even when things occur that were never one's intention. *C'est la vie,* as the French say.

CHAPTER 55

"How Did You Start Collecting Art?"

Pierre Théberge, 2006

ART HAS ALWAYS HAD a place on my walls, ever since I started living on my own. At first just pictures that caught my fancy, ripped out of magazines and hung up with Scotch tape. Later, I became more sophisticated and would carefully extract pictures from an art book and have them framed. I even did this at school with two Yousuf Karsh portraits—one of Albert Schweitzer and the other of Bertrand Russell. But the acquisition of original art had to wait until my 1962 marriage, after which the walls started to reflect many of the works Tunya painted at the UBC night school and New York City's Art Students League. Tunya's output was uneven but sometimes accomplished.

When I was a college student, a status I occupied for nearly a decade, we had little money to spend on art, but I recall buying a bill bissett drawing and a Michael Morris oil from a Vancouver dealer, Eric Christmas, in the early 1960s.

After I had a secure job, in the late 1960s, my art acquisition became more frequent. Although living in Ottawa, my work frequently took me across the country. Someone must have told me that the Isaacs Gallery, on Toronto's Yonge Street, was a good place to shop for art. I recall that before I ventured in the first time, I fortified myself with a couple of double Scotches at lunch at a nearby French restaurant. At first I didn't see anything I liked, and then I spotted a painting on the floor, propped up against a wall at the back of the gallery. It was of a farm scene that looked surprisingly familiar.

"That's by one of my framers, a man named William Kurelek," Av Isaac said.

"I recall seeing that scene somewhere before," I replied.

Av told me that it must have been on the National Film Board film that had been made about William Kurelek's life. A few minutes later I ended up buying the painting for $1,500, a sum that Av kindly allowed me to pay off over three years.

My next acquisition was an arresting Claude Breeze canvas from his *Lovers in the Landscape* series, which I saw at the Vancouver Art Gallery. I just phoned up the artist directly and made a deal to buy it, being ignorant about the protocol of going through a dealer.

When we moved back to Vancouver in the early 1970s, I started to patronize the Bau-Xi Gallery, occasionally acquiring work by Vancouver artists. In the late 1970s there were few art purchases due to the personal financial challenges that I was experiencing, and my purchases in the 1980s were sporadic and purely Vancouver based.

After my initial enthusiasm for William Kurelek's work (I ended up buying half a dozen of his paintings), I turned my attention to British Columbia modernists such as Jack Shadbolt. Shadbolt's vibrant colours, combined with First Nations overtones, particularly fascinated me, as did the marvellous abstract collages created by Toni Onley. B.C. Binning's nautical themes, though somewhat formalist for my taste, were also a target of acquisition; similarly, E.J. Hughes's almost superrealism of the early 1960s and early 1970s.

Visitors to our home were usually surprised by the eclecticism of the work on the walls. Emily Carrs hung next to old First Nations works, and one might even encounter the work of Quebec's Automatiste School and Mexican modernists.

As noted earlier, I became attracted to First Nations art at an early age after watching Kwakwa̲ka̲'wakw master carver Mungo Martin at work in Victoria's Thunderbird Park, but I never gave much thought to collecting it until well into the twenty-first century, when by chance I met Donald Ellis, considered by many to be the premier dealer in North American Indigenous art.

Donald is an extraordinary character. He left school (near a Mohawk reserve in Ontario) while still young to pursue a career as an art dealer. After eventually acquiring years of experience on *Antiques Roadshow*, he travelled incessantly in search of Indigenous art treasures to bring to the attention of his clients, always with the idea that, whether they be Hopi, Inuit, Iroquois or Haida, the best of them were works of art equal, if not of a superior calibre, to those made by distinguished artists of European origin. I had started to collect old Northwest Coast works on my own, and on one occasion apparently bid against Donald Ellis for a superlative Tsimshian chest at Sotheby's.

It wasn't until he co-curated an exhibition at Vancouver's Equinox Gallery that I met Donald. Since then he has been responsible for the acquisition of all our historic masks, which he has sourced across the length and breadth of North America and Europe.

My enthusiasm for Quebec's Automatiste School dates back to a visit I made to the public library in Peterborough, Ontario, when I was sixteen, where I saw a small group of Jean Paul Riopelle's abstract paintings. Eventually, in the early 1990s, I was fortunate enough to purchase a major Riopelle at Sotheby's in Toronto, and subsequently I have acquired others from his early 1950s period. Riopelle was one of the first artists to work purely with a palette knife rather than a brush, and my own view is that his paintings from that period have more vigour than the works of Jackson Pollock, an artist to whom Riopelle is often compared.

The decision to acquire works by Riopelle's colleague Paul-Émile Borduas was a more difficult one, though it was Borduas who was the author of the Automatistes' 1948 manifesto, *Refus Global* (*Total Refusal*), which denounced traditional Quebec cultural strictures and defined the new direction in which Quebec artists were striking out. But a challenge with Borduas is that his very desirable 1950s works, completed in France and New York, are fragile and tend to experience a lot of paint loss.

Visitors to our home tend to be surprised by our many Mexican Modernist works—in fact, we are told ours is the leading collection of this type in Canada. "How on earth did you become interested in collecting Mexican art?" is a regular question.

Actually, it stemmed from my interest in Mexico City's decorated walls, which I became acquainted with as a teenager, from a *National Geographic* article. This led me to buy a Greyhound bus ticket to Mexico City with earnings from a summer job in Victoria. So at the age of seventeen I spent several weeks in a cheap hotel, living on tacos and tequila. When I wasn't gossiping with the would-be writers and artists who hung out at my lodging, I would trot around the city, riding the "peso taxis," as they were called, looking at works by Los Tres Grandes: Diego Rivera, José Clemente Orozco and David Alfaro Siqueiros.

Strangely enough I never focused on the work of Rivera's wife, Frida Kahlo, or imagined that she would eventually become such an internationally celebrated artist. Kahlo died in 1954, the year before my visit, and before her home, La Casa Azul, in Coyoacán, was turned into a museum. It was not until the early 1980s that Frida Kahlo's work was extensively exhibited outside Mexico. Then she achieved enormous fame, helped by the 2002 biographical movie *Frida*, which I have yet to view.

When I am asked whether our collection includes a Frida Kahlo work, the answer is usually, "No, but I did have the honour of being the under-bidder on one of her works at Sotheby's in New York, which I understand was won by Madonna."

CHAPTER 56

"All You Old White Men Look the Same"

Yoshiko Karasawa, 2010

IT WAS A CRISP fall morning when I trooped into Rideau Hall, the Governor General's Ottawa residence, with Yoshi and my daughters, Fenya and Kyra, to be made an Officer of the Order of Canada. While I appreciated the recognition, being awarded the Order of British Columbia a couple of years prior actually held more significance to me, as my family had been part of the fabric of British Columbia for two decades before the province even joined Confederation.

One of those curious things about Canada is that at times it is difficult to decide whether we have a deeper attachment to, say, Newfoundland, Quebec or BC than to our country. Are we regionalists first? But abroad, of course, we are all proud to attach those maple leaf labels to our backpacks to identify us first and foremost as Canadians.

My own attachment to British Columbia partly stems from how good the province has been for my family. When my great-great-grandfather Robert Dunsmuir landed in Fort Rupert, on Vancouver Island, on August 9, 1851, after a seven-month voyage by sailing ship from Glasgow, he must have wondered how he was going to earn a better living than in the coal-mining valleys of his native Scotland. There was a small clearing, in which the tree stumps were still evident, and a tiny two-room Hudson's Bay Company cabin awaiting his family. He and his fellow miners were a small minority at the edge of a large 'Na̲mgis First Nation village, the scourge of smallpox having not yet devastated the Indigenous population.

The story of how Robert Dunsmuir built an empire and became one of the largest private landowners in the world has been told elsewhere. My father wrote *From Coalmine to Castle* (which set off a round of legal wrangling within the family), and there is Terry Reksten's more authoritative work *The Dunsmuir Saga*.

As I mentioned earlier, when I was young I was not particularly proud of my family's history and took pains to avoid identifying with it. But when I eventually entered the business community, I began to respect the economic prosperity created by daring entrepreneurs who risk their capital and expertise to create new job-producing industries. Thus, my admiration for Robert Dunsmuir and his son James began to grow, particularly when I realized that they were not only businessmen but were prepared to take a role in the political affairs of the young colony of Vancouver Island, which later joined with the mainland to eventually become Canada's westernmost province. Robert Dunsmuir served as a long-time MLA, and James Dunsmuir as both premier and Lieutenant Governor.

British Columbia has also been good to me. It really seemed a land of plenty when I arrived as a boy over seventy years ago from war-torn Europe, and as I believe I have indicated in these pages, it was during my years as a student at the University of British Columbia that I achieved a degree of confidence and happiness that I had not earlier thought possible.

To top it off, if I was to go into the property development business, I likely could not have picked a better town to do it in than Vancouver. While the ups and downs of the housing market have always been very cyclical, the company that I and my partners built has survived and prospered, even though we never aspired to be BC's largest home builder or to grow our company beyond the boundaries of Greater Vancouver. Our focus has always simply been on providing well-designed and well-constructed homes of good value for our customers.

A successful business is all about people, and Polygon has been fortunate to benefit from having some of the brightest and most honest people in the business, including John Northey, who in the early days ran our development operation; my young partner Rick Genest, who left this world too early; and Ralf Schmidtke, who for over twenty-five years looked after the financial side of the company. Now, there is a new generation, headed by our president and chief executive officer, Neil Chrystal, who is widely respected as one of our province's most prominent business leaders.

One day, sitting in my office, I received a telephone call from the prime minister's office saying that I had been appointed to the National Gallery of Canada's board and asking if I could get to a meeting scheduled ten days later in St. John's, Newfoundland. I expressed my surprise and said I would really have to consider whether such an appointment was something I might want to accept. In discussing it over the weekend with Yoshi, she was adamant that I should do the job, because she told me that she had immigrated to Canada, not just to British Columbia, and she was thankful for the quality of life that her new country had offered her.

I accepted the appointment, and as I started to learn about the way the National Gallery functioned, it didn't take me long to understand that for over 130 years it had played a vital role in the cultural life of our country. For example, there is no other national gallery in the world that consistently tours its collection to the extent that ours does. This is of tremendous assistance to small and regional art museums throughout the land. And after seven years on the board, as a trustee and then chair, I began to appreciate the significance of the great Canadian experiment, which stretches our small population base across 5,514 kilometres, from sea to sea. So in the end, I felt honoured to be recognized by our nation.

At Rideau Hall we attended a colourful investiture ceremony in which about sixty people received the insignia of the Order of Canada. The only recipient that I knew was Dr. Larry Goldenberg, the prominent University of British Columbia urologist. Of course, Governor General David Johnston made quite a few moving remarks, saying that this was the first Order of Canada investiture that he had presided over since his appointment as Canada's twenty-eighth Governor General.

That evening Yoshi and I returned to Rideau Hall for a very pleasant black-tie dinner. To my surprise I was seated at the Governor General's side, while Yoshi was accommodated at another of the round tables that had been set with splendid silver and china in the ballroom. Midway through the meal, the amiable Governor General excused himself to go from table to table, personally greeting all the guests.

Later, when I met up with Yoshi again, her tablemate, Canadian astronaut Dr. Roberta Bondar, said to me, "Your wife is a real joker. She didn't even know who the Governor General was when he came to our table! She said, 'My goodness you have a lot of medals, do you work here?'"

On the way back to the hotel in the taxi I said to Yoshi, "How could you not recognize the Governor General? He was up on the stage all morning presiding at the investiture. You saw me have my photo taken with him."

In her own inimitable way, Yoshi replied, "Very sorry, darling, but all you old White men look the same."

CHAPTER 57

"Some People Might Consider It Selfish That You Never Share Your Art with the Public"

Ian Thom, 2011

BACK IN THE EARLY 1990S we were astonished to receive a request from Mrs. Frank Sinatra to entertain a group from the Palm Springs Art Museum. She had been told that the art in our home was quite remarkable. We replied that, regretfully, our house was not open for viewing, a policy that we instituted after hosting a fundraiser for the Vancouver Symphony Orchestra, during which one prominent board member accidentally grazed his head from an encounter with an open casement window and commented, "I hope your insurance is up to date."

For Yoshi and I, our home had always been a very private place. Guests were welcome, but we were never keen on taking on the obligations that come with charity events and opening one's home to tours by people one doesn't know. The Americans seem to be very generous in this respect, as we have been welcomed to visit remarkable collections in Dallas and New York homes.

What sparked the idea of perhaps sharing our art collection with the public was a visit to the south of France in 1995. The visit started in a rather stressful fashion, as we were hosting some friends of Yoshi's sister for lunch at the Alain Ducasse restaurant in nearby Monaco's Hotel Paris.

Not having previously met Count and Countess d'Angerville, I selected the Alain Ducasse restaurant for lunch thinking it might be the style to which the Monaco residents were accustomed. However, the irascible old Englishman quickly told me he considered the restaurant far too expensive and that on Sundays you could get a much better deal at a hotel buffet down the street. When it came to ordering, Yoshi and Hisako opted for Alain Ducasse's famous menu of young vegetables, but Howard proved troublesome. He didn't look at the menu, and just ordered a Dover sole. When the maître d'hotel apologized for not having one available that day, he replied, "Then just bring me fish and chips."

The maître d' apologized again, now in a grovelling manner, and started to perspire profusely, as did I. A couple more of the count's menu suggestions were rejected, with the chef having to assist before a compromise was reached with a mushroom omelet, after which Howard started to regale us with his life experiences.

One story he told us was that Georges VI had made him a baronet for keeping his eye on King Peter II of Yugoslavia during the war. But, as no one subsequently wanted to retain him to do the same thing for another monarch, the count said that he was reduced to publishing an annual registrar of European aristocracy that he sold for a pittance, making him "the poorest man in Monte Carlo."

The meal safely concluded, Howard asked if we would care to go for a drive with him. We gladly accepted, assuming that he meant in his wife's small Toyota, which he explained she used for shopping.

Instead, to our surprise, at the front door of the hotel was a large Bentley driven by an Australian chauffeur. As we clambered in, a flag was unfurled on the front fender, and tourists began to snap our picture. It turned out that the car had previously been owned by Charlie Chaplin and that our destination would be a villa in nearby Villefranche-sur-Mer. Later we learnt that it was quite common for Monaco residents to have a home for relaxation purposes in nearby France. What was crucially important, though, was that they return to their Monaco abode, usually an apartment, by midnight in order to avoid losing their Monaco tax status.

The next day we visited the Fondation Maeght, situated in the ancient village of Saint-Paul-de-Vence, which is about eighteen kilometres east of Nice. I had never previously been to such a small art museum. We were able to view wonderful paintings and sculptures so intimately, in an almost residential setting. It was a revelation. The small museum was not overwhelmed by urban buildings but situated peacefully on a southern hillside overlooking the village and surrounded by the wild maquis—that combination of drought-resistant shrubs and small trees that clads the Riviera hillsides.

The museum was founded by Marguerite and Aimé Maeght in 1964. Maeght was an important Parisian art dealer who decided to share his personal collection with the public by collaborating with artist friends to build a small museum close to the village he loved: Saint-Paul-de-Vence. Catalan architect Josep Lluis Sert was retained to do the overall design, with Alberto Giacometti handling the furniture and courtyard, and Georges Braque designing a pool and a stained-glass window.

Outside were mosaics by Marc Chagall and a Joan Miró labyrinth filled with sculptures and ceramics. Within the museum were situated important works by these artists, as well as works by Pierre Bonnard, Alexander Calder, Fernand Léger, Anthony Caro, Ellsworth Kelly, Joan Mitchell and Jean Paul Riopelle. The art collection isn't huge as far as museums go, but the important thing is that each and every work exhibited is an important example of the artist's oeuvre. The Maeghts not only had an excellent eye, but also the ability to carefully select from the artists they exhibited in Paris. Today, the Fondation Maeght's temporary exhibition gallery is dedicated to introducing new artists to their visitors.

What Yoshi and I felt was so important about the museum was the marvellous integration between the building and the natural landscape, with the added bonus that for much of the year the doors could be kept wide open, allowing effortless transition from one stone-clad building by the courtyard to another. The tour buses were parked far away.

I suppose that part of the Fondation Maeght's appeal to me was that it is essentially suburban. As a boy, whether in England, Ireland or Canada, my parents had always favoured country homes suitable for dogs romping amid flower-clad gardens, and usually with room for horses, chickens and pigsties. When it was time for Yoshi and I to buy a home, after some experiences on traffic-clogged streets, we opted for the comparative tranquility of suburban West Vancouver. Our home is on a quiet, narrow lane shielded by a grove of very tall Douglas fir trees. We have neither lawn nor garden, just natural landscape patrolled by free-roaming dogs.

And size matters. A relatively modest expanse of wall space allows a person to focus better on the art and escape the intellectual constipation that can come from tramping through acres of museum galleries. Yes, smaller is better when it comes to museums.

That evening, as we retired to bed at the nearby Château Saint-Martin, Yoshi and I reviewed our experience and agreed that if we ever got around to building a museum of our own, it would be a small one with an atmosphere similar to what we had experienced that morning.

The years went by, and though our art collection grew, we never revisited our fanciful musings about building our own museum. We had decided that our art should eventually go to the Vancouver Art Gallery, which was planning to relocate to a larger site where more of its own collection could be regularly exhibited.

What re-sparked Yoshi's and my interest in building a museum was actually a surprise invitation from Vancouver Art Gallery director Kathleen Bartels to exhibit some of our collection. We mulled the idea over for several months, focusing on what we saw as the negative implications: the loss of the art in our home, possible damage to the works, and above all, potential security problems associated with the collection's public exposure.

I mentioned to Yoshi one Sunday morning that VAG curator and our good friend Ian Thom had advised, "As you don't allow tours at your home, some people might consider it selfish that you never share your art with the public."

After a long pause, Yoshi said, "Well, let's look on the bright side. It could be an opportunity to have our living room repainted."

In late 2011 the exhibition went ahead with the title *Shore, Forest and Beyond: Art from the Audain Collection* despite the Occupy Vancouver movement being briefly camped downtown next to the gallery. To our delight the exhibition garnered a strong audience and many positive comments, particularly about the historic First Nations works. But obviously you can't please everyone. One comment I particularly enjoyed came from an artist friend who said, "I was so pleased to see some contemporary photography after all that brown wood downstairs!"

Once our art collection was safely installed back home, Yoshi and I continued to ruminate about its future. We thought that our Mexican works could go to the National Gallery of Canada, because it has such a fine track record of sharing its collection with local art museums across the country. But what of the British Columbia collection, which ranges from late-eighteenth-century First Nations works to photo-based conceptual art?

The relocation of the Vancouver Art Gallery to a new building is something that we believed would eventually happen, but given the scale of the project and the paucity of BC government funding for cultural projects, the timing was uncertain. We began to wonder if there was some way to realize our dream, from twenty years back, of building our own museum.

Yoshi and I decided that if we were going to build something it had to be on a naturally well-treed site with good public transit access. So we started to put the word out and look around. Our first preference was to build on a beautiful oceanfront location in Pender Harbour, on the Sunshine Coast. Our cottage is located there and we love the area. I also thought it would be good for the local economy, which had lost so many jobs over the years in the fishing and logging industries. The major challenge to that location, however, was that visitors would likely only arrive in the summer months—what would be done with the collection through the gloomy, wet winters?

The Emily Carr University of Art and Design was keen for us to locate in their new Vancouver campus, but while that sounded appealing, the site would be a very tight one and the timing not immediate. And like other Vancouver area sites we came across, it was devoid of natural landscape.

Knowing that our museum would house one of the most important collections of Emily Carr's work, having tree cover on the site was important to us. I felt that in some curious way the surrounding environment should relate to the art. After all, much of the art by Canada's most famous female artist, particularly her late work, had a lot to do with trees. To my mind, Carr is indisputably the best portrayer of the tree-clad West Coast landscape, and arguably one of the world's more accomplished painters of trees, whether standing in sunlit glades or in the dark spaces of the deep forest. And, of course, for the original peoples of the Northwest Coast, life would have been impossible without the forested coastlines that for thousands of years supplied materials for their sustenance and art.

Then, one evening while dining at Pender Harbour's Painted Boat Resort, our good friend Jim Moodie, a retired urban development consultant, said, "Hey, if you come up to Whistler, I can show you a whole bunch of sites. Surely one of them might fit the bill?"

I was dubious after having tramped in the snow around Whistler the previous spring on a visit to the Squamish Lil'wat Cultural Centre, a fine building but one without a sufficiently large audience to demonstrate that the resort town could support an art museum. Nevertheless, on September 21, 2012, Moodie drove me up to Whistler, where to my surprise Mayor Nancy Wilhelm-Morden, Councillor Duane Jackson, Chief Administrative Officer Mike Furey and senior staff were waiting at the municipal hall.

The mayor explained that an art museum was completely in line with her council's policy to diversify Whistler's economic base from a reliance solely on outdoor sports to a more cultural experience. So, without further ado, we jumped into a couple of vehicles and drove around, getting out to walk a couple of the more promising sites.

When we returned for a sandwich lunch at the hall, Mike Furey asked me which of the sites had the most appeal, to which I immediately replied, "If you will give me the three-acre site right across the street from here, I will build you a museum on it."

"What do you like about it?" he asked.

"Well," I said, "I believe it's got everything going for it. It's flat and looks relatively easy to build on. It borders Fitzsimmons Creek. It's currently owned by your municipality, so we shouldn't have to pay for it, and best of all it is beautifully treed with impressive Englemann spruce."

After a short discussion, it was agreed that this particular piece of land had the best attributes for a museum, and the only thing that remained was whether the municipality could sell it.

"If we leased it to you for, say, ninety-nine years, would that work?" asked Furey.

"Yes, if you will put a 'one' in front of that ninety-nine," I responded.

In all my years in the development industry, I have never done business so quickly with a municipality. Of course, that was not the end of the story. Numerous council meetings and lengthy negotiations ensued, but the Resort Municipality of Whistler was extraordinarily co-operative in arranging both the land disposition and eventually the required rezoning and architectural plan approvals. Besides being the chap who lured me up to Whistler, Jim Moodie was also the man who maintained liaison with the municipality throughout the process.

Oh, yes, someone did ask me about a feasibility study. My thought was that you just build an interesting museum and the people will come. I am not sure that Marguerite and Aimé Maeght commissioned a feasibility consultant fifty years ago for their successful venture in Saint-Paul-de-Vence. Not being a skier, however, I knew so little about Whistler that I thought it wouldn't do any harm to learn what an expert thought, so we commissioned Lord Associates, the international museum consultants, to take a look at what we were planning.

Ted Silberman, the Lord consultant assigned to the project, was at first skeptical about the viability of the museum in a community of only 10,000 people. But once he got up to Whistler and hoofed it around the resort, talked to concierges and all and sundry, Ted changed his mind. He realized that while the local population is small, if the museum was of a sufficient calibre it should attract art lovers from Vancouver and beyond, perhaps as well as skiers looking for something to while away the hours on a rainy afternoon. In the meantime, it was full speed ahead to retain an architect.

Retaining an architect wasn't tough. Although I had a number of personal friends who were architects, I wasn't convinced that any would want to tackle the complexities of designing an art museum to contemporary environmental standards and associated intricacies. BC fortunately has many outstanding architectural firms, so we decided to give an hour to eight of them during a single day. This worked except for one firm's unavailability on the particular day we chose. To interview the firms and rate their suitability I roped in Jim Moodie, Polygon CEO Neil Chrystal, architect Ray Letkeman, curator Ian Thom, and Yoshi. And what an outstanding group of presentations we had.

All the firms seemed excited and competent to handle the commission. Who were we going to pick? Using a rather crude weighing scale, we narrowed it down to two firms, including one headed by John and Patricia Patkau, who had received over fifteen Governor General's Awards for their work. I really was impressed with the Patkaus, but confided to the selection committee that they somewhat terrified me.

"Why don't we invite them over to the house for tea to see whether we can get more comfortable with them," Yoshi suggested.

So that's what we did. The Patkaus came on Sunday afternoon, despite my being apprehensive as to what they would think about our suburban Craftsman-style home, so different from the originality of their architectural projects.

"We should at least tidy up our living room before they arrive, and perhaps we should put the dogs away?" Yoshi suggested.

When the Patkaus arrived, they expressed mild surprise about the scale of the art, which Yoshi says overpowers our living room, but they politely sipped green tea and turned their attention to discussing the details of Japanese art museums they had visited.

I explained to John Patkau that I was leery of working with such famous architects for fear that their design might overwhelm the site and possibly be neither welcoming nor functional for the art. I said this based on photographs I had seen of earlier Patkau projects.

In response, John said, "Well, if that's the case we wouldn't be doing our job. We believe the site is fabulous and, if anything, the trees should be the main feature of what gets developed there. We obviously don't have any plans yet, but in my mind I see a Zen-like building situated within the forest.

After they left, Yoshi told me that that statement alone completely sold her on the Patkaus, though two days earlier she had been leaning towards another firm. It is not a decision that we have regretted.

The Audain Art Museum opened on March 12, 2016. The opening celebration dinner was presided over by the Honourable Judith Guichon, Lieutenant Governor of British Columbia, who to my surprise read out a letter from the Queen:

> I send my warm good wishes to you all as you gather in this magnificent building on the occasion of the opening of the Audain Art Museum in Whistler.
>
> I understand that the art in the Museum represents exquisite centuries-old Pacific Northwest Coast art, with historical and contemporary First Nations artists being exhibited together with a broad range of British Columbian artists whose works span the last 100 years.
>
> My sincere congratulations to all who have been involved in this remarkable project. The generous benefactors and the many supporters assembled here today can be very proud of what they have achieved. I hope you have an enjoyable and memorable evening, and that the Museum will be enjoyed by many visitors in the years to come.
>
> Elizabeth R.

I believe that the large crowd at the Fairmont Chateau Whistler was impressed, but I was personally stunned to hear that message. I know our small gallery opening in faraway British Columbia must have been brought to the Queen's attention by others, possibly Gordon Campbell, Canada's High Commissioner to the United Kingdom, but it would have been her decision to respond.

The Queen's remark in her 2016 Christmas broadcast about ordinary people doing quite extraordinary things really hit home with me, and I think could be adopted as a kind of summary comment on my own meanderings. She said, "I often draw strength from meeting ordinary people doing extraordinary things: volunteers, carers, community organizers and good neighbours, unsung heroes whose quiet dedication makes them special."

Indeed, that's what I have found in life. People who might never suspect that they had the capacity to do something brilliant quite often rise to do noble things, if not extraordinary ones, on some level or another. You don't have to be born a prince or princess—it's something that we all have the potential to do.

In my own case, I regard myself as a very ordinary human being who, though judged a failure in my early life, has occasionally gathered the courage to take the risk of stepping outside my comfort zone to try my hand at something new, whether in business or the community.

CHAPTER 58

"That Bear Had a Message for You"

Dr. Soma Ganesan, 2014

UP THE BRITISH COLUMBIA coast, I was sitting alone in a sunlit glade by the swift-flowing river as I listened to the dark gurgling water and watched for signs of trout. It was a good place to relax and let my mind wander.

All of a sudden I smelt a strange, pungent odour. Without moving my body, I lifted my eyes from the water and glanced to the left, straight into the huge saucer-shaped face of a grizzly bear, whose sounds of approach must have been muffled by the water's noise.

What could I do other than freeze when confronted with the face of this huge animal so close to mine? With my heart beating rapidly I waited, staring into the large brown eyes. But a moment or two later the animal's head shifted and it started to amble around the log that I was sitting on. It squatted down on its haunches about four metres away and stared intently at the river.

Then I woke up in my bed in our Tokyo apartment. It was the morning of March 23, 2014.

The dreams that you remember are the ones that occur just before you wake up. They are often nightmares. Even though I had been petrified in the dream, the bear seemed to have simply accepted me and been glad of my company.

I left on a short business trip to Bangkok that morning, completely mystified concerning the origin of the dream, because I knew little about grizzly bears and had never particularly given much thought to them. There had been no grizzlies on Vancouver Island, where as a boy I hunted and fished with my father. The smaller black bears were what we were familiar with, as they were abundant throughout BC, even in suburban Vancouver.

I wasn't much interested in the interpretation of dreams, but I was glad to bump into Dr. Soma Ganesan, then chief of psychiatric medicine at Vancouver General Hospital, when changing planes in Tokyo for my flight back to Vancouver. I recounted the dream to Soma and asked him if he had any opinion concerning what it meant. He reminded me that the First Nations of the Northwest Coast have long believed that the spirit of the bear plays an important role in their culture, adding, "For you I don't exactly know, but one thing is for sure: that bear had a message for you."

In the weeks that followed, motivated by the dream, I became determined to learn something about grizzly bears. The bears migrated about 50,000 years ago from Asia to North America, where once they roamed the continent, from the Arctic to northern Mexico, and from the Pacific Ocean to the East Coast. What seems to have happened is that, with the advent of the repeating rifle the bears had been exterminated throughout most of the continent, to the point that sustainable populations of grizzlies remain only in British Columbia and Alaska. In the continental United States, the grizzly is listed as an endangered species and therefore is not hunted, whereas in British Columbia, the provincial government would license foreigners and residents to participate in the spring and fall hunt, despite the grizzly being considered a species at risk.

I also learnt that grizzly bears are considered by biologists to be a "keystone" species, because when grizzly bears flourish the remainder of the environment is healthy. Also, somewhat to my relief, I learnt that while grizzly bears are omnivorous, they subsist most of the year on plants, and eat meat (mostly fish) opportunistically. Human beings are not among their natural prey.

As I read more about the species, I became determined to actually see some in the wild. So in September Yoshi, my daughter Kyra and I, with our friends Jim and Doria Moodie, embarked on a brief trip arranged by Chantal Shah, our family foundation executive director, to the Spirit Bear Lodge, located at a small First Nations settlement in the midst of what has become known as the Great Bear Rainforest.

Decked out in rain gear, we were whisked away on a fast boat to the estuary of the Mussel River, a territory whose access is controlled by the Kitasoo/Xai'xais band. Our guide led us along a trail to the riverside, where we were told we would be stationed for the next few hours in order to see some bears if they came along. As our small group sat on a log, I couldn't help but reflect on the similarity between this scene and the one that had occurred in my dream. The river was almost the same width, and there was a convenient log to sit on in a treeless glade—but instead of warm sunshine there was continuous rain. "Well," I thought to myself, "I'm glad at least something is different," because I didn't want to repeat the proximity to the bear that I encountered in my dream.

We saw the occasional bear at some distance, including an amusing scene of a mother bear and three cubs surfing on their backs down the river, partly obscured by a shrub-covered island that lay between us. As the afternoon wore on, we ate the sandwich lunches that we had packed that morning, and we began to feel the discomfort that a day in the cold rain can bring. Thoughts arose about how pleasant a hot shower would be on our return to the lodge. Suddenly, our guide said, "Don't move—just sit still." To our amazement, the mother grizzly appeared with three cubs trailing her. The mother gave our unfinished lunches a glance but continued ambling up the trail, not five metres away from us, with her cubs in tow.

That evening all of us who witnessed that moment with the mother bear and cubs agreed that it was magical. For me it strengthened my conviction that I have a curious affinity for this huge animal that predated the arrival of human beings on our continent. And it was this experience that led to a meeting with Stuart McLaughlin, operator of the Grouse Mountain Resort and Wildlife Refuge, which had adopted and raised two orphan grizzlies.

After some discussion, Stuart and I determined to commit ourselves to the long-term welfare of the bears by forming the Grizzly Bear

Foundation. We roped in to our board wildlife veterinarian Ken Macquisten, former provincial deputy minister Suzanne Veit, and chief counsellor Douglas Neasloss, whose band operates the Spirit Bear Lodge and who has done so much to end the trophy hunting of grizzly bears on the central coast.

In my grizzly bear orientation process, I was indebted to environmental organizations that have long campaigned to bring a halt to BC's trophy hunt. For education, Chantal Shah arranged for me to receive briefings from Chris Genovali of the Raincoast Conservation Foundation, which is headquartered in Victoria and has been involved in many research projects concerning wildlife conservation in the Great Bear Rainforest, and also Dr. Faisal Moola of the David Suzuki Foundation, a biologist with a remarkable knowledge of the role that grizzlies play in the environment.

In 2016, when the Grizzly Bear Foundation received its charitable status, the board appointed Stuart McLaughlin, Suzanne Veit and I to consult widely throughout the province concerning how British Columbians feel about their grizzly bears, and what policies should be adopted by government concerning the species, including what role our foundation could play in the bears' long-term welfare. The Grizzly Bear Foundation's Board of Inquiry Report was released in February 2017 to considerable public interest, and in December 2017 we were elated when the newly elected provincial government of NDP premier John Horgan terminated the sport of hunting grizzly bears in our province, a long overdue action that I was told our foundation helped bring about.

Until now, when I have been asked what originally spawned my interest in grizzly bears, I've always just referred to the wonder of seeing that mother and three cubs walking by in close proximity. I have been shy about mentioning the strange dream that occurred that early morning in Tokyo, for fear of not being taken seriously. But now that we have an organization that is starting to engage thousands of people in being concerned about the long-term welfare of these animals, I believe that I no longer have a reason to be so wary. The bear spoke to me in its own way and I listened.

CHAPTER 59

"Isn't It Strange That It Takes Someone from Vancouver to Get Us Together"

André Desmarais, 2019

AS I ADVANCE INTO my eighties I continue to resist the temptation to just sit by and play bingo, or reminisce in the nineteenth hole of the golf club. I seem to have no trouble finding things an old man can do.

I confess that attempting to engage in cultural activities in the province of Quebec at my age is not something I would have considered likely or advisable, but as it turns out that is what I have been spending much of my time doing recently.

It is all the fault of Jean Paul Riopelle. I mentioned earlier that Riopelle's paintings first caught my eye when I was in my teens, but it was over forty years before I was finally able to own one of his works, a glorious large triptych from 1954 in which the colours red and black predominate. Twenty-two years later, when we donated much of our British Columbia art to the museum in Whistler, Yoshi and I were left with many blank walls in our Vancouver home. Instead of continuing to collect regional art, we decided that perhaps it was time to branch out, and acquiring more Riopelle works made sense since we both loved the one we had lived with for so many years.

For me it was time to learn more about Riopelle, and I long ago had determined that the best way to do so was not by looking at images in books or on an iPad, but rather by viewing the original works, which enables the artist to communicate with no interference. I suppose that I had already been doing that for some years in Riopelle's case. The Power Corporation, a Quebec industrial behemoth headed by the Desmerais family, has a magnificent collection of Riopelles that I was able to spend time with during a visit to corporate headquarters in 2014. I had also long admired the sumptuous Riopelle in Ottawa's National Gallery, titled *Pavane*, which continues to be a feature of their permanent collection.

I am not going to bore you here with all the reasons why I believe Riopelle happens to be one of the greatest artists of the twentieth century. I have come to learn some things about art, in part to appreciate acquisitions we've made after the fact, but the main consideration that guides us in choosing to collect any given piece is simply whether or not we like it. This may account for the reputed eclecticism of our collection. It turns out we like a lot of different things, and we really like Jean Paul Riopelle. Some have been surprised to find so many Riopelles alongside our Emily Carrs, E.J. Hugheses and Mexican realists, because Riopelle is typically classed as an abstractionist. During his signature period in the 1950s he created complex, brilliantly hued works upon which he layered faceted pigment laced with splashes that are often compared to the works of celebrated American abstract expressionist Jackson Pollock. Riopelle's best works from this period have a power that entrances viewers, even those who think they don't like abstract art.

As a matter of fact, Riopelle rejected the "abstract" label and insisted he painted from nature. Living surrounded by his work I have come to appreciate what he meant by that statement, and now see him as a painter of nature in the tradition of a great many predecessors, perhaps starting with Leonardo da Vinci. Riopelle's unique talent was that he painted nature in a way that it had never been painted before. He was able to do this, he said, by going into nature rather than abstracting from it. This is how he created his magnificent mosaic paintings of the early 1950s, which were so enthusiastically received by the art world.

Like most great artists, Riopelle was not content to replicate one style. For instance, his gorgeous watercolours of the late 1940s, before he ever took up a palette knife, are really sublime, and his Arctic paintings of the late 1970s depict that world of snow and ice with a uniqueness no painter has equalled before or since. Riopelle's bronze works, many of which relate to the natural world of northern Quebec, are outstanding, as is his great masterwork, the 40-metre-long *L'Hommage à Rosa Luxemburg,* with its spray-can-painted images in which wild birds predominate. The piece was created as a memorial to his long-time partner, the acclaimed American abstract expressionist Joan Mitchell. Installed today in the Musée national des beaux-arts du Québec, it is a fitting finale to a great artistic career.

At the peak of his fame Riopelle had greater worldwide recognition than any other Canadian artist, and he is still, together with the photo-conceptualist Jeff Wall, one of the Canadian artists of greatest international reputation. One might think there would be little need for a tyro like me to weigh in on Riopelle's behalf but, as with so many great Canadians, his recognition at home has suffered from prophet-in-his-own-land syndrome.

When a poll in 2017 asked a thousand Canadians if they could name a Canadian painter, living or dead, only 52 per cent of respondents managed to do so. The leading artist named was Emily Carr, followed by members of the Group of Seven. I suppose that one shouldn't have been surprised by the survey results, and it is wonderful that Emily Carr has become so well known in the world of Canadian art, especially considering that much of the eastern cultural establishment traditionally overlooks contributions from the West. As much as one might like to think Carr's high profile is due to her mastery of West Coast iconography, with its powerful rainforests and Indigenous themes, it is likely that her compelling personal story is also partly responsible. The saga of a young woman struggling against the disdain of her family and fellow Victorians—boating unaccompanied up and down the remote reaches of the coast in the days when it was not customary for women to travel on their own, and persevering in her artistic vision—resonates in an era when the accomplishments of pioneering women are being appreciated anew.

Yet, while Emily Carr has been widely exhibited and collected in Canada, she remains little known abroad. This is the reverse of Riopelle, whose reputation is generally higher abroad than in Canada—with the exception of Quebec, where he was identified by 47 per cent of respondents in the 2017 survey. One might be forgiven for assuming the Canadian art elite would be enthusiastic about him, but that is not universally so. For example, in his book to celebrate the 150th anniversary of Confederation, National Gallery of Canada director Marc Mayer failed to include Riopelle in his introduction highlighting important Canadian artists. To the best of my knowledge, the National Gallery has not put on or scheduled a Riopelle exhibition between 1963 and 2023, though during that time retrospectives were hosted at Quebec venues as well as the Musée National d'Art Moderne, Centre Georges Pompidou, in Paris; the Museo de Arte Moderno in Mexico City; the Museo de Arte Contemporáneo de Caracas; and the State Hermitage Museum in St. Petersburg, to name a few. This neglect in Riopelle's own land was no mere oversight.

At a Rideau Club lunch in 2018 I heard a senior official of the National Gallery tell a staff member who suggested a Riopelle exhibition, "That's not going to happen on my watch." Later he told me that he thought Riopelle's early mentor Paul-Émile Borduas was a considerably better artist than Riopelle, a contrarian view that belies Riopelle's immensely greater output, greater artistic range, more extensive international holdings and higher prices, but it's one which I have heard repeated elsewhere in Canadian curatorial circles.

I had been told that the Montreal Museum of Fine Arts boasted a fine Riopelle collection, and in 2017 I visited Montreal to see it for myself. To say that I was disappointed would be an understatement. Yes, they had several beautiful Riopelles, but they were surrounded by lesser quality works, and all situated in a low-ceilinged basement gallery that was titled, in English, *The Age of the Manifesto*. It was an apparent reference to *Refus Global* (*Total Refusal*), the 1948 manifesto of Quebec's Automatiste School, often billed as Canada's first true modernists. A bold call for artistic independence from the church-dominated strictures of Quebec society, *Refus Global* was mainly attributed to Paul-Émile Borduas, though Riopelle designed the cover and signed it along with fourteen other artists.

The Automatiste group was certainly important as one of the cultural precursors of Quebec's Quiet Revolution, which so profoundly changed that province in the 1960s. But besides the insult of relegating Canada's most internationally renowned artist to an out-of-the-way basement space, there were other things that annoyed me. First, it is wrong to characterize Jean Paul Riopelle as solely a Quebec Automatiste. Yes, he studied and exhibited with those artists in his very early days, but he made his real reputation after moving to France in 1947, where he was variously described as a surrealist, a tachist, a lyrical expressionist, or simply as a member of the École de Paris, even though he personally identified with none of those labels.

The other extraordinary thing about the basement gallery is that the curators had populated it with random Quebec painters, such as Guido Molinari, who had never claimed any affiliation with the Automatistes. There was even an E.J. Hughes painting from British Columbia, looking strangely out of place.

I left the museum that day wondering how a painter of Riopelle's stature, whose works were in art museums around the world, could be treated so insensitively by the principal art institution in his hometown. Had his reputation fallen so low that his works were no longer valued, despite one of Montreal's most prominent public spaces being called Place Jean-Paul Riopelle?

Fashions in visual art come and go, as in other areas of life. And given the lack of solo Riopelle exhibitions in recent years, it would seem that the once-sought-after artist is no longer of great interest to museum curators and other arbiters of good taste, whereas in the 1950s and 1960s museums all over Europe were clamouring for his work. Despite this trend, if auction records are any indication, there has been a fairly steady demand for Riopelle's work from private collectors, though his prices have continued to be very modest in comparison to those of his New York contemporaries, such as Jackson Pollock and Franz Kline, to say nothing of his long-time companion Joan Mitchell.

Despite my advanced age and my location out on the West Coast, I began to wonder if I could do anything to improve Riopelle's standing in his native land. It was all very well to acquire some of his remarkable paintings to live with, but what could a private person like me do to help Canadians realize that we had living among us one of the greatest painters of all time?

While pondering all this in 2017, I received an invitation to an exhibition called *Mitchell/Riopelle: Nothing in Moderation* at the Musée national des beaux-arts du Québec. As mentioned, Mitchell was Riopelle's partner during his twenty-five-year period in France, and a major artist in her own right. When I visited the exhibition in the beautiful new Pierre Lassonde Pavilion I was greatly interested to meet staff members from the Joan Mitchell Foundation, based in New York City. One of them told me that they were surprised that there was not a similar foundation in Canada to document, celebrate and perhaps promote the work of Jean Paul Riopelle.

That evening, in Quebec City, I had an opportunity to meet Yseult Riopelle, the artist's daughter. I quickly arranged a follow-up lunch with her in Montreal to see if she would be interested in establishing a foundation. When we met at Maison Boulud restaurant, Riopelle told me that it had indeed been her father's intent in the early 1980s to establish a foundation to not only focus on his own art, but to help young people learn the basic techniques of art-making, including printmaking and metalwork.

Riopelle, a slight, intelligent woman known for wearing a backpack 365 days a year, seemed somewhat taken aback that someone from the West Coast would be sufficiently interested in her father's work to undertake the job of organizing a foundation, but she warily indicated her support.

Around that time I was also contacted by Nathalie Bondil, the dynamic director of the Montreal Museum of Fine Arts, who had somehow heard that a Riopelle collector from British Columbia was making noises about forming a foundation. She invited me to a delightful dinner with the board's incoming vice-president, Michel de la Chenelière. Nathalie told me that she had been thinking about mounting an exhibition that would be a "new take" on Riopelle, who she acknowledged to be our country's most famous artist. This time she felt there could be an opportunity to celebrate his encounter with northern Canada and interest in Indigenous art. Would this be something that our family foundation might be interested in sponsoring? When I replied in the affirmative, subject of course to learning more details about the exhibition, Nathalie immediately organized a visit to Vancouver—where she seemed visibly shocked at the scale of the Riopelle collection Yoshi and I had built.

Things moved fairly swiftly after that in terms of getting the foundation underway, with mega Riopelle collectors André Desmarais, the deputy chair of Power Corporation, and Pierre Lassonde, the former chairman of Franco-Nevada Mining Corporation, becoming founding directors, along with Yseult Riopelle and myself.

After an exploratory meeting at the Montreal airport in October 2018, the first official meeting was held at the downtown Sofitel Hotel in February 2019, followed by a celebratory lunch at the Mount Royal Club, where we were joined by Yoshi and Chantal Shah, the Audain Foundation's executive director.

It took about six months to obtain charitable status, but during this time we expanded the board to include John Porter, the former director of the Musée national des beaux-arts du Québec, and Senator Serge Joyal, an enthusiastic supporter of the arts. Meanwhile, things were auguring well for Riopelle's reputation. In 2019 the new director of the National Gallery of Canada, Sasha Suda, announced that the gallery had decided to mount a Riopelle retrospective exhibition in 2023 to celebrate the centenary of the artist's birth. She told me on a visit to Vancouver that there is hope that this show will travel internationally.

Also in 2019, the Jean Paul Riopelle Foundation hired its first executive director, Manon Gauthier, a former member of Montreal City Council with strong government connections, who had been deeply immersed in cultural affairs. The new foundation was now looking like it was really on its way.

I confess that attempting to engage in cultural activities in the province of Quebec at my age has been a challenge, especially as I seem to have lost most of the French language that I picked up over sixty years ago, but it has been a challenge that I have welcomed, as it is so refreshing to engage with fresh faces and customs. There is no doubt that Montreal is a unique city on the North American continent, one which fortunately does not seek to emulate either Paris or New York City, but just to express its own vibrant language and culture. Any hesitancy Quebecers might have had about a western anglophone meddling in their affairs evaporated once I had a chance to express my enthusiasm for Jean Paul Riopelle. A high point in the whole experience occurred after our first board meeting, when I overheard those two pillars of Quebec society, André Desmarais and Pierre Lassonde, murmur to each other, "Isn't it strange that it takes someone from Vancouver to get us together?"

Of course I am unlikely to provide long-term leadership for the Riopelle Foundation, but I believe that with our excellent board and strong executive director, we can hopefully play a role in not only elevating the status of this iconoclastic artist in this country and abroad, but also help our citizens to grow more aware of the cultural heroes who have been nourished by the soil of this great and beautiful country called Canada.

A POSTSCRIPT

EVEN TODAY, IN MY ninth decade, I still have many goals to pursue before I meet the Creator, so I normally prefer to get on with what I have on my plate rather than analyze my past. But perhaps the anecdotes recounted in this book reveal something of me that I have been unaware of myself. And hopefully it will demonstrate that, even though people may experience troubled times as youngsters, it needn't rule out one day having a fulfilling life.

As I put down my pen from writing these tales, I am conscious that we in Canada, as elsewhere in the world, are just starting to recover from a pandemic that I am sure many people will view as their life's toughest experience. It is already apparent that there will be a plethora of books and films about the pandemic, its roots and how we all fared. So many have lost their aged loved ones, to say nothing of their livelihoods and dreams for the future.

I recall my stepfather, George Carmichael, telling me in the 1950s that when someone standing in a London pub started spouting off about his experiences during the Blitz, the others would just edge away and turn their backs on him, because all had gone through a similar experience. I believe it will be the same with the pandemic. Those who lived through it, and especially those who have suffered grievously, will want to put those dark days behind them and move on. Therefore there are no pandemic tales in this book, other than noting that while Yoshi and I were comfortably secluded in our seaside home, we were so greatly impressed with how others in our lives simply carried on. I am thinking especially of Neil Chrystal and his talented team at Polygon Homes Ltd.; Curtis Collins, director of the Audain Art Museum in Whistler; Audain Foundation executive director Chantal Shah; and Manon Gauthier, executive director of the Jean Paul Riopelle Foundation in Montreal; all of whom stayed at the helm forging ahead with those activities that are very close to my heart. And, of course, I am particularly grateful to my own personal support staff, Barbara Binns, Laura Chanyan, Vanessa Watson and Georges Dordor, all of whom have admirably lived up to the World War II motto "Keep Calm and Carry On."

I owe a special debt to publisher Howard White, a man whom I have long admired for being such a great champion of British Columbia history as well as an artful spinner of Sunshine Coast folk lore. Without Howard's constant encouragement, these tales wouldn't have been written, let alone made it into print.

As an unhappy child, I often dreamed of what the future might bring, and while I cannot report that all my early dreams have come true, it has still led to a fairly eventful life—but not one I have journeyed on alone. I am very thankful for the support and companionship of so many of my fellow men and women, and especially the love and companionship of my wives, Tunya and Yoshi; my children, Fenya and Kyra; my grandchildren, Cameron, Aidan, Desmond and Beatrice; as well as, of course, the twelve wonderful Labrador retrievers with whom I have shared my life.